MORE PRAISE FOR *SOCIAL SECURITY WORKS!*

"It is about time that facts not propaganda influence public debate about Social Security. . . . Millennials as well as aging baby boomers have a crucial stake in preserving the one source of universal financial security. Altman and Kingson provide a public service in explaining why." —Fernando Torres-Gil, director, UCLA Center for Policy Research on Aging and former U.S. Assistant Secretary on Aging

"*Social Security Works!* shows why expanding Social Security is a top priority for MoveOn.org's millions of members." —Anna Galland, executive director, MoveOn.org Civic Action

"*Social Security Works!* is the most important book that any policy maker, voter, or concerned citizen can read in preparation for November 2016. . . . Social Security does indeed work. There is no reason to cut benefits—for anyone. Moreover, as these brilliant authors prove beyond any reasonable doubt, Social Security will work even better if it is substantially expanded." —Max J Skidmore, professor of political science, University of Missouri at Kansas City and author of *Securing America's Future: A Bold Plan to Preserve and Expand Social Security*

"A spirited defense of our Social Security system. Although they write with commitment and passion, [Altman and Kingson] take the time to look at the data in a rigorous manner. The result is a useful work of policy analysis with which all participants in the Social Security debate will need to reckon." —Edward D. Berkowitz, professor of history and public policy, George Washington University, and author of *Mr. Social Security: The Life of Wilbur J. Cohen*

"In *Social Security Works!*, two of our nation's leading policy experts explain in a clear and concise fashion how Social Security benefits are calculated, why Social Security is so important to all Americans, and what can be done to ensure that it is there for future generations." —Jill Quadagno, Mildred and Claude Pepper Eminent Scholar in Social Gerontology, Florida State University, and author of *One Nation, Uninsured*

Scholars, policy advisers, and political activists who are nationally known for their work on Social Security, **Nancy Altman** and **Eric Kingson** founded the not-for-profit organization Social Security Works in 2010 and co-chair the Strengthen Social Security Coalition, comprised of more than 320 of the nation's leading national and state seniors', union, women's, disability, civil rights, netroots, and other organizations. Both served as staff to the 1982 National Commission on Social Security Reform, the bipartisan commission that forged the consensus leading to the enactment of the 1983 Amendments to the Social Security Act. On the organizing committee of the National Academy of Social Insurance in the mid-1980s, they later served on the academy's founding board of directors. Both also served in 2008 on the advisory committee to President Barack Obama's Social Security Administration transition team.

Altman, a lawyer, is the author of *The Battle for Social Security*. A member of the faculty of Harvard University's Kennedy School of Government from 1983 to 1989, she also taught courses on private pensions and Social Security at the Harvard Law School. Currently on the board of the National Academy of Social Insurance, she also chairs the board of directors of the Pension Rights Center. She lives in Bethesda, Maryland.

Kingson, a professor at Syracuse University's School of Social Work, writes about the politics and economics of aging. Director of the Emerging Issues in Aging Program of the Gerontological Society of America in 1984–85, he also served as senior adviser to the 1994 Bipartisan Commission on Entitlement and Tax Reform. Author of *Lessons from Joan: Living and Loving with Cancer*, he lives in Manlius, New York.

David Cay Johnston is an investigative journalist and the winner of a 2001 Pulitzer Prize for uncovering loopholes and inequities in the U.S. tax code. He is the president of the 4,900-member Investigative Reporters & Editors and the author of the bestselling trilogy *Perfectly Legal*, *Free Lunch*, and *The Fine Print*. He is the editor of *Divided: The Perils of Our Growing Inequality* (The New Press). He teaches at Syracuse University College of Law.

ALSO BY NANCY J. ALTMAN

The Battle for Social Security: From FDR's Vision to Bush's Gamble

ALSO BY ERIC R. KINGSON

Lessons from Joan: Living and Loving with Cancer, A Husband's Story

The Generational Equity Debate
(ed. with J.B. Williamson and D. Watts-Roy)

Social Security in the 21st Century (ed. with J.H. Schulz)

Social Security and Medicare: A Policy Primer (with E.D. Berkowitz)

Ties That Bind: The Interdependence of Generations
(with B.A. Hirshorn and J.C. Cornman)

SOCIAL
SECURITY
WORKS!

WHY SOCIAL SECURITY ISN'T
GOING BROKE AND HOW
EXPANDING IT WILL HELP US ALL

NANCY J. ALTMAN

AND

ERIC R. KINGSON

THE NEW PRESS

NEW YORK
LONDON

To the late Robert M. Ball (1914–2008), whose enduring legacy continues to improve the lives of many millions of people every day. Social Security was his calling. For seven decades, he tirelessly devoted his extraordinary intellectual, political, organizational, and personal gifts to advancing Social Security, which he understood to be an instrument of social justice, human dignity, and civility.

© 2015 by Nancy J. Altman and Eric R. Kingson
Foreword © 2015 by David Cay Johnston

Published in the United States by The New Press, New York, 2015

Distributed by Perseus Distribution

ISBN 978-1-62097-037-9 (pbk.)
ISBN 978-1-62097-047-8 (e-book)
CIP data available

The New Press publishes books that promote and enrich public discussion and understanding of the issues vital to our democracy and to a more equitable world. These books are made possible by the enthusiasm of our readers; the support of a committed group of donors, large and small; the collaboration of our many partners in the independent media and the not-for-profit sector; booksellers, who often hand-sell New Press books; librarians; and above all by our authors.

www.thenewpress.com

Book design and composition by Bookbright Media
This book was set in Bembo and Gotham.

Printed in the United States of America

10 9 8 7 6 5 4 3

CONTENTS

Part Five: Next Steps

ACKNOWLEDGMENTS

We have dedicated this book to the late Robert M. Ball, our mentor, role model, adviser, teacher, colleague, and friend. Without his wisdom, insight, and inspiration, this book would never have been written.

There are others without whom this book would never have come to be. Primary among them is David Cay Johnston—Pulitzer Prize–winning journalist, best-selling author, and Distinguished Visiting Lecturer at Syracuse University, whose recent book, *Divided: The Perils of Our Growing Inequality*, is also published by The New Press. David, also the author of our book's foreword, provided a generous introduction to Ellen Adler, publisher of The New Press.

That introduction began an outstanding, productive relationship not only with Ellen, but also with assistant editor Jed Bickman. Both Ellen and Jed provided careful, thoughtful editing of our manuscript, as well as guidance through the process. Everyone at The New Press was extremely able and helpful: Julie McCarroll, director of marketing and publicity, Christy Johnson, sales and marketing manager, Meredith Sheridan, publicity and marketing assistant, and Bev Rivero, publicist, lent their collective creative genius to the book's design, marketing, and distribution; and Sharon Swados, director of sales and rights, and Nikki Marron, manager of foundation relations, ably and efficiently helped with the technical business aspects of the relationship, including promotion of the book. Also, thanks to Daniel Gaetán-Beltrán and Ebonie Ledbetter, production managers at Bookbright Media, who capably shepherded the manuscript through copyediting and galleys, to Jill Becker, the copyeditor, and to Alana Cash, who developed the index. We are privileged to be published by The New Press, a nonprofit trade publisher and unionized press with national reach and a social justice mission.

We especially want to thank the entire staff of Social Security Works, with particular thanks and appreciation to Alex Lawson and Ben Veghte, PhD. Alex, executive director of Social Security Works, first suggested that we write this book and then lent his considerable enthusiasm and talent to facilitating its writing and dissemination. Ben, the organization's research director, invested countless hours providing invaluable research, analysis, editing, drafting of charts, fact-checking assistance, and much more. He spent nights and weekends to help us complete the manuscript as quickly as we did. He has earned our very deep gratitude. Others on the staff who also provided masterful assistance are Stephanie Connolly, legislative and policy associate, and Linda Benesch, communications associate, who assisted Ben; Molly Checksfield, legislative director, and Jasmine Jefferson, legislative associate, who helped with questions about current legislation; Lacy Crawford, communications director, who helped to develop a plan to publicize the book; and Michael Phelan, deputy director, who provided invaluable technical assistance.

We also wish to thank the Office of the Chief Actuary of the Social Security Administration, with special thanks to Stephen C. Goss, chief actuary, and Alice H. Wade, deputy chief actuary of the Office of Long-Range Estimates. Steve and Alice were always generous in providing technical assistance. Thanks also to Virginia Reno, vice president for income security policy at the National Academy of Social Insurance, for insightful comments on the manuscript. A huge thanks also to economist Dean Baker, co-director of the Center for Economic and Policy Research, who generously provided insights and information regarding several important points. Our appreciation extends too to Patricia E. Dilley, professor of law, Levin College of Law, University of Florida, and Pamela Perun, senior policy consultant to the Initiative on Financial Security, Aspen Institute, who provided advice on obtaining a sample treasury bond. We also thank W. Andrew Achenbaum, professor of history and social work, University of Houston, and

Amanda Torre-Norton, health and long-term care quality consultant, for their extremely helpful suggestions.

Eric would like to acknowledge his colleagues at the Syracuse University School of Social Work, especially professor Alejandro Garcia, for their considerate support, as well as Syracuse University, which generously allowed him to take academic leaves that supported his work with Social Security Works and the Strengthen Social Security Coalition, leading in turn to the writing of this book.

On a substantive note, we want to alert readers that, while some of the stories related in the book are drawn from real people, some, as mentioned in the pertinent endnotes, were created as illustrative. We also want to acknowledge that some material that appears in this book builds on and was drawn from earlier publications of the authors, as listed in the first endnote to chapter 1.

This book came out of our work as the founding co-directors of Social Security Works and co-chairs of the Strengthen Social Security Coalition, which involves many organizations and wonderful people. We do not thank by name the many dedicated people engaged with the coalition, though we owe a debt of gratitude to each and every one of them. We do discuss in appendix D some of the organizations that have been working in a variety of ways to protect and advance the American people's Social Security.

We also thank, with appreciation, the funders of Social Security Works: the Atlantic Philanthropies, Retirement Research Foundation, CREDO Action, and the individual donors who supported and advanced Social Security Works and the Strengthen Social Security Coalition. We also appreciate the support of organizations that have previously served as administrative homes and fiscal intermediaries for Social Security Works—The Tides Advocacy Fund, Campaign for America's Future, and the Pension Rights Center—and now the Alliance for Retired Americans, who, among other valuable assistance, provide donated office space at the national headquarters of the AFL-CIO.

We would be remiss if we did not highlight the special role the Atlantic Philanthropies, its board of directors, and its staff have played in funding and shaping the organizational work that led to our writing this book. In 2009, the Atlantic Philanthropies had the foresight to recognize that the future of our Social Security system would soon emerge on the national agenda. Concerned that policymaking might proceed without adequate input from those most directly affected, the Atlantic Philanthropies asked us to develop a plan and then proceeded to generously fund Social Security Works and the coalition's work, which grew from that plan. Atlantic's staff, especially Stephen R. McConnell, director of United States programs, as well as Laura Robbins and Stacey Easterling, our grant officers, provided advice, guidance, enthusiastic support, and friendship over the past five years as we engaged in work which led to the writing of this book.

Finally, but most importantly, we want to thank our families, without whose love and support our work would be impossible. Eric lovingly thanks his wife, Nancy, and his children, Aaron, Johanna, and Sarah. Nancy lovingly thanks her husband, Chip, and her children, Toni, Adam, Jennifer, and Michael. We both thank our grandchildren—Samuel, Ezekiel, Kylie, and Beatrice— whose love enriches our lives and whose very presence provides a window into the future. It is for them and all generations, now and in the future, for whom we and many others work to expand Social Security.

FOREWORD

Social Security stands for a simple proposition: no matter how life works out, whether prosperity or ruin, no one will be left penniless in old age or because of disability or being orphaned.

Social Security is by far the most popular federal government program, the best funded federal program, and the strongest remaining piece of our badly frayed system of social benefits. It is also under relentless attack by those who would kill it.

In their new book, *Social Security Works!*, Nancy J. Altman and Eric R. Kingson set the record straight. Altman and Kingson are scholars who served on the staff of President Ronald Reagan's 1982 National Commission on Social Security Reform. They have studied the program ever since and now, as co-directors of the nonprofit organization Social Security Works, work to preserve and improve this vital program that reduces risks for individuals and helps businesses prosper.

Altman and Kingson explain that although Social Security's primary goals are not alleviating poverty or income inequality, the program does more to rectify income inequality and prevent poverty among older Americans than any other program, public or private, while also providing crucial protection for orphans and the disabled. More important, they prove that the widely made claims that Social Security adds to the federal government's perennial budget deficits have no basis in fact.

The fact is that Social Security works efficiently and effectively.

With only tweaks to adjust for demographic and economic changes, Social Security can remain financially sound so long as the United States of America endures. In this, Social Security is no different than our Constitution, which we amended twenty-seven times in the 203 years from when the Bill of Rights was adopted through 1992, when the rules on congressional pay raises were clarified.

NATIONAL INSURANCE

Social Security is a form of national insurance, its premiums paid with a dedicated tax on what the law calls *compensation for services.* This includes wages, including bonuses, salaries, and stock option profits, up to the annual salary cap on earnings subject to tax, which was $117,000 in 2014. Compensation above that level is not taxed and is not counted in calculating benefits.

Today more than 44 million retirees, spouses, and their survivors collect a monthly benefit. For another 9 million workers disabled by injury, illness, or violent crime, the same protection is provided. Then there are children whose father is killed in an accident, whose mother is felled by sickness, whose parents are murdered. Because of Social Security's orphan benefits, the heartless gods of chance do not ruin their future prospects.

Social Security shows that Americans care for their fellow Americans and willingly share in the risks, and burdens, that come with building a strong and economically vibrant nation of free people. Numerous polls show that not only do Americans love the freedom from want Social Security insurance guarantees, but by overwhelming majorities they declare their willingness to pay more taxes to expand these benefits. Indeed, a solid 62 percent majority of Republicans favor increasing Social Security benefits, as Altman and Kingson detail in the pages ahead.

Those who collect a benefit each month are not the only ones who benefit from America's Social Security system. We *all* do.

A CUSHION IN HARD TIMES

In hard times Social Security's steady, reliable flow of funds to those who earned their benefits, and to their dependents, cushions a general economic collapse. The monthly checks that more than 58 million Americans collected in 2014 kept the beneficiaries clothed, fed, and sheltered. And spending that money also kept others working. But for these leveling effects as Social Security payments are spent, many millions more would have lost their jobs and their homes, adding to the burdens taxpayers endured during the Great Recession and the much too slow recovery from it. Many more small businesses would have failed but for sales to people who received Social Security checks every month.

In every future recession Social Security will provide the same cushioning benefit whenever the economy contracts temporarily, provided that we maintain the program's financial strength.

This broad benefit in the Great Recession and recovery—keeping money reliably circulating through the economy—came despite modest Social Security benefits. The average retiree's checks roughly equal the gross pay of someone working full time at the federal minimum wage. The disabled generally collect less.

Social Security also prevents America's child poverty rate, by far the worst among modern industrialized countries, from worsening. Among America's 74 million children under age eighteen, more than one in ten live in a household where they or someone else collects Social Security benefits. Social Security lifts more than a million children out of poverty, recent annual reports by the Social Security trustees show.

Among older Americans poverty was endemic from the founding of the country through the Great Depression. Starvation and ill health from not having enough to stay safe and warm in old age worked together as advance agents for the Grim Reaper, bringing millions to premature and often ugly deaths. No more, thanks to Social Security.

In our time, thanks to Social Security and the increases in benefits adopted by Congresses under both parties over the past seven decades, only one in eleven older Americans remains mired in poverty. Take Social Security benefits away, though, and every other older American would be in poverty. Among black Americans the poverty rate would triple.

Despite overwhelming popular support, sound economics, and reduction in anxiety as well as poverty, Social Security remains under relentless attack by those who would replace it with costly, unreliable, and inefficient schemes. The opponents would shift the risks to each individual, instead of spreading risks among all of us. The ardent public opposition to president George W. Bush's attempt to privatize Social Security, however, did not quell the program's enemies, who are well funded to continue their assault for decades to come.

Unable to win popular support with proposals that would have diverted vast amounts of tax money from Social Security to Wall Street, the opponents try to lure people into their tent with promises of riches for all by privatization and "ownership" of one's retirement account. These plans defy the laws of simple arithmetic, as you will read in the pages ahead. They also carry the same risks as the Individual Retirement Accounts and 401(k)s that promoters claimed would make everyone rich but instead enriched Wall Street.

By distorting, obscuring, and flat-out lying, the enemies of Social Security have succeeded in persuading many millions of people that Social Security is on the verge of collapse, threatening to bring down the whole economy. Using big numbers, out of context, they scare those who do not understand the economics of public finance, which is almost everybody. They do not tell people that the trillions of dollars of benefits owed over the next seventy-five years, but not fully paid for under the current rules, equal only a tiny fraction of economic output over those decades. They don't tell people that the difference amounts to a tiny 1 percent of expected economic output over the next seventy-five years or even to infinity. And they never apply the same scare tactics to government programs without a dedicated tax. The unfunded future costs of national security and public education far outstrip Social Security with its dedicated taxes.

Artful deceptions have been used to attack Social Security from its inception. Despite this, overwhelming majorities in Congress voted for it in 1935. The House tally was 372 to 33, and the Senate vote 77 to 6.

In 1936, Alf Landon's campaign for president called Social Security a "cruel hoax" and "a fraud on the workingman." His campaign tried to scare people with baseless claims that an army of federal bureaucrats would be snooping into their lives. Americans responded by giving Franklin D. Roosevelt a second term and 61 percent of their votes.

COUNTERING THE BIG LIE

Today the distortions and lies about Social Security are so widely and so often repeated on television, in the newspapers, and in magazine that many younger Americans accept as uncontestable truth the dire predictions that they will be taxed all their working lives for benefits they will never collect.

Nothing could be further from the truth.

Social Security has robust trust funds, valued at $2.8 trillion and growing as of summer 2014. That surplus is expected to keep growing until 2020 or so when—as planned—it will be drawn to pay benefits to the baby boomers born during the nineteen years between the start of 1946 and the end of 1964.

Where will the money come from to pay benefits financed from the trust funds, which is basically money we have saved through our government? Easy—the government will simply exchange Social Security bonds for Treasury bonds, not unlike the way that corporations refinance their debt and homeowners refinance houses.

Benefits beyond the continuing flow from the dedicated tax and the surplus can be paid through a slight increase in the tax rate. The flow of funds into Social Security would surge if our federal government adopted new policies that resulted in many more jobs at higher wages than we have experienced since wage stagnation set in at the turn of the millennium.

Who are these Social Security opponents? A few are motivated by greed. The prospect of fat fees for managing individual retirement accounts, making the system less economically efficient, naturally draws ravenous supporters.

Most of the opponents, though, are driven not by greed but by alarm that Social Security is a success. That it works undermines their ideology that government should be small, weak, and focused on the common defense and law enforcement, not on making sure everyone has some insulation from the harsh realities of the economy. These opponents would ignore that one of the six noble purposes written down in the preamble to our Constitution is to "promote the general Welfare." That capital W is in the original.

Many opponents think Social Security is *socialism*. These same opponents rarely, however, express disgust with, or seek to privatize, America's socialized police, fire, and prosecution services or our socialized system of roads, canals, and national parks, not to mention our socialized military.

BEFORE SOCIAL SECURITY

Before the Social Security Act of 1935, life in the United States was perilous. Economic self-sufficiency depended on being healthy and young enough to work. The prospect of a disabling injury or sickness hung over all but the rich like a modern sword of Damocles. One industrial or automobile accident, one fire, one errant bullet from a bank robber or a drunk could ruin a whole family. Such events were the equivalent of clipping the single horsehair that kept a sword from falling point first into the head of the citizen who an ancient Syrian king let sit on his throne to enjoy the experience while also appreciating the dangers and risks.

The risk of economic ruin served no purpose. It was a risk we did not need, as many Americans recognized in the depths of the Great Depression. The easing of those risks is a tribute to president Franklin Roosevelt and, especially, to the dedication of one woman whose focus and hard work led to the creation of a system of national insurance so that most of us could be protected against economic ruin. A key to this success was a general understanding that those who played by the rules and worked hard could nevertheless be wiped out if age, death, or disability ended their ability to earn.

Frances Perkins became the fourth secretary of labor and in 1933 the first woman to serve in any president's cabinet. When she arrived at the Labor Department, she found in her office some two thousand ideas from citizens proposing ways to end the Depression and help older Americans left destitute by the economic collapse.

Perkins understood that severe lack of money destroys families. During the Great Depression many teenage boys and girls left home simply because they there was not enough money for food to feed their younger siblings. This altruism was not a rare occurrence. Many thousands of young people left home, some ending up in jail for stealing food when they were starving, some in prostitution for the same reason, some finding menial work that kept them fed, and a few going on to great things after this awful experience.

America can continue to go on to great achievements of the human spirit if we strengthen, expand, and protect Social Security. Nancy Altman and Eric Kingson show what you need to know to stand up for this most popular, most valuable, and best funded of all federal government programs.

David Cay Johnston
Rochester, New York
September 2014

PART ONE

THE FACTS

1

THE CHANGING CONVERSATION

*This is no time, this is the last time, to be talking about cutting
Social Security. This is the moment when we talk about
expanding Social Security.*

—Senator Elizabeth Warren
The Rachel Maddow Show
November 20, 2013

WHETHER YOU ARE A MEMBER OF THE SILENT GENERATION
or a baby boomer, whether a Gen Xer or a millennial, this book is
for you.[1] It makes the case for why and how we can and must expand our Social Security system. Why doing so is excellent policy,
excellent politics, and, most importantly, excellent for all Americans—young and old, women and men, people of all races and
ethnicities.

For the many readers who have heard for decades that Social
Security is going bankrupt and won't be there in the future, the
idea that it's not—and that there's a movement to expand it—may
come as a shock. If you are one of those readers, it is essential to
your own and your family's well-being that you free yourself from
what you think you know about Social Security.

Armed with misinformation and half-truths, a three-decade-
long, well-financed campaign has sought to dismantle Social
Security, brick by brick. This campaign has been remarkably successful in undermining confidence in Social Security. In fact, the

younger you are, the less confident you are likely to be that Social Security will exist when you need it.

The campaign has also been successful in convincing prominent politicians of both political parties that Social Security must be radically changed, or at least scaled back. The mainstream media has aided and abetted the campaign by uncritically accepting and advancing a panoply of misconceptions, while largely ignoring the facts.

While the campaign against Social Security has been successful in those ways, its hundreds of millions of dollars have failed to en-act anti–Social Security legislation. Standing in the way, resolute, are the American people.

Politicians and the media decry how polarized our nation's politics are. Electoral maps, depicting red states and blue states, provide a pictorial representation of that polarization. Hot-button topics like abortion, same-sex marriage, and immigration reform divide the electorate. But there is one issue about which Americans are overwhelmingly united: they support Social Security. Poll after poll reveals this. The findings of a recent online survey of two thousand adults, ages 21 and over, conducted by Matthew Greenwald and Associates in collaboration with the nonpartisan National Academy of Social Insurance, is a good example, as figure 1.1, summarizing the findings, shows. A large majority of Americans believe that Social Security is more important than ever, do not mind contributing to Social Security because it provides security and stability, and believe that consideration should be given to expanding its benefits.[2]

Numerous polls show that Americans of all political affiliations —Republicans, Independents, Democrats, self-proclaimed Tea Partiers, union households, and progressives—support our Social Security system by large majorities. Conservatives may disagree with progressives about most political issues, but not about the importance of Social Security. Those from the Northeast may differ with those from the Deep South about many issues, but both groups support Social Security.[3]

Virtually all demographic groups support Social Security. Men and women support Social Security. So do African Americans, Hispanics, European Americans, and other racial and ethnic

AMERICANS OVERWHELMINGLY AGREE ABOUT SOCIAL SECURITY

Percent Agreeing with Statements

Respondent characteristics	Social Security benefits are more important now than ever	I don't/didn't mind paying Social Security taxes because it provides security and stability to millions	We should consider increasing Social Security benefits
Total	89%	84%	75%
Generation			
Silent	93	88	72
Baby boomer	93	86	76
Generation X	87	85	74
Generation Y	84	79	74
Family Income			
Less than $30,000	89	83	80
$30,000 to $49,999	93	90	78
$50,000 to $74,999	89	82	70
$75,000 to $99,999	87	82	71
$100,000 or more	88	86	67
Party Affiliation			
Republican	81	74	62
Democrat	94	91	84
Independent	91	86	71

Data from National Academy of Social Insurance survey, September 2012.

Source: Jasmine V. Tucker, Virginia P. Reno, and Thomas N. Bethell, "Strengthening Social Security: What Do Americans Want?," National Academy of Social Insurance, January 2013.

Figure 1.1

groups. Every age group supports Social Security as well. Even younger Americans, who have bought the lie that Social Security won't be there for them, nevertheless support the program for their parents and grandparents, and don't want to see it cut.

And the support is not just widespread; it also runs very deep. Feelings for Social Security are so strongly held that one well-respected pollster, Celinda Lake, president of Lake Research Partners, says this support is not just an indication of preference, but of deeply held values.

This view of the overwhelming majority of the American people should come as no surprise. The America we know today would not be possible without Social Security. This institution undergirds the economic security of virtually every American. And it gives expression to the American people's best instincts—caring for our parents, children, and neighbors; working hard and contributing; engaging in self-help and mutual aid; respecting the dignity of each person; managing resources conservatively and prudently; and understanding that together we stand stronger. Old-fashioned ideas, perhaps, but still valuable, and fundamental to advancing strong families, communities, and our nation.

The current campaign to undermine Social Security is not a new battle. Although the moneyed interests and conservative ideologues have hated Social Security and battled against it since before it was enacted, the will of the people has always ultimately prevailed. The intensity of the battle and fields of engagement may ebb and flow, but the battle lines are always drawn. The current campaign against Social Security is simply the latest skirmish in that ongoing war. It's a war we, the people, can and must win.

THE CONTINUING BATTLE OVER SOCIAL SECURITY

The fight for Social Security has been part of a larger struggle over worker security. It is also part of the ongoing struggle between those who view poor Americans, even those who have worked for their entire adult lives, as undeserving, versus those who understand that each of us deserves to be treated with dignity, especially when unemployment, health problems, old age, or other circumstances undermine our ability to support ourselves and our families. At base, it is a struggle over the role of government in improving our lives. And it is a struggle about our responsibilities to our families, neighbors, and selves.

At the beginning of the twentieth century, with the growing industrialization and urbanization of the United States, increasing numbers of Americans became dependent on wage income. To ensure a living wage, and to protect those workers in the event of the loss of those wages, a variety of workers' movements arose. These various movements sought minimum wages and maximum hours, workers' compensation for industrial accidents, health insurance, unemployment insurance, disability insurance, survivors' or life insurance, occupational safety, an end to child labor, the freedom to unionize, and old-age annuities.

Older workers were particularly vulnerable. When older workers lost employment, they could seldom find new work. Indeed, want ads often plainly stated that the old need not apply. Older people, no matter how frugal, generally had insufficient savings to last until death. Those unable to work routinely moved in with their children. Those who had no children, or whose children were unable or unwilling to support them, often wound up in the poorhouse. The poorhouse was not some Dickensian invention; it was an all-too-real last resort for the desperate and destitute old. The vast majority of the residents were elderly. Most of the "inmates," as they were often called, entered the poorhouse late in life, having been independent wage earners until that point. Fear of the poorhouse was always lurking in the background, haunting people as they aged.

Prior to the Great Depression, most of the efforts to address worker insecurity and old-age dependency took place at the state level. The movements had varying degrees of success. The drive for statewide programs of workers' compensation, for example, was highly successful, but minimum wage and maximum hour laws were held unconstitutional by the Supreme Court. Some states established very modest programs for groups deemed "worthy"—the indigent old, the blind, and dependent children. Once the Great Depression began, though, these states were generally not capable of sustaining their programs without federal aid.

With the onset of the Great Depression and the election of Franklin D. Roosevelt, a highly progressive president, the leaders of these progressive movements focused more intensely on achieving nationwide legislation at the federal level. One of the leaders in pushing for worker security was Frances Perkins, a social worker from New York and close, longtime confidante of Roosevelt's. Upon his election, Roosevelt quickly appointed Perkins to be his secretary of labor, making her the first woman in the nation's history to become a member of a president's cabinet.

The start of the Roosevelt administration was focused on the emergency caused by the Depression. Roosevelt's record-setting first one hundred days in office resulted in more than a dozen historic pieces of legislation aimed at relieving distress, getting people back to work, promoting economic recovery, and reforming the nation's banks and stock exchanges.

THE SOCIAL SECURITY ACT OF 1935

President Roosevelt's next priority was to enact measures to ensure that Americans would be protected in good times and bad. To develop legislation, Roosevelt established the Committee on Economic Security (CES), an interagency group of five high-ranking members of the administration, chaired by Secretary Perkins.

Given only six months to complete its work, CES's mission was extraordinarily broad. It worked on national health insurance, unemployment insurance, disability insurance, life insurance, accident insurance, retirement annuities, and public assistance (i.e., welfare) for the aged, the blind, and dependent children, as well as family and maternity benefits. Not all of those elements made it into the actual legislation; Roosevelt, for example, held back the national health insurance piece out of concern that it might sink the entire legislation. Still, the president's Economic Security Act—later renamed, in the course of congressional deliberations, the more alliterative "Social Security Act"—was introduced at the start of the 1935 congressional session. It was met with stiff opposition. Some thought it did not go far enough, but many others thought it went much too far. Much of the attack focused on the provision of old-age annuities in retirement, the part of the legislation generally known today as Social Security.

Some of the opposition's rhetoric was truly colorful. One member charged that the measure was "placing a financial lash upon the backs of the people whose backs are breaking under a load of debt and taxes."[4] Another insisted, "The bill opens the door and invites the entrance into the political field of a power so vast, so powerful as to threaten the integrity of our institutions and to pull the pillars of the temple down upon the heads of our descendants."[5] Others simply called it "socialism."[6]

Despite the opposition, the Social Security Act of 1935 was signed into law on August 14, 1935. It established two insurance programs, Unemployment Insurance and Old Age Insurance. (The latter, with subsequent statutory improvements, is what people generally refer to today as Social Security.) The legislation also included three welfare programs—Old Age Assistance, Aid to Dependent Children, and Aid to the Blind—as well as several public health and social service programs. In his signing statement, the president was clear that the new law was just a first step, albeit a very significant one, in the march toward economic security—a framework upon which future generations should build:

> We can never insure one hundred percent of the population against one hundred percent of the hazards and vicissitudes of life, but we have tried to frame a law which will give some measure of protection to the average citizen and to his family against the loss of a job and against poverty-ridden old age.
>
> This law, too, represents a cornerstone in a structure which is being built but is by no means complete. . . . It is, in short, a law that will take care of human needs and at the same time provide the United States an economic structure of vastly greater soundness.[7]

DEFENDING SOCIAL SECURITY: THE EARLY YEARS

The enactment was not the end of the fight. Social Security became a major issue in the 1936 presidential election. Republican presidential nominee Alf Landon denounced Social Security as "a fraud on the workingman" and "a cruel hoax." He claimed that

Social Security's reserves were mere IOUs. He sought to scare Americans about "federal snooping" by a "vast army" of bureaucrats who would be collecting information.[8]

Just days before the election, the Republican National Committee mailed millions of posters, pamphlets, and pay envelope inserts, all attacking Social Security, to employers across the nation. Employers all over the country put up the posters, handed out the pamphlets, and, most egregiously, added the inserts in the envelopes of each employee's pay that week. Each insert, which was designed to look like an official government notice, alarmingly declared:

> Effective January, 1937, we are compelled by a Roosevelt "New Deal" law to make a 1 per cent deduction from your wages and turn it over to the government. . . . [T] his may go as high as 4 per cent. You might get this money back . . . but . . . [t]here is NO guarantee. Decide before November 3—election day—whether or not you wish to take these chances.[9]

In response, the next night President Roosevelt addressed the nation in a live broadcast from Madison Square Garden. Warning against the powerful, moneyed interests, he explained:

> It is an old strategy of tyrants to delude their victims into fighting their battles for them.
> Every message in a pay envelope, even if it is the truth, is a command to vote according to the will of the employer. But this propaganda is worse—it is deceit. . . . When they imply that the reserves thus created . . . will be stolen by some future Congress, diverted to some wholly foreign purpose, they attack the integrity and honor of American Government itself.[10]

EXPANDING SOCIAL SECURITY:
1939 TO THE MID-1970S

The battle did not end with Roosevelt's landslide re-election, either. To guard against similar attacks in 1940, and to build on the structure now begun, Congress moved the date monthly benefits started from 1942 to 1940 and eliminated the anticipated buildup of reserves by increasing the benefits of those close to retirement and adding new important benefits.

The Social Security Amendments of 1939 addressed the economic insecurity that the death of a working parent could leave children and spouses without a steady income. Before Social Security, it was not unusual for widows and widowers to give up their children simply because they no longer could support them financially. For example, in 1914, an estimated 2,716 children lived in New York State's orphanages, mainly because their widowed mothers could not support them.[11] But, thanks to Social Security, beginning in 1940, surviving wives of deceased workers with young children became eligible to receive benefits, protections that were extended to widowers in 1950.[12] Parents struggling to maintain their children after the death of a working spouse now have income they can count on.

For the subsequent thirty-five years, the Social Security structure continued to be improved, brick by brick. Social Security was expanded to cover millions of additional workers, including those in hard-to-regulate occupations, such as domestic and migrant employment. And new benefits were added. The Social Security Amendments of 1956 established disability insurance protections for workers aged 50 to 64, extended in 1960 to include workers under age 50. Still more was to come in the nation's march to a more robust Social Security system. In 1965, the nation added two very significant programs to the architecture of the Social Security Act: the Medicare and Medicaid programs. The Medicare program provides health insurance to nearly all Americans age 65 and older, as well as to people with disabilities. Medicaid, targeted to the poor, provides similar medical services and also long-term care services to low-income seniors, people with disabilities, and others.

During these same years, benefits were regularly increased to keep pace with inflation and America's improved standard of living. Some liberal supporters of Social Security were concerned that, while inflation is ongoing, benefit adjustments tended to occur every other year, just before elections. At the same time, conservatives who supported a modest Social Security program were concerned that the tendency of politicians was to expand Social Security too much, in these pre-electoral enactments. The two joined forces to support the enactment in 1972 of automatic, annual cost-of-living adjustments.

None of these improvements occurred without opposition. The fight only rarely fell along strictly partisan lines. Both Republican and Democratic presidents have fought for Social Security. In every generation, though, fighting on the other side have been libertarians and other conservative ideologues, backed by moneyed interests.

President Harry S. Truman sought to expand Social Security by including disability and sickness insurance, as well as national health insurance. Congress, which switched to Republican control in November 1946 for the first time since Herbert Hoover was president, ignored the calls, however. Instead Congress enacted, over Truman's vetoes, legislation shrinking the number of workers covered by Social Security. Running hard against the Republican-controlled Congress, Truman issued one of the vetoes during a whistle-stop train tour, proclaiming, "If our Social Security program is to endure, it must be protected against these piecemeal attacks."[13] The skirmish fit perfectly with his campaign theme that Congress was "the worst in [his] memory," favoring the wealthy over ordinary Americans.[14]

Truman won the election, despite polls showing that he would lose, and Congress was returned to Democratic control. The election paved the way for the expansions of Social Security that occurred in 1950 and 1952.

The election of president Dwight Eisenhower in November 1952 gave new hope to opponents of Social Security. Holding elective office for the first time in his career, Eisenhower had never been forced to take a stand on the issue. Under the urging of the U.S. Chamber of Commerce, the leadership of Congress, now back in Republican control, appointed representative Carl Curtis, an outspoken opponent of Social Security, to chair a subcommittee instructed to "conduct thorough studies and investigations of all matters pertaining to our Social Security laws."[15] But by August of his first year in office, President Eisenhower revealed his strong support for Social Security in a message to Congress accompanying proposed legislation to expand coverage:

> Retirement systems, by which individuals contribute to their own security according to their own respective abilities, have become an essential part of our economic and social life. These systems are but a reflection of the American heritage of sturdy self-reliance which has made our country strong and kept it free; the self-reliance without which we would have had no Pilgrim Fathers, no hardship-defying pioneers, and no eagerness today to push to ever widening horizons in every aspect of our national life.
>
> The Social Security program furnishes, on a national scale, the opportunity for our citizens, through that same self-reliance, to build the foundation for their security. We are resolved to extend that opportunity to millions of our citizens who heretofore have been unable to avail themselves of it.[16]

With the clear, unequivocal support for Social Security by a Republican president, opposition to the basic program became increasingly marginalized. During these years, opponents of Social Security did not disappear, but they became a negligible, minority voice.

FINANCING ISSUES DOMINATE THE SOCIAL SECURITY AGENDA: MID-1970S TO 1983

A number of factors in the mid-1970s breathed new life into the cause of those who wanted to dismantle Social Security.

In 1973, Egypt and Syria attacked Israel. The Organization of Petroleum Exporting Countries (OPEC) announced that its members would ship no oil to the United States or any other country supporting Israel in the war, and would quadruple the price of oil worldwide. Lines at gas stations around the country grew long, sometimes snaking for miles, and prices of everyday goods skyrocketed. The price of food jumped 20 percent.[17] Inflation overall climbed steadily and rapidly, to 11 percent in 1974.[18] Meanwhile, unemployment rates soared. By 1975, unemployment reached 8.5 percent,[19] the highest since before World War II.

For the first time in its history, Social Security was projecting deficits.

Although critically important for helping stabilize the incomes of the old, disabled, and surviving family members, the automatic cost-of-living adjustments enacted in 1972 made the financing of the program more sensitive to economic change. Never before had the nation experienced simultaneously double-digit inflation, sluggish wage growth, and high unemployment brought on by the shock of the OPEC oil embargo. These conditions caused Social Security's income to grow more slowly than projected, while at the same time increasing the program's outgo more than had been projected. Social Security started to project a short-range shortfall. Moreover, demographic changes, including declining birthrates, increased life expectancies, and the aging of 76 million baby boomers,[20] while well understood and anticipated by experts, nevertheless resulted in long-range shortfalls that had to be addressed at some point. To make matters worse, the long-range shortfall was very large due to a technical flaw introduced in 1972, when the cost-of-living and other automatic adjustments were implemented.[21]

Sensational headlines proclaiming the impending bankruptcy of Social Security, together with the declining trust in government as a result of the recent Watergate scandal, gave opponents of Social Security the opening they were looking for.

Around this same time, a conservative infrastructure of think tanks, conservative campus newspapers, and other organized outreach efforts, backed by large sums of money, was built. The "bankruptcy" of Social Security was an inviting focus for this new infrastructure.

Giving added hope to these organized opponents of Social Security was the election of Ronald Reagan as president in 1980. Like Barry Goldwater, whom he had supported for president, Reagan had been an outspoken critic of Social Security. But he understood the politics. When called out on his position by president Jimmy Carter in a presidential debate during the 1980 election,

Reagan stated, "I, too, am pledged to a Social Security program that will reassure these senior citizens of ours that they are going to continue to get their money."[22]

Reagan remained a hero of the newly invigorated conservative movement, but his statement recognized reality. Social Security was so widely and deeply supported that in the early 1980s, a senior aide to Speaker of the House Tip O'Neill dubbed Social Security "the third rail of politics," a reference to the electrified subway rail that results in instant death when touched.[23] The reference implicitly warns politicians that opposing Social Security will result in political death.

By April 20, 1983, at a ceremony signing into law the Social Security Amendments of 1983, which eliminated Social Security's short- and long-range projected shortfalls, President Reagan, no longer calling for radical reforms to Social Security, declared: "This bill demonstrates for all time our nation's ironclad commitment to social security. It assures the elderly that America will always keep the promises made in troubled times a half a century ago. It assures those who are still working that they, too, have a pact with the future. From this day forward, they have our pledge that they will get their fair share of benefits when they retire."[24]

OPPONENTS FIND NEW TACTICS: EARLY 1980S TO THE PRESENT

President Ronald Reagan's signature on the 1983 amendments to the Social Security Act was disheartening to opponents of the program. The legislation and Reagan's signing statement highlighted for opponents what they had known for a while. They had to change their tactics.

Unlike the early years, when Social Security was just getting started, it had now proven its worth. Built to provide a basic floor of protection in good economic times and bad, by the mid-1980s it had been working well for four decades. Today, eight decades after its enactment, Social Security is so fundamental to the well-being of the nation's families that it is almost impossible to imagine its absence. It is the nation's largest children's program, providing support directly or indirectly to nearly 11 percent of the nation's children,[25] as well as insuring almost all of the nation's children against lost income in the event of disability, death, or old age of a working parent.[26] It is the nation's largest disability program, providing support to nearly 11 million permanently and seriously disabled workers and their families, while insuring the wages of nearly all workers and their families in the event of their loss as the result of serious and permanent disability.[27] And as half or more of the income of almost two out of three senior beneficiary households,[28] and more than seven out of ten disabled beneficiaries,[29] Social Security provides the nation's foundation for what should be a secure and dignified retirement after a lifetime of work. Even in the midst of the nation's 2007–2009 Great Recession, Social Security's earned benefits were paid on time and in full.

The 1983 legislation was perhaps a wake-up call for opponents. Aware of the powerful support that Social Security generates, they realized that instead of objecting to Social Security on ideological grounds, they needed to undermine public confidence in the future of the program.

Just two months after President Reagan signed the 1983 amendments, a libertarian think tank held a conference on Social Security, and then published the resulting papers in its fall volume. A particularly revealing piece was entitled "Achieving Social Security Reform: A 'Leninist' Strategy," which outlined a plan and strategy to dismantle the Social Security system.[30] The plan appears to provide a blueprint for almost exactly what has unfolded over the subsequent thirty years: neutralize the support of older Americans by reassuring them that their benefits will be untouched, undermine the support of younger Americans by convincing them that the program is unsustainable and that they can do better investing on their own, and convince Wall Street to get involved to increase their profits.

Opponents, with the aid of the well-financed conservative think tanks and other infrastructure, began attacking Social Security, seemingly in an effort to see what might stick. They claimed that Social Security is unfair to the poor because it wastes benefits on those with higher incomes, unfair to the rich because they could do better investing on their own, unfair to African Americans because they have shorter lives on average than whites and so will collect retirement benefits for fewer years, unfair to children because too much is being spent on seniors, and unfair to every other group for whom they could conjure up an ostensibly plausible argument. (All of these claims are refuted in chapter 10.)

In the 1990s, when Social Security began to project a manageable shortfall, decades away, these same forces latched onto the news, proclaiming that Social Security was once again going bankrupt. A wonderful program, some claimed, but badly in need of modernization. In its present form, though, they asserted, it just was not sustainable.

And in 2000, opponents of Social Security saw the election of a president who, unlike Reagan, would seek to radically change Social Security. Once safely elected to a second term, president George W. Bush employed these new tactics and pulled one very old tactic out of mothballs. Just like Alf Landon's 1936 attack, he asserted that Social Security's reserves were nothing more than IOUs—just paper, backed by no "real" assets—and were no guarantee that future benefits would be honored. (This charge too is refuted in chapter 10.)

Following the Leninist strategy to the letter, Bush told those age 55 and older that they would get their benefits, but advocated that the program allow young workers to divert some of their Social Security contributions into individual private accounts. Though his privatization proposal would have ended Social Security as we know it, he called Social Security "one of the greatest achievements of the American government, and one of the deepest commitments to the American people."[31] He justified dismantling it as his effort to "strengthen and save [it]."[32]

Today, many prominent politicians are proposing to dismantle Social Security to "save" it. Many may not even understand the implications of what they are proposing. They, like the American people, may be convinced that Social Security is unaffordable. But they nevertheless understand the dangers of grabbing this third rail of politics.

Today, even politicians who may not see that they are undermining Social Security nevertheless talk about cutting it in veiled language. Social Security, Medicare, and Medicaid in today's parlance are generally referred to as "entitlements," a change in language purposely advanced by the opponents of Social Security. The word is not well understood by the general public and so offers a code for engaging in opaque discussions about cutting these programs. The word also hides from view that it is not spending on seniors, but rising health care costs, private as well as public, and large tax cuts benefiting the very well-off that are the causes of our long-range budget deficits. The word, which started as a neutral budget term and as a description of programs where the right to a benefit is established under the law, has a subtle pejorative undertone to it as well. Sounding like a government handout to those who consider themselves entitled, and insinuating that Social Security and Medicare benefits are not earned compensation, the word serves to undermine the dignity of people receiving benefits from these programs.

For more than three decades, the conversation about Social Security in Washington and across the mainstream media has been disconnected both from the facts and the preferences of the American people. It has become conventional "wisdom" that Social Security is unaffordable, headed for bankruptcy, and that it will not be around for younger workers.

Everyone knows, say the elites, that the problem is that people are not saving enough or working long enough. Everyone knows, says the same inner circle, that spending on the old is crowding out spending on the young and burdening them with crippling debt. And everyone knows that, with the aging of the population, resulting in more beneficiaries receiving Social Security and relatively fewer workers paying into the system, Social Security is unsustainable.

Left unexplained is the reality that we remain the wealthiest nation in the world, capable of investing in both the young and the old. Left largely unspoken in questions about Social Security are the impacts of rising income and wealth inequality, stagnant wages, growing health care costs (private as well as public), and a tax system that has encouraged larger percentages of wages to be paid in deferred and noncash forms. Also largely unstated by most politicians is that today's military expenditures and tax benefits for the well-off dwarf those in the 1950s and 1960s. Left unexplained is that today's children stand to lose the most if the proposals advanced by those seeking to cut the program become law. Also left unexplained is the reality that, notwithstanding recessions and slowed economic growth, the nation's per capita income (after adjusting for inflation) is more than twice as large today as it was forty years ago, and that after-tax income is expected to grow substantially in the decades to come. Most fundamentally, what rarely gets mentioned is that whether Social Security benefits should be cut, expanded, or left alone is a matter not of demographics or math, but of our priorities, of what kind of a society we want for ourselves, our children, and our grandchildren.

The everyone-knows "facts," which aren't facts at all, and the accompanying failure to entertain differing views have resulted in a distorted debate: not about whether, but how to cut Social Security, given the public's overwhelming support for the program. It is no surprise that the debate has had this flavor. It has resulted from a deliberate campaign, backed by hundreds of millions of dollars. But the efforts have not been successful, because the premises are false and the policy solutions fly in the face of what Americans want; because this institution is deeply valued.

Understanding how wide and deep the support for Social Security is, these forces have, in recent years, tried to enact changes to Social Security through expedited procedures and comprehensive pieces of legislation, dubbed a "Grand Bargain." Because they understand how popular Social Security is, they claim "crisis" where none exists, and seek to cut the program behind closed doors and without significant public review.

These forces have held center stage—until now—and they have had far too much influence on the conversation. Experts who disagree have written dozens of books that have gone largely unread. Analysts have pointed out the factual errors in blog posts that have been ignored by the mainstream media. The insularity of the debate over Social Security is the result. But the time has come to let new voices into the debate.

THE PENDULUM BEGINS TO SWING BACK

Fortunately, at the time of this writing, the conversation is beginning to shift. Powerful forces have taken notice, though, and begun to push back. When senator Sherrod Brown, from the swing state of Ohio, gained press attention with his co-sponsorship of a bill to expand Social Security, the *Washington Post* immediately decried the idea by pointing out that "the rich have finite resources" (though failing to ever make a similar point about the poor and middle class whose benefits the *Post* regularly urges be cut).[33] When senator Elizabeth Warren of Massachusetts went to the Senate floor and the airwaves talking about the value of expanding Social Security, the *Wall Street Journal* ran an op-ed slamming her for her support of expansion and warning Democrats against "follow[ing] Sen. Warren . . . over the populist cliff."[34]

But this genie will not easily be put back in the bottle. Nor should it.

The truth is that an expanded Social Security system is an important step in addressing serious challenges facing America's workers, their families, and the nation. These challenges include: the economic insecurity of a majority of today's seniors; the nation's looming retirement income crisis, which is threatening today's workers; the increasing financial pressure on families and family caregivers; and growing income and wealth inequality.

Whether the American people through their elected officials use Social Security to address these challenges is a matter of politics and choice. In the chapters that follow, we invite our readers—concerned citizens, the general public, politicians, activists, policy experts, and journalists alike—to consider how much is at stake for you, your family, your neighbors, and the nation. And we invite you to think about what can and should be done to expand Social Security, and about what we can do together to build on this uniquely American institution that those who preceded us left as a legacy for us and those who will follow.

2

SOCIAL SECURITY WORKS FOR
ALL GENERATIONS

GENERATIONS OF AMERICANS BUILT OUR SOCIAL SECURITY system, and they constructed it extremely well. Social Security has worked efficiently for nearly eighty years, never failing to meet its obligations, even during the deep recession that followed the near-collapse of the economy in 2008. And, if the public's will is respected, it will be with us as long as there is a United States.

The importance of Social Security cannot be overstated. The most reliable source of retirement income for seniors and working Americans, Social Security is also the primary disability and life insurance protection for the vast majority of Americans, including the nation's children. Each month, 165 million workers make Social Security contributions,[1] and over 58 million receive earned benefits totaling $834 billion during 2014.[2]

Whatever age you are now, you, every member of your family, your neighbors, and every American alive today benefits from Social Security. We benefit individually, starting with the first day of life. We benefit together as a result of the kind of country Social Security has helped create.

Perhaps you are a new parent, aware of the promise and vulnerability of the baby you hold in your arms, the financial responsibility to provide, the moral responsibility to nurture. Social Security can't advise you on how to rear your child, but it can, and does, provide the nation's most important life and disability insurance for

21

your family in case the unimaginable happens. If a working parent of dependent children dies or is so seriously and permanently disabled that he or she is unable to work, Social Security is there.

Though premature death or severe disability may seem unimaginable, those tragedies happen all too often. We do not like to think about our mortality or the potential onset of severe disability, but the reality is that a 20-year-old worker has a more than one in four chance (27 percent, to be precise) of becoming disabled and a one in eight chance of dying before reaching age 67.[3]

If a 30-year-old worker who is married with two young children and who earns around $30,000 a year were to die, Social Security would provide the surviving family the equivalent of roughly $550,000 in life insurance. If that same 30-year-old did not die but became so seriously and permanently disabled that he or she could never work again, Social Security would provide benefits equivalent to disability insurance with a face value of about $580,000.[4]

Or perhaps you are middle-aged, helping your kids through college, and anticipating retirement ten to fifteen years in the future. Social Security cannot assure that you will meet your financial goals, but it is the floor of protection upon which you build for your retirement years.

Reflect on some of the people you know, on family members who live in dignity in old age because they can count on a monthly Social Security check that they or another family member earned. Older persons—maybe you, your mother, father, grandmother, grandfather, aunt, or uncle—who outlived modest savings, or possibly never had much to begin with, continue to live independently thanks to Social Security. Think of friends whose family relied on Social Security to pay the bills when a working parent died or was seriously disabled.

Consider that by providing an orderly way for individuals to contribute during working years, in exchange for financial protections against premature death, disability, and old age, Social Security takes some of the tension out of family life and reinforces the independence and dignity of many. Knowing that one's parents have Social Security often frees up the generation in the middle to direct more family resources toward their own children.

Think, too, of how Social Security, like the nation's highway system, is so embedded in the everyday life of our nation's families, communities, and economy that it is barely noticed. When focused on, it is virtually impossible to imagine an America without this institution running seamlessly, day in and day out, protecting the economic life of our families and communities. Think of the nation before Social Security, when growing old was something to dread, when death or disability could leave families to beg on the streets, and think of the nation that Social Security has created: one in which loss of wages does not result in destitution, but in a secure, guaranteed source of income that each of us has earned.

Social Security transformed the nation. It eradicated what once was a primary anxiety for the vast majority of Americans: the terror of growing old penniless, dependent, and vulnerable. It provided basic economic protection not previously available to most households. It enabled, as historian Andrew Achenbaum observed, "ordinary workers to take advantage of relatively worry-free time" in their older years, something "that the wealthy took for granted."[5] It ended the complete destitution that often accompanied the death or serious injury of a breadwinner. Again, its importance cannot be overstated.

This chapter briefly explains how Social Security works, the vision on which it is based, and the enormous good it does for everyone in our diverse yet United States of America. (A more complete description of the details of how Social Security works can be found in appendix A.)

A PRACTICAL, TIME-TESTED MEANS OF PROTECTING ALL GENERATIONS

Some talk about the need to modernize Social Security, but its fundamental structure is thoroughly modern. Just as in 1935, when Social Security was enacted, most Americans today are dependent on wage-paying jobs to afford the necessities of life. To be economically secure, workers and their families must have insurance against the loss of those wages. To protect against the loss of wages when laid off and unable to find immediate new employment, workers need unemployment insurance. To protect against lost wages due to disability, they need disability insurance. In case they die leaving dependents, they need life insurance for their families. If they are fortunate enough to live to be very old, they need old-age annuities that they cannot outlive. Social Security is insurance against the loss of wages in the event of disability, death, or old age. (Unemployment insurance, which is wage insurance in the event of unemployment, was part of the Social Security Act of 1935, but is not generally called Social Security.)

Throughout its history, many have described Social Security as forced savings, but it is not. It is easy to confuse wage insurance in the event of old age on the one hand, and retirement savings accounts on the other, because both are focused on protection in old age—a state virtually all of us hope to reach, and most of us will. However, this similarity obscures fundamental differences.

Retirement savings are, at best, poor substitutes for wage insurance. Most workers in this country find that they have insufficient savings for even short-term needs. But even if a worker was willing and able to sacrifice current consumption in order to maintain his or her standard of living in retirement, he or she would confront unanswerable questions: How much savings is enough? How much is too little? How much is more than necessary? If too little is saved, one risks destitution if wages are lost. Even if complete destitution is avoided, saving too little may force people to sell their homes, move from their neighborhoods, and cut all expenses drastically. If too much is saved, one needlessly reduces one's standard of living decades in advance of the contingent event, which may never occur.

Workers who, over their working lives, want to save the amount needed to replace their pre-retirement wages each and every year until their deaths would have the impossible task of trying to predict all sorts of eventualities that actuaries know for groups, but that no one can know for an individual. Those worker-savers would have to know in their late teens or 20s, at the start of their working lives, what their wages will be at the time of their retirement, at what age they will retire and whether they will have worked and saved every year until that retirement date, or whether they will have had periods of no wages or even periods of dissaving for more immediate expenses, such as child care, medical costs, and other necessities. They would also have to know their rate of spending in retirement. Extensive medical costs or the need for long-term care can result in the rapid drawdown of savings.

Those saving for retirement also have to accurately predict how long they will live, since, if they do not live until retirement, they will not need to save anything for that eventuality. On the other hand, if they are fortunate enough to live to the age of 105, they will have to save substantial amounts—twenty more years of support than they would have needed if they died, for example, at age 85.

Such uncertainties—easily estimated for groups, but impossible to determine for individuals—require an insurance solution, not savings. Wage insurance such as Social Security, where the benefit is explicitly designed to replace wages, is precisely geared to this goal and, in the case of Social Security, provides protection in the event of death or disability before reaching retirement. Wage insurance, not savings, is the most effective way to protect workers and their families when wages are lost as a result of disability, death, or old age. Savings are fine as a supplement—for those who are able to save—but not as a substitute.

Wage insurance, not simply savings, and not just welfare, as we elaborate in chapter 7, is what is needed to prevent economic devastation and mitigate economic hardship. Where welfare programs seek to relieve extreme financial problems and require that participants be poor, Social Security, in addition to helping to maintain the standard of living of its beneficiaries, prevents extreme financial distress in the first place. Built on the principle of universal coverage, it provides a social means of pooling risks. In exchange for making relatively modest work-related contributions over many years, this wage insurance provides individuals and their families with a floor of protection against predictable risks.

In addition to the mistaken view that Social Security is savings or welfare, some view Social Security simply as a government spending program, undifferentiated from other federal spending, and the employer payments and deductions from wages that support the program as merely a payroll tax, undifferentiated from other taxes. But Social Security is, more accurately, group insurance, supported primarily by premiums paid by workers and their employers.

SOCIAL SECURITY'S FINANCING

Social Security insurance contributions or premiums (often called payroll taxes) have always been and, under current law, always will be the primary source of money from which Social Security's benefits are paid. A second, smaller source of revenue is investment income. From the beginning, in any year that Social Security has more income than it needs to cover all benefits and related administrative costs, the surplus is held in trust and invested in interest-bearing treasury bonds, backed by the full faith and credit of the United States: the safest investment on the planet. (If you have heard that the trust funds aren't real and the bonds are worthless IOUs, you will want to read chapters 8 and 10!) In addition to premiums and investment earnings, Social Security has had a third revenue source—income generated every year since 1984 from treating a portion of Social Security benefits as taxable income. (Unlike revenue from the taxation of other income, the revenue that is generated by the taxation of Social Security benefits is dedicated to Social Security and goes into its trust fund accounts, rather than into the general operating fund of the government.)[6]

Social Security is conservatively financed and managed. Employers often pay all the costs of private pension benefits, but Social Security requires every worker to contribute as well. Benefits cannot be paid unless Social Security has sufficient revenue to cover not only the cost of those benefits, but the cost of administering them as well. As figure 2.1 shows, Social Security ran a $32 billion surplus in 2013 (the most recent year for which there is data at the time of this writing), which was added to its accumulated and growing reserve of $2.8 trillion.[7] (Again, if you have heard this money has already been spent, please read chapter 10.)

SOCIAL SECURITY'S BENEFITS

Because Social Security is insurance, workers and their families are only eligible for benefits if workers have made sufficient contributions to be insured. Social Security benefits, whether claimed as the result of retirement, disability, or old age, rely on the same benefit formula.[8] The formula determines the amount of monthly

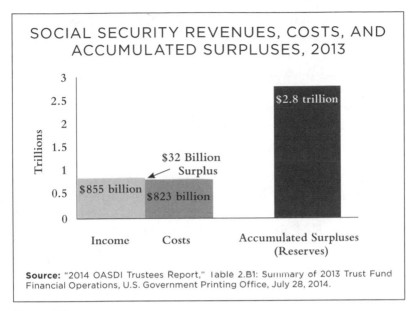

Figure 2.1

benefits workers get if they claim their retired worker benefits at their statutorily defined retirement age, also known as a worker's "full retirement age" or "normal retirement age."[9] If workers become disabled or die before retiring, they are treated as if they died or became disabled on their full retirement age.[10]

The full retirement age was 65 for most of Social Security's history, but as a result of changes enacted in 1983, Social Security's full retirement age is gradually increasing to age 67. Workers may claim their retired worker benefits as early as age 62, but their benefits will be permanently reduced for every month receipt begins before their full retirement age. Similarly, workers may claim their retirement benefits after full retirement age, in which case their benefits will be permanently increased for each month they delay receipt up to age 70.

Social Security's benefit formula is one of its most ingenious and important features. The more you earn and the more you contribute, the higher your benefit in absolute dollars. In recognition, though, of the fact that those with lifetimes of lower earnings generally have less discretionary income, the formula yields benefits that are a larger proportion of the wages of those with lower earnings. Those lower earnings could be the result of a lifetime of low-wage jobs. They also could be a function of years with no wages as the result of unemployment, illness, uncompensated caregiving, or other factors. Figure 2.2 shows the larger dollar amounts received in 2014 by those with higher earnings, and the larger proportionate amounts received by those with lower earnings.

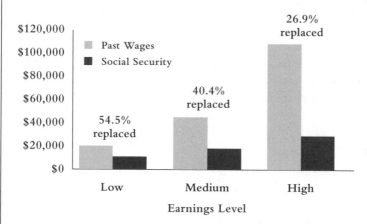

HIGHER EARNERS RECEIVE LARGER DOLLAR AMOUNTS, LOWER EARNERS RECEIVE HIGHER BENEFITS IN RELATION TO PRIOR EARNINGS

Replacement Rates for Workers Retiring in 2014 at Age 65

Note: "Medium" earners, whose career-average wage-indexed earnings ("Past wages") were about equal to Social Security's Average Wage Index (AWI: $45,128 for 2013), and who retired at age 65 in 2014, received $18,251 in Social Security benefits in 2014. "Low" earners, whose past indexed wages averaged 45 percent of the AWI ($20,308), received $11,077. "High" earners, whose past wages were at or above the Social Security contribution cap for each year from age 22 onward (averaging $108,570), received $29,209 in Social Security benefits in 2014. (Earnings in excess of the maximum contribution cap are excluded from these calculations.)

Source: Michael Clingman, Kyle Burkhalter, and Chris Chaplain, "Replacement Rates for Hypothetical Retired Workers," *Actuarial Note* 2014.9, Social Security Administration, July 2014.

Figure 2.2

Social Security also recognizes that even when workers have earned the same wages, those with families generally have less discretionary income than those without dependents. Consequently, based on the same benefit formula, benefits are provided to spouses; divorced spouses, when the marriage lasted at least ten years; dependent children, including adult children who became disabled prior to age 22; and, in some cases, benefits for grandchildren and parents of workers.

Social Security's benefits are essential but modest in amount. Figure 2.3 shows the average benefit levels of representative beneficiaries.

Social Security's wage insurance includes a number of valuable features that are not found in the private sector. For example, private sector annuities and defined benefit pensions reduce the monthly annuity amount of the primary insured or worker if a spouse is added. In contrast, Social Security's annuities provide add-on benefits for spouses, without reducing by a penny the worker's own benefit. Moreover, if the worker has been divorced after having been married ten years, there are add-on spouse and widow(er) benefits for the divorced spouse, again without reducing the worker's benefit. Very importantly, benefits are annually increased to offset the effects of inflation, without limit, regardless of the rate of that inflation.

AVERAGE MONTHLY SOCIAL SECURITY BENEFITS, DECEMBER 2013

All retired workers	$1,294
Aged couple with both receiving benefits	$2,111
Widowed caregiving parent and two children	$2,593
Aged widow(er) alone	$1,243
All disabled workers	$1,146
Disabled worker, spouse, and one or more children	$1,943

Source: "Fact Sheet on the Old-Age, Survivors, and Disability Insurance Program," Social Security Administration, February 4, 2014.

Figure 2.3

NOTHING DOES IT BETTER THAN
SOCIAL SECURITY

Change the title of Carly Simon's 1977 hit song "Nobody Does It Better" to "Nothing Does It Better" and you have a good summary statement of how exceptional Social Security is. Social Security is not just good insurance; it is the best.

First, it is the most secure insurance available. Current benefits are funded largely from the contributions paid by current workers, with the promise—held together by the power and authority of the federal government—that current workers will themselves receive benefits when they become eligible.

Unlike private insurance companies or employers, the federal government will never go out of business. Moreover, it has the power to tax. Legislative oversight, annual reports by program officials, and reviews by actuaries and independent panels of experts provide an early warning system for financing imbalances that will arise from time to time. The authority and taxing power of government, as well as the self-interest of political leaders and the public to protect promised benefits, guarantee the continuity and financial integrity of Social Security. (As for Social Security going "broke," don't believe it. Read chapters 8 and 10 for discussions of that claim.)

It is also the most efficient insurance around. Insurance works best—that is, it is most cost-effective and efficient—when the risk pool is as broad as possible and there is no "adverse selection." Adverse selection is when those who are most at risk purchase the insurance, creating an unusually expensive pool that results by necessity in more expensive insurance. For example, if everyone who has been diagnosed with a terminal illness buys life insurance when they receive the diagnosis and no young, healthy people buy it, the cost of that insurance will be much more expensive. The risk pool for wage insurance is broadest when all wage earners are covered. Adverse selection is virtually impossible when participants must pay premiums starting at the moment they first start earning wages, receiving their first paychecks.

Only the federal government can mandate coverage of all workers, and require participation as soon as they enter the workforce and begin to earn wages. Because the federal government is not competing for market share, there are no advertising costs, broker fees, or other marketing costs. Overhead is lower because it is administered by civil servants, not highly paid CEOs, and there is no money taken out for profits. Not surprisingly, Social Security's administrative costs are far lower than private sector insurance and pensions. Less than a penny of every Social Security dollar collected and spent is used for administration.[11]

Social Security is also the most universal insurance, covering such hard-to-reach workers as household employees, farm workers, other intermittent and seasonal workers, part-time workers, full-time workers working part-time for multiple employers, independent contractors, other self-employed workers, and all employees of small businesses, irrespective of the size. And Social Security is extremely fair in its distribution of benefits, seeking to address the twin concerns of individual fairness and social adequacy.

Today, nearly all workers—93 percent—are covered by Social Security.[12] Social Security is completely portable from employer to employer, but imposes few administrative costs on employers. It is carried from job to job; records are kept seamlessly by the Social Security Administration (SSA) through the use of Social Security numbers. Wages from all covered employment are automatically recorded by the Social Security Administration and used in the calculation of benefits. No adverse selection is possible, because every covered worker must pay Social Security insurance contributions or premiums as soon as they start to earn wages. This universality and pooling of risks to which we are all exposed are part of the vision that underlies Social Security.

PUTTING MORAL AND RELIGIOUS VALUES INTO ACTION

Social Security is a trust based on broadly shared civic and religiously based principles: concern for our parents, for our neighbors, for our children and for the legacy we will leave those who follow. The program combines individual responsibility—benefits are based on individual work effort—with a deep understanding that our nation is strongest when we share both our prosperity and our risks.

President Franklin Roosevelt understood that government is nothing other than all of us working together. In a fireside chat explaining his plan for Social Security, Roosevelt described the program as self-help, in which Americans were "to use the agencies of government to assist in the establishment of means to provide sound and adequate protection against the vicissitudes of modern life—in other words, social insurance."[13]

The president's secretary of labor, Frances Perkins, also understood this. She spoke of how America "evolved the ethical principle that it was not right or just that an honest and industrious [person] should live and die in misery." "[T]he people are what matter to government," she explained, and "a government should aim to give all the people under its jurisdiction the best possible life."[14]

A practical solution that provides protection to all of us, Social Security reflects the solidarity across generations that is integral to a well-functioning society. Our needs and capacities vary throughout life. Early on, we receive more than we give; during working years, this balance shifts; and in later years or in disability, the balance may shift again. No matter who we are or how able we are, we are interdependent. Our lives are intricately bound to our families and others, and to the institutions that support us during our lives. An embodiment of this interdependence, Social Security balances individualism with an understanding that individuals thrive in the context of families and communities. Social Security unites generations.

Douglas Brown, an architect of the Social Security Act, put it another way. He spoke eloquently of an "implied covenant," arising from a deeply embedded sense of mutual responsibility that "rests on the fundamental obligation of the government and citizens of one time and the government and citizens of another time to maintain a contributory social insurance system."[15] Indeed, its financing and functioning are based on a mutual interest and interdependence, since how one generation fares in retirement will directly depend upon how the next generation is doing in its working years.

SOCIAL SECURITY WORKS FOR OUR DIVERSE NATION

This chapter ends where it began. Social Security works for all of us. Today, 165 million working Americans earn Social Security's disability, survivor, and retirement protections for themselves and their families.[16] Social Security pays $834 billion in benefits to more than 58 million beneficiaries—nearly one in five Americans (18.1 percent).[17] Figure 2.4 shows how Social Security is not only a program for retirees; it is, more accurately, a family protection plan.

With 38 million retired workers and nearly 9 million people with severe disabilities receiving monthly benefits, it comes as no

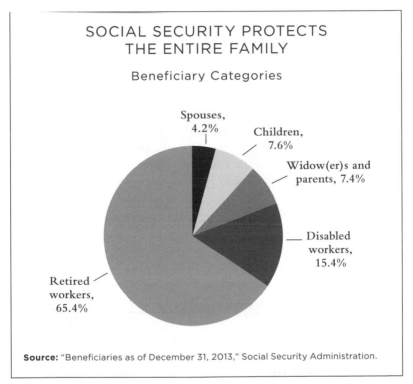

SOCIAL SECURITY PROTECTS THE ENTIRE FAMILY

Beneficiary Categories

Spouses, 4.2%
Children, 7.6%
Widow(er)s and parents, 7.4%
Disabled workers, 15.4%
Retired workers, 65.4%

Source: "Beneficiaries as of December 31, 2013," Social Security Administration.

Figure 2.4

surprise that Social Security works for seniors, disabled workers, many spouses, widows, and widowers.[18] Less well understood:

- **Social Security works for young and middle-aged families.** Many people do not realize the full importance of the life insurance and disability protections workers earn for themselves and their families. There is no more secure life and disability insurance available. When unexpected tragedy strikes, these benefits go a long way toward enabling families to maintain their living standards. And as today's young and middle-aged workers age, Social Security will be every bit as important to them in old age as it is for their parents and grandparents.

- **Social Security works for children.** Social Security is the nation's largest and, despite its modest benefits, most generous children's program. Its protections are by far the most important life and disability safeguard available to virtually all of the nation's 74 million children under age 18.[19] Each month, 4.4 million dependent children—about 3.4 million under age 19 and 1 million adults disabled before age 22—receive Social Security checks totaling about $2.5 billion.[20] Another 4.8 million children live in homes where all or part of the household income comes from Social Security.[21] So it is not surprising that, in addition to protecting the children of middle-income workers, Social Security lifts 1 million children out of poverty.[22] And it is the single most important source of income for the 7.8 million children being raised in a household headed by a grandparent or other older relative.[23]

- **Social Security works for people of color.** Having less savings and less supplemental pension protection, people of color generally rely on Social Security more than white, non–Hispanic Americans.[24] According to the Commission to Modernize Social Security, people of color do not use Social Security in the same way as whites do, relying more on disability and survivors' protections, often due to such disadvantaged circumstances as higher rates of disability and health problems, and holding more physically arduous employment.[25] Because their average income tends to be lower, people of color benefit more from the way Social Security's benefit formula provides a disproportionately larger benefit for low-wage workers and their families.

- **Social Security works for women.** As Terry O'Neill, president of the National Organization for Women, said, "Social Security is a 'women's issue.'" Indeed, the majority (55 percent) of adults receiving Social Security are women.[26] Women live longer than men and are less likely to have pension income.[27] They need to count on a steady stream of income for more years, especially in advanced old age when health expenditures may have depleted their other assets.

- **Social Security works for veterans and their families.** In serving those who serve our nation, Social Security pays benefits averaging more than $16,000 a year to more than 9.6 million veterans[28]—about four in ten veterans. Nearly all of those who are not Social Security beneficiaries today will be so in the future. And very importantly, Social Security provides critical frontline protection for family members dependent on those who have served or are serving to protect our nation. As a 2011 report titled "Social Security: Serving Those Who Serve Our Nation" explained, "the vast majority of the Active Duty community's [709,776] spouses and 1.2 million children, and the Total Selected Reserve community's [400,991] spouses and [731,632] children, are eligible for Social Security's disability and life insurance benefits if a service member retires, becomes severely disabled, or dies."[29] That's why nearly 5,000 children who lost a parent in the Iraq and Afghanistan wars are now receiving survivors benefits,[30] and many more of the children of the roughly 771,000 wounded servicemen and service women are receiving disability dependents benefits.[31]

- **Social Security works for same-sex couples and their families.** Until recently, there was no way for lesbian, gay, bisexual, and transgender (LGBT)[32] persons in committed same-sex relationships or marriages to receive the same spousal, widow(er)s', and family-related benefits for children as everyone else. Fortunately, discriminatory barriers

are falling due to the Supreme Court striking down significant portions of the Defense of Marriage Act on June 26,
2013. Same-sex couples married and living in states that
recognize their marriages as legal are now eligible for the
full range of Social Security benefits. Serious barriers still
exist but, in time, full recognition of the civil rights of these
Americans seems inevitable. In the meantime, legislation
has been introduced to expand Social Security to same-sex
married couples, irrespective of the state in which they reside. (As appendix C notes, such legislation has been introduced in both the Senate and the House of Representatives.)

For those interested in knowing more about how Social Security
works in your state and county, take a look at the fifty state and six
related jurisdiction reports (e.g., Puerto Rico, Guam) published
each year by Social Security Works, available for download at
www.socialsecurityworks.org.

As important as Social Security is today, its importance is likely
to be even greater in the future. The next four chapters identify
a number of challenges facing the nation. An expanded Social
Security system is a solution to all of them.

PART TWO

THE CHALLENGES

3

THE PRECARIOUS LIVES OF TODAY'S OLD

FALSE, DEROGATORY STEREOTYPES ABOUT OLDER AMERI-
cans abound. Former Republican senator Alan Simpson (R-WY)
has given particularly ugly voice to the noxious stereotype that seniors are self-centered retirees, driving luxury cars, enjoying endless
rounds of golf, and leaving mountains of debt for their grandchildren by fighting cuts to Social Security benefits they don't need. He
routinely calls seniors and national senior organizations who object
to cutting Social Security "greedy geezers," "old cats 70 and 80
years old . . . who live in gated communities and drive their Lexus
to the Perkins restaurant to get the AARP discount."[1] Despite polls
showing that the overwhelming majority of Americans oppose Social Security benefit cuts, he categorizes opponents as follows:

> Who are the people howling and bitching the most?
> The people over 60. This makes no sense. You've got to
> scrub out [of] the equation the AARP, the Committee
> for the Preservation of Social Security and Medicare,
> the Gray Panthers, the Pink Panther, the whatever.
> Those people are lying. . . . [They] don't care a whit
> about their grandchildren . . . not a whit.[2]

Senator Simpson's vitriolic attacks should be ignored as ignorant ravings of little consequence. Unfortunately, as co-chair of
President Obama's 2010 deficit commission, Simpson was given a

megaphone along with a gavel. And he's enjoyed using that mega-phone. "I've made some plenty smart cracks about people on Social Security who milk it to the last degree," he proudly proclaimed. "You know 'em too. . . . We've reached a point now where it's like a milk cow with 310 million tits!"[3]

Instead of correcting such false and disparaging stereotypes, the media, more often than not, have given Simpson and his less flam-boyant comrades-in-arms a pass. For example, *Washington Post* op-ed columnist Dana Milbank wrote that Simpson "deserves some slack when he speaks about 'greedy geezers,'" and praised his com-ments for "being colorful, provocative and *honest* in an arena that discourages all three."[4] (Emphasis added.)

But pejorative stereotypes about the old (or any other group) are unacceptable and undermine civil discourse. Further, the informa-tion conveyed by these stereotypes is just plain wrong. So we cor-rect the record in this chapter.

HOW FARE TODAY'S OLD?

It is false that most older Americans are on "easy street." A very small percentage are; many more are poor, or near poor. Some seniors maintain a very modest middle-class lifestyle, often strug-gling to make ends meet. Others, often those employed or retired with significant pension and savings, may be very comfortable in the moment. But that can change with loss of employment, death of a spouse, costly illness, drops in housing prices, or precipitous declines in stock portfolios.

Numbers provide a snapshot of how today's old are doing at just one point in time. Over time, the finances of any of us—even those who were well-off at younger ages—can, and often do, change dra-matically and for the worse. Take, for example, the story of Emma and James M., retired in 1993 at ages 64 and 62, respectively.[5]

An accountant and nurse with good work histories, Emma and James had accumulated $350,000 in their company-sponsored 401(k) retirement plans and had another $75,000 in savings and in-vestments, plus their Social Security. With their Columbus, Ohio, home paid off and their children through college, they looked for-ward to enjoyable retirement years. The first ten years were just that—travel, civic involvements, friends, and grandparenting—notwithstanding James' diagnosis in 1997 of Parkinson's disease, controlled fairly well with medication.

Unfortunately, by 2003, James showed further deterioration—slurred speech, memory loss, depression, and difficulty managing personal hygiene. By 2005, taking care of her husband's needs had become too hard for Emma to do alone. She contracted with a home-care agency to provide personal care and chore services three days a week, expanding to seven days, before James entered a nursing home in 2008 as a private pay patient, costing roughly $70,000 a year. Besides James and Emma drawing heavily on their joint resources, the deep recession and drop in housing prices further diminished their resources. When James died in 2013, Emma, then 82, had very little other than her home and Social Security. She worries how she'll get by if she needs support one day. If the roof needs to be replaced.

Even more dramatic, Neil Friedman's story, as reported in the *Wall Street Journal*, shows that Social Security is important for everyone, even the wealthiest Americans. Ponder how life can change in an instant.

Neil Friedman saw virtually all of his life's savings vanish on the morning of December 11, 2008, when investment adviser Bernie Madoff's Ponzi scheme was revealed. Friedman had invested $4 million with Madoff, including his pension. He never had an inkling that Madoff's investments were fraudulent until the day he learned that the money was gone. Now 79 and widowed, he relies completely on Social Security to get by, supplemented only by the meager income he earns selling notecards each Sunday at a flea market in Palm City, Florida. The notecards he sells bear witness to the prosperous lifestyle he and his wife lived prior to the disappearance of their nest egg—photos of trips to Antarctica, Australia, and many other destinations. Fortunately for him, he still has Social Security.[6]

DEFINING ECONOMIC WELL-BEING IN TERMS OF POVERTY AND NEAR-POVERTY

The economic well-being of older Americans can be measured in a number of ways. One measure involves subsistence: whether or not people have enough income to purchase the bare necessities of life. Widely used for fifty years and adjusted annually for inflation, the Census Bureau's official U.S. poverty index establishes poverty thresholds for households, adjusted for such factors as number of people, presence of children, rural/urban location, and age. Ironically, it sets a higher poverty line for adults under age 65 than for those over 65—$11,945 for individuals under age 65 compared to $11,011 for those over age 65 in 2012; $15,374 for couples under age 65; $13,878 for couples over 65.[7]

Why the difference? The short explanation: the measure assumes that older people eat less![8]

Figure 3.1 shows how many seniors live in poverty or in "near poverty," defined as between 100 percent and 125 percent of the official poverty line. When you look at the chart, keep in mind just how low the official poverty line in 2012 was for seniors ($11,011 for individuals and $13,878 for couples).[9] And the "near-poor" line, defined as 125 percent of poverty, is not much more: just $13,764 for individuals and $17,348 for couples.

Responding to criticisms of the official poverty measure, the Census Bureau and the Bureau of Labor Statistics worked with other federal agencies to develop a new measure, the Supplemental Poverty Measure, first used in Bureau reports in 2011.[10] The new index, which is not used for official purposes, but is instructive, is a much more refined measure, incorporating items left out of the official measure—including out-of-pocket health expenses, work expenses, child care, the value of noncash benefits such as housing assistance, taxes paid, tax credits, housing type, and geographic differences in the cost of housing. Under this more refined measure, the poverty rates of the old jump from 9 percent to 15 percent in 2011.

Even more striking is how many people are at significant economic risk. Defining persons below the Census Bureau's Supplemental Poverty Measure as poor and those between 100 percent and 200 percent of this measure as having very modest income, at any one point in time, nearly half (48 percent) of senior households, age 65 and over, live in poverty or very modest circumstances.[11] In other words, nearly half are either already unable to meet some

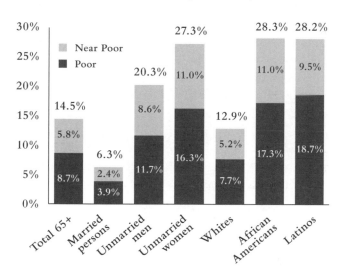

SENIORS IN POVERTY OR NEAR POVERTY BASED ON OFFICIAL POVERTY MEASURE

Based on Family Income, 2011

Legend: Near Poor, Poor

Category	Total value	Near Poor	Poor
Total 65+	14.5%	5.8%	8.7%
Married persons	6.3%	2.4%	3.9%
Unmarried men	20.3%	8.6%	11.7%
Unmarried women	27.3%	11.0%	16.3%
Whites	12.9%	5.2%	7.7%
African Americans	28.3%	11.0%	17.3%
Latinos	28.2%	9.5%	18.7%

Note: "Near poverty" is defined as 125% of the poverty line, which for seniors in 2011 was $10,788 for one-person households (near-poverty threshold: $13,485), and $13,596 for two-person households (near-poverty threshold: $16,995).

Source: "Fast Facts and Figures about Social Security, 2013," Social Security Administration, August 2013, p. 9.

Figure 3.1

basic needs such as food, clothing, and shelter, or are one serious economic setback away from not being able to do so. The percentage of women in this category of economic vulnerability is even higher. More than one out of two—52.6 percent—are poor, or economically vulnerable and at risk. For African Americans over age 65, the percentage is higher still—63.5 percent. For Hispanics, the percentage is 70.1 percent.[12]

Moreover, this economic vulnerability increases with age. Fifty-eight percent of those age 80 or over are poor or just one shock away from becoming poor. An astounding three-quarters of African American and Hispanic women age 80 or over are also very much at risk! These percentages are summarized in figure 3.2.

Despite the stereotype of wealthy seniors, the economic security of even those seniors who do not fall into the various categories of economic vulnerability is not assured. Their incomes are likely to decline considerably as they advance in age; as they leave work; as inflation bites into their assets; as they draw down savings, which

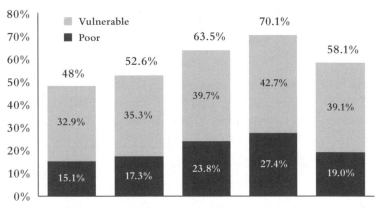

NEARLY HALF OF ALL SENIORS ARE ECONOMICALLY VULNERABLE

Incomes in 2011 Under 200% of New Supplemental Poverty Measure

Note: Data on poverty (defined as having income less than 100% of the SPM threshold) are for 2011; data on vulnerability (defined as having income less than twice the SPM threshold) are averaged from 2009–2011. All data are based on family income.

Source: Vulnerable seniors: Elise Gould and David Cooper, "Financial Security of Elderly Americans at Risk," Appendix Table 1, Economic Policy Institute, June 6, 2013. Poor seniors: Benjamin Bridges and Robert V. Gesumaria, "The Supplemental Poverty Measure (SPM) and the Aged," Table 6, *Social Security Bulletin* 73, no. 4, June 13, 2014.

Figure 3.2

will accelerate if their or a spouse's health declines; or if investments falter or unexpected financial expenses arise.

DEFINING ECONOMIC WELL-BEING IN TERMS OF MAINTENANCE OF STANDARD OF LIVING AND WEALTH

Another measure is not whether people can remain out of poverty—quite a low bar—but whether they can maintain their standards of living when wages are lost. Even if not in dire poverty, most people do not want to be forced to alter the way they have been living (e.g., put off necessary repairs or sell their homes). Consequently, financial planners and economists often measure income adequacy of the old based on the idea that the goal of retirement income planning for individuals should be to maintain their standard of living no matter how long they live. They talk about "replacement rates," the percentage of pre-retirement income that needs to be replaced by post-retirement income—sources such as Social Security, private pensions, and income from assets. Most suggest that this level varies between 65 and 85 percent, with higher-income persons having to replace less because they generally, among other things, move into lower tax brackets when they leave work; no longer need to save and, indeed, have savings to draw on; and sometimes have paid off their home mortgages. But, again, conditions can change.

Social Security, which, as we discuss below, is the main source of income for most seniors, replaces only about 40 percent of an average worker's wages, as figure 2.2. in chapter 2 illustrates. Moreover, these already modest replacement rates are gradually declining, as chapter 4 discusses. In addition to having the means to cover current expenses, financial advisers generally emphasize how critically important it is to protect against costly contingencies, such as illness, inflation, and longevity. You may not think you will live to age 100 or even older, but consider that, in 2010, 53,364 Americans were over age 100[13] and that the Census Bureau estimates there will be 690,000 centenarians in 2060.[14] You may someday be among them!

Another important measure of how older households are faring is wealth. To many it may seem that the old are doing well when newspapers report that the median net wealth of older households was $170,516 in 2010. But such reports only tell part of the story. When the value of home equity is excluded, it reveals that the median wealth is just $27,322—seemingly having much more in common with an empty nest than a nest egg.[15]

No matter how measured, older Americans, on average, are doing better today than they were in 1960, when living standards were lower, Social Security benefits were smaller, and Medicare and Medicaid did not exist. Investments in the economy and social programs, along with hard work, have yielded greater economic security for today's older adults. The poverty rates of persons age 65 and over dropped from 35.1 percent in 1959 to 9.1 percent in 2012, according to the official poverty measure. The median income for elderly households—the dollar amount that half of older households are below and half above—rose from $23,124 in 1960 to $34,832 in 2013 (in 2013 dollars).[16]

But, contrary to the claims of those who want to cut your Social Security, facts such as these do not mean today's seniors are living high on the hog. Drilling down into these measures shows that only the rare outlier has income that we commonly associate with being rich, as figure 3.3 shows.

This should not come as a surprise because, for the large majority of older households, Social Security is the single most important source of income, and its benefits are modest at best.

THE IMPORTANCE OF SOCIAL SECURITY

Among beneficiary households with at least one person age 65 or older, almost two-thirds receive at least half of their income from Social Security. More than one-third receive all, or almost all, of their income from Social Security.[17] That's why, when some politicians call for "little tweaks" in Social Security's level of benefits or argue that they are simply advocating giving a small "haircut" to Social Security benefits, the amounts may sound small to those with higher incomes, but not to those seeking to get by primarily or exclusively on Social Security.

And that is most seniors. Figure 3.4 underlines the importance of

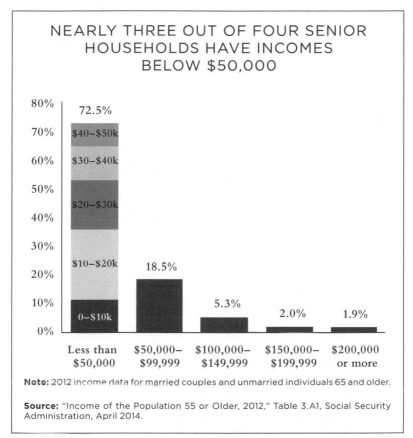

NEARLY THREE OUT OF FOUR SENIOR
HOUSEHOLDS HAVE INCOMES
BELOW $50,000

Note: 2012 income data for married couples and unmarried individuals 65 and older.

Source: "Income of the Population 55 or Older, 2012," Table 3.A1, Social Security Administration, April 2014.

Figure 3.3

Social Security to the finances of older people. More than 75 percent of the income going to the bottom 60 percent of senior households—those with less than $35,493 in income in 2012—comes from Social Security. Social Security is also, by far, the most important income source going to the 20 percent of senior households with incomes between $35,493 and $63,648.[18]

An uptick since the mid-1990s in the labor force participation of seniors, especially those age 65 to 75, is increasing the importance of earnings, but as figure 3.4 shows, the benefit of earnings flows mainly to better-off and, likely, younger senior households.

In looking at this figure, it is important to remember, as Emma

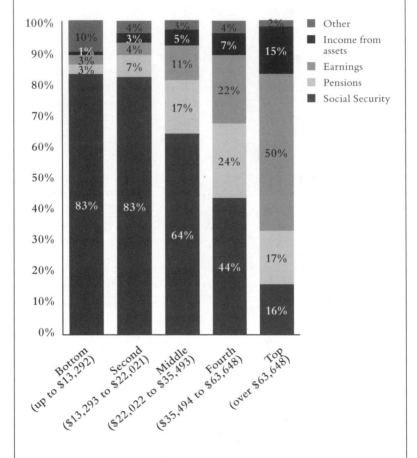

SOCIAL SECURITY IS BY FAR THE LARGEST PART OF THE INCOME OF THE VAST MAJORITY OF SENIORS

Shares of Total Income for Households Age 65+ by Income Quintile, 2012

Source: "Income of the Population 55 or Older, 2012," Table 10.5, Social Security Administration, April 2014.

Figure 3.4

and James M.'s story exemplifies, that this breakdown is just a snap-shot in time, revealing income in a single year. It does not show how the fortunes of the old can change over time—how some start off their older years in very comfortable financial circumstances but later face major difficulties.

So keep in mind that many of those represented by the bar that is farthest to the right in figure 3.4—the top one-fifth of senior households, those with more than $63,648 in income—are still working. They are still receiving a large proportion of their incomes from earnings and have often not yet begun drawing down assets.[19] Once they leave work, however, their earnings will disappear, and their incomes are likely to shrink. Over time many will join the ranks of those senior households with lower annual incomes.

Through good times and bad, Social Security has been, and remains, the most important source of income going to people age 65 and over. Indeed, it is more important today than it was in the 1960s and 1970s.[20]

SENIORS AT GREATEST RISK TODAY

As important as Social Security is for virtually all of today's older Americans—and will be in the future—there is still much to be done to achieve the promise of economic security in old age. Expanding Social Security is important for all of us, but it is especially important for older women, people of color, the LGBT community, low-wage workers, many early retirees, and the oldest old.

Women: Women are at greater risk, even with Social Security, than men are of suffering large declines in income in old age, and possible impoverishment. Persistent gender gaps in wages, societal expectations that women will leave work to perform caregiving duties (for both children and aging parents), greater longevity, and lower rates of private pensions and savings compared to men all contribute to this increased risk. Because of their longer average life expectancies, women are also at greater risk of outliving their resources, as well as having them greatly erode in value, since—with the exception of their Social Security—what supplemental pensions they do have are generally not protected against inflation.[21]

Women comprise 56 percent of Social Security beneficiaries age 62 and over, and almost 67 percent of beneficiaries age 85 and older. Single women age 65 and older received 50.4 percent of their income from Social Security, compared to 35.9 percent for elderly single men and 32 percent for elderly couples.[22] Without Social Security, the poverty rate among older women, according to the official poverty measure, would increase from the current 11 percent to 48 percent.[23] But, as the upcoming story of Theresa B. illustrates, even *with* Social Security, the economic status of women can be precarious, especially for those who are single as a result of divorce, the death of a spouse, or never marrying.[24] The poverty rates for such women are among the highest for any subgroup in the country. While the poverty rate for a married couple (over age 65) is only 5.4 percent, the poverty rate for a woman living alone (over age 65) is 18.9 percent.[25] Take the case of Theresa:

Theresa is a 59-year-old college-educated white woman living in Rainbow City, Alabama. She married at age 25 but was divorced at 30. She remarried at 33 and has two children from that marriage. Her husband, a building contractor, left her eight years later. She managed to get child support and half their savings of $25,000, which helped her get by while the children were young. She has worked as a preschool teacher and also selling cosmetics at a department store. However, she has not held a full-time job since 2000, when her mother developed cancer and required Theresa's full-time care. Her mother is now deceased, but Theresa still lives with her father, a former mechanic who is 92 and requires constant care. As Theresa approaches her own retirement years, she has no savings and no supplemental pension. Her father receives a monthly Social Security benefit of $1,100. (In 2014, his Medicare Part B premium, which is deducted directly from his check, reduced his monthly benefit by $104.90, and out-of-pocket health care costs take a bigger bite each year since they are outpacing his annual cost of living increases.) Because Theresa was not married to either of her former spouses for at least ten years, she is ineligible for spousal benefits and must qualify for Social Security solely on her own limited earnings record. According to her most recent Social Security earnings statement, Theresa's Social Security would be $985 a month if she waits until age 66 to start her benefit, but less than $738 a month if she takes her Social Security when she turns 62, which she thinks she will need to do.[26]

People of color: Similarly, Social Security is extremely important to African Americans, Hispanics, and other people of color. Disadvantaged minority populations are more likely to have lower lifetime earnings, due to a variety of factors, including lower educational attainment, employment discrimination, physically challenging employment, and higher rates of unemployment. They are also more likely to suffer disabilities. Social Security is designed to provide economic protection against these disadvantages. It especially benefits those who have lower lifetime earnings and longer periods of unemployment. Moreover, Social Security protects workers and their families economically against the risks of disability and premature death.[27] Social Security is also particularly important to minority workers and their dependents because they have far lower rates of employer-provided retirement, life, and disability insurance coverage.[28]

In 2012, among beneficiary households with at least one person age 65 or over, Social Security provides at least 90 percent of the income for 46 percent of African Americans, 53 percent of Latinos, and 44 percent of Asians.[29] Without Social Security, the poverty rate among African American seniors would triple, from 17 to 50 percent, and the poverty rate among Hispanic American seniors would rise from 19 to 50 percent.[30] Because of their poorer health and more physically demanding jobs, these groups tend to rely more heavily on Social Security's disability and survivor protections as well.

LGBT community: Because members of the LGBT community also suffer discrimination in the workplace, Social Security is particularly important to them as well. Indeed, as a result of the so-called Defense of Marriage Act, members of this community who were committed to each other nevertheless were not entitled to the spouse, divorced spouse, and widow(er) protections that heterosexual couples enjoyed. Thanks to the recognition of same-sex marriages in more and more states, together with the 2013 Supreme Court case holding unconstitutional major parts of the Defense of Marriage Act, these protections are now increasingly available for this segment of the American community.

Low-wage workers and many early retirees: Many of today's seniors who accepted permanently reduced Social Security benefits are also at special risk. The vast majority of Social Security retirees in 2009—2 million out of 2.7 million—accepted permanently reduced benefits before reaching the full retirement age of 66. Nearly half, 1.3 million, accepted these benefits at age 62, when benefit reductions are largest.[31] Many who have accepted reduced benefits over the years had little or no choice due to health and employment circumstances. Twenty-seven percent of all workers age 60 to 61 report a "work-limiting health condition," with higher percentages reported for minority workers—36.5 percent of African Americans and 31.5 percent of Latinos.[32] Moreover, 45 percent of workers age 58 and older work in jobs that are either physically demanding or have other difficult working conditions.[33] These older workers are likely to have great difficulty holding a job and are primed to become disadvantaged retirees.

Social Security's companion program, Supplemental Security Income (SSI), plays an important role in assisting the most low-income elderly persons. In 2014, SSI provided a federal income guarantee of up to $721 a month for individuals and $1,082 for couples[34] to roughly 8.4 million low-income, severely disabled, blind, or aged (65 and over) people.[35] Some states provide modest supplements on top of the federal guarantee. Even so, SSI fails to provide income that permits more than the bare necessities.

The oldest old: The reliance on Social Security is even greater as people age and exhaust other sources of support. For beneficiary households with at least one person age 80 or over, three out of four rely on Social Security for half or more of their income. For almost one out of two—47 percent—Social Security constitutes 90 percent or more of their income.[36] For widowed, divorced, or never-married women, and for people of color, the percentages are even higher at those ages.[37]

HEALTH AND LONG-TERM CARE EXPENSES PLACE SENIORS AT RISK

As vital as Social Security is, past policymakers understood that it is necessary, but not sufficient, to insure against loss of earnings in old age. They understood that seniors would remain economically vulnerable as long as they were one serious illness away from bankruptcy. That recognition led to the enactment of Medicare and Medicaid, institutions that have gone a long way in protecting older families.

Medicare has done much to protect the finances of older persons (and persons with severe disabilities) and open up access to hospital-based care, important physician and outpatient services, limited rehabilitation services, and pharmaceutical services. Many elders have supplemental Medigap insurance or other forms of insurance that provide additional protection. Medicaid, in turn, finances hospital and outpatient medical care, long-term care services in nursing homes, and limited long-term care services at home for low-income elders, some who have always had low incomes and others who have expended their resources.

Even so, today's seniors remain exposed to very significant out-of-pocket health expenses. Adjusted for inflation, out-of-pocket expenditures of seniors grew from $3,865 in 1992 to $5,197 in 2010, consuming more than one-third, or 37 percent, of the average Social Security benefit by 2010.[38] Worse yet, Fidelity Investments estimates that a 65-year-old couple retiring in 2013 will, on average, spend $220,000 out-of-pocket for medical expenses, consuming "61 percent of their Social Security payments by 2027."[39] And this estimate does not include the cost of long-term care, which in a nursing home today tops $80,000 a year![40]

While Medicare and Medicaid have expanded access to health care for seniors, today's elders, even upper-middle class elders, remain very much at risk because of uncovered health and long-term care expenses.

THE RIGHT TO DIGNITY IN OLD AGE

No one who has worked hard throughout life and played by the rules should face poverty or fear of financial calamity in old age.

That's why it is time for the nation's leaders to take a sober look at the reality of old age in America, and not be seduced by shrill, ignorant claims about so-called greedy geezers. Notwithstanding how critically important Social Security, Medicare, and Medicaid are, almost one out of two seniors still are economically vulnerable today, as shown above in figure 3.2. And if Social Security is not expanded, tomorrow's seniors are likely to be even more threatened, as we explain in the next chapter.

4

THE COMING RETIREMENT INCOME CRISIS

YOU'VE HEARD ABOUT BOOMERANG KIDS—ADULT CHILDREN in their 20s and 30s who have returned to live in their parents' homes. Well, get ready for boomerang parents, formerly independent middle-aged people who—ten, fifteen, twenty years hence— will have no choice but to move into their adult children's homes because they cannot afford to maintain their own.

While politicians and journalists have been distracted for years by a faux crisis in Social Security, a very real crisis has gathered momentum and threatens to undermine the plans and hopes for a secure retirement of tens of millions of today's workers.

Congressional champions are beginning to sound the alarm. Retired senator Tom Harkin (D-IA) warns that the "retirement crisis is worse than most people realize. . . . [The] difference between what people have saved for retirement and what they should have at this point—is a staggering $6.6 trillion, and half of Americans have less than $10,000 in savings."[1]

"Add up . . . the dramatic decline in individual savings and the dramatic decline of guaranteed retirement benefits and employer support," explains senator Elizabeth Warren (D-MA), "and we're left with a retirement crisis—a crisis that is as real and as frightening as any policy problem facing the United States today."[2] And President Obama has weighed in, explaining, in his 2014 State of the Union address, that, "Today, most workers don't have a pension. A Social Security check often isn't enough on its own."[3]

But Washington is just catching up to what too many Americans have already discovered the hard way—that the American Dream of maintaining one's standard of living in retirement after a lifetime of work—never a reality for millions of workers—is endangered for nearly all but the wealthiest among us.

Testifying before the United States Senate Special Committee on Aging, Joanne Femino Jacobsen, age 63, talked about why she cannot ever see herself retiring, even though she has worked her entire life—eighteen years with AT&T while earning a college degree at night, twelve years with Verizon until being laid off at age 52, and then learning a new trade leading to positions in real estate appraisal, sales, and training, and as a town tax assessor.[4]

But it's not just workers in their early 60s who are worried. Currently a temporary worker, Karen O'Quinn, age 46, explains: "I worked for corporate America for many years and after being laid off, I had to re-create myself. I ,like millions of people in this country, have no retirement and no savings for retirement. I do not know how I am going to make it."[5]

Small business owner Brian Edwards, age 39, says, "I have a 401(k), but now that I am self-employed nothing else is getting put into it. It is basically sitting there."[6]

Childbirth educator Alana Rose, age 29, explains that at "this time, I am not able to save for retirement. My business is not profitable enough to pay all my bills and save for retirement." David Muse, a 53-year-old audio technician, warns, "You work until you either fall apart, your health totally crumbles, or you die." And C. William Jones, a retired executive, age 79, worries that his "kids and grandchildren are really going to have a difficult time, because as of right now, I don't know what kind of pension they can depend upon."[7]

These are but a few examples of Americans caught in the crosshairs of the nation's emerging retirement income crisis. As we explain in this chapter, the crisis is most acute for those in their mid-40s, 50s, and early 60s—those nearing retirement age—whose prospects for a secure retirement have been greatly diminished by already enacted cuts to Social Security, the declining availability of occupational pensions, the inadequacy of 401(k)s and other retirement savings vehicles, the loss of savings as the result of the Great Recession, and the stagnation of wages. And, depending on how things play out, the crisis is likely to affect those just entering the workforce as much as, or even more than, today's older workers.

THE RISE AND FALL OF RETIREMENT SECURITY

Before Social Security, growing old was widely feared. In 1912, Lee Welling Squier, a pension expert, described this fear:

> After the age of sixty has been reached, the transition from non-dependence to dependence is an easy stage— property gone, friends passed away or removed, relatives become few, ambition collapsed, only a few short years left to live, with death a final and welcome end to it all—such conclusions inevitably sweep the wage-earners from the class of hopeful independent citizens into that of the helpless poor.[8]

The fifty years following the enactment of the Social Security Act of 1935 ushered in what some, a bit too effusively, called the golden age of retirement in America. Rising wages, improving standards of living, Social Security, Medicare, Medicaid, home ownership, senior housing, congregate meals, Meals on Wheels, other federally funded social services, and employer-sponsored pensions meant that most Americans could count on at least a modicum of economic security in old age, leaving them free to choose to continue or discontinue work, pursue new interests, recreate, give to family and community, and live with their children or by themselves. Not that aging in America was without problems. Yet from 1935 until near the end of the century, things appeared to be moving in the right direction.

Although not a reality for everyone, the promise of the 1950s and 1960s was that Social Security would provide a secure foundation upon which workers could build a secure retirement from a combination of Social Security, employer-provided pensions, and personal savings. Those workers could look forward to the possibility of a period of leisure after a life of hard work.

Unfortunately, fewer and fewer workers today feel confident in that ability. While no one thinks that a return to poorhouses and the mass insecurity in old age that preceded Social Security is around the corner, working-age Americans are increasingly worried about their ability to maintain their standards of living in retirement. Allianz Life Insurance Company reported, from its 2010 survey of 3,257 people, that "an overwhelming 92%" answered that they absolutely (44%) or somewhat (48%) believe that the nation faces a retirement income crisis, with "more than half (54%)" of persons ages 44 to 49 saying they are "totally unprepared" for retirement.[9] In its 2013 retirement confidence survey of 1,003 workers, the Employee Benefit Research Institute (EBRI) found that only "13 percent are very confident they will have enough money to live comfortably in retirement," the lowest ever reported in the twenty-three years of conducting this annual survey.[10]

During the so-called golden age of retirement, a metaphor for secure retirement income became popular: a three-legged stool, with the three legs representing Social Security, employer-provided pensions, and savings. Coined in 1949 by a prominent actuary who worked for the Metropolitan Life Insurance Company,[11] the stool was a useful image for those promoting private pensions. But it was never accurate, because the legs were never equal. Even for the half of the workforce fortunate to have employer-provided pensions, Social Security was generally the most important and secure source of retirement income. A more apt picture of the patchwork of retirement income would have been a pyramid, as in figure 4.1.

But recent events and trends render even the more accurate pyramid image irrelevant. Indeed, Peter Brady, an economist with the Investment Company Institute, suggests that "instead of a stool" most Americans "have a pogo stick: Social Security" to negotiate their retirement years—which goes a long way in explaining why working Americans are increasingly fearful.[12] Although Social Security is much more stable than a pogo stick, the three-decade-long, billionaire-funded campaign to undermine confidence in the program, discussed in detail in chapter 9, may make the receipt of

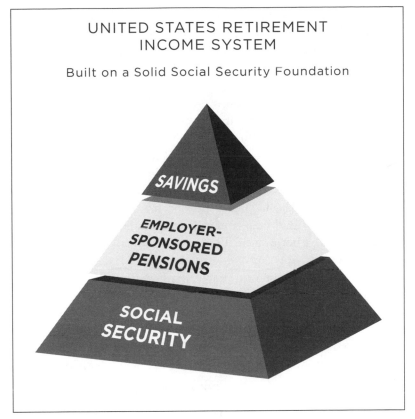

Figure 4.1

benefits feel less secure than it is. Moreover, the benefits by themselves are inadequate, and diminishing.

SOCIAL SECURITY'S BENEFITS HAVE ALREADY BEEN CUT

Not widely recognized, the Social Security foundation is gradually weakening. Social Security benefits have been chipped away, and will be roughly 24 percent lower for workers born after 1959.[13] Here's why.

In 1983 Congress passed legislation that included significant reductions in benefits. Very importantly, the 1983 legislation raised

Social Security's full retirement age from age 65 to 67, a change that is still being phased in.[14] The 1983 amendments set full retirement age at 66 for those born in 1943 through 1954. It will then gradually increase to age 67, fully phased in for those born after 1959.

For those not thoroughly immersed in how Social Security benefits are calculated, increasing Social Security's "full" retirement age sounds like just a small, reasonable adjustment for changes in life expectancy. But that is not right. Rather than a single, fixed retirement age, it is more accurate to think of Social Security as having a band of ages. Workers may claim benefits as early as age 62. For every month they delay, benefits are increased to take into account that they will be received for one month less.

Consequently, because of the way that Social Security benefits are calculated, raising the age defined in the Social Security Act as the "retirement age" by one year is mathematically indistinguishable from about a 6.5 percent cut in retirement benefits, whether one retires at age 62, 67, 70, or any age in between. Raising the statutorily defined retirement age sounds like it should mean that if you work longer, you will eventually get what you would have gotten. But you never actually do catch up. If the definition of retirement age is changed to be an older age, you always get less than you would have without the change.

This point is complicated and not well understood, even by some experts. Because the use of the phrase "full retirement age" lends to confusion, please, as you read, keep in mind that the important thing to understand about retirement age increases is that for every year that Social Security's "full retirement age" is raised, benefits are cut by 6 to 7 percent.[15] It does not matter when someone first claims benefits—at 62 or 70, or somewhere in between. The 1983 enactment, which gradually phases in a two-year increase in the full retirement age from age 65 to age 67, has already lowered benefits by around 6.5 percent. When fully phased in, the change will cut the benefits of those born in 1960 or later by around 13 percent.

In addition to increasing the full retirement age, the 1983 legislation delayed the annual automatic cost of living adjustment by six months, from June to January. Again, it's a bit complicated to understand without knowing the details of benefit calculations, but this delay translates into a 1.4 percent cut for everyone, now and in the future.[16] Finally, decisions made in 1983 and 1993 to treat a growing portion of Social Security benefits as taxable income effectively will have lowered benefits (i.e., net after-tax benefit income) by 9.5 percent in about thirty-five years.

Prior to the 1983 legislation, Social Security benefits were tax free. Since 1984, up to 50 percent of Social Security benefits have been counted as taxable income for individuals with incomes in excess of $25,000; $32,000 for couples. Since 1993, additionally, up to 85 percent of Social Security benefits have been taxed for some individuals with incomes in excess of $34,000; $44,000 for couples.[17] Because these thresholds are not adjusted for inflation, the reduction in effective benefits increases over time.[18] The effective cut is, on average, 6 percent in 2012, 8.8 percent in 2030, and 9.5 percent in 2050.[19]

The result of all these cuts together is that Social Security—by far the most important retirement asset that most working Americans have—is on a trajectory to replace less and less pre-retirement earnings. Even so, it remains the most widespread, effective, secure, and significant source of retirement income for today's workers and those who will follow. This is why it is so important for Social Security's retirement protections to be expanded, especially because, as the discussion that follows shows, the prospects for relief from other quarters are slim to none.

TRADITIONAL PRIVATE-SECTOR PENSIONS ARE DISAPPEARING

Traditional private-sector pensions, also called defined benefit plans, have been disappearing at a rapid rate. Structured to pay employees a pension that generally reflects number of years worked and average earnings, defined benefit plans stand in contrast to defined contribution plans, to which workers, and sometimes employers, make regular, specified (i.e., defined) contributions to a retirement savings plan, but without any guarantee regarding the amount of savings or the monthly benefits that can be derived from those savings if annuitized. The advantage of defined benefit plans for employees is that their employer generally funds it (or most of it) and bears the financial risk of investments and other funding decisions. While employees still carry some risk (e.g., company bankruptcy, unscrupulous raiding of plans, loss of coverage when transferring jobs), anticipated pension income is far more predictable and does not fluctuate with stock market returns.

Even at their height, employer-sponsored defined benefit plans had serious shortcomings. Because they are voluntary arrangements, they have never covered more than about half the workforce. Because, even when available, they vary from employer to employer, they have never been portable—able to be carried from job to job. That has a number of disadvantages. Primary among them is their inadequacy for mobile workers, who might be entitled to benefits based only on the low pay earned at the start of their careers. In addition, private sector defined pension plans, which promise annuities not payable for decades, are inherently insecure. The plan may have insufficient funds when the time for payment arrives, and the employer sponsoring the plan may no longer be around.

The Employee Retirement Income Security Act of 1974 (ERISA) sought to improve the security of private sector defined benefit plans, yet the government regulation has made them less attractive to employers. These arrangements must be funded in advance and must meet minimum standards. Federal fiduciary responsibilities are imposed on those who have responsibility for the plan operation and assets. Benefits are required to be insured by the Pension Benefit Guaranty Corporation. To the extent that private sector employers must conform to federal requirements, defined benefit pension plans are less attractive to those employers.

Other factors have played a role in the disappearance of these arrangements. They generally have been offered where unions could demand them. As regulation of traditional private pensions has increased, as accounting rules have changed regarding how pension liabilities are to be reported, and as unions and manufacturing have declined, employers have increasingly terminated, frozen, or closed their plans to new employees. Today, those plans are nearing extinction in the private sector. Where in 1979, nearly four out of ten private sector workers participated in these plans, in 2011, it's just one out of seven (14 percent).[20] Rather than carry financial costs and risks that come with defined benefit pension plans, many employers have dropped or frozen out new employees from participation, and, in the case of the vast majority of new employers, not ever established defined benefit plans.[21]

PUBLIC PENSIONS ARE UNDER ATTACK

The one place where traditional pensions remain is in the public sector, but they are under sustained, ideological attack. If successful, this attack will have caused a destructive race to the bottom.

With the decline in unions representing private sector workers, private sector traditional pensions have declined. Public sector unions remain strong, and public sector workers continue to have strong pensions. Utilizing a divide-and-conquer strategy, those seeking to dismantle public employee unions and benefits play workers against each other by seeking to turn some workers, labeled "taxpayers," against other workers, labeled "public employees," though, of course, public employees are taxpayers, too.

An Economic Policy Institute report reveals that the "champions of anti-union legislation often portrayed themselves as the defenders of non-union workers—whom they characterized as hardworking private-sector taxpayers being forced to pick up the tab for public employees' lavish pay and pensions."[22] Why should public employees receive "plush pension benefits," they argue, when so many taxpayers do not? Never mind that these benefits were negotiated and earned, that many have forgone more lucrative private sector jobs for public service, and that some are in harm's way every day. Or that the budgetary problems of many states and localities are caused by imprudent tax cuts and the Great Recession. Rather than face up to real problems, it's easier to scapegoat public employees—the first responders, teachers, sanitation and public health workers, community and state college employees, prison personnel, social and mental health service providers, and other civil servants.

The large majority of state and local government employees —78 percent in 2011—and nearly all federal workers still participate in defined benefit plans, but their pensions are increasingly threatened. While some state and local pensions need to be financially buttressed, the attack on public employee defined benefit plans is fueled and driven by ideology and anti-union animus. In fact, the largest cutbacks in state public employee pensions did not take place in states with the largest unfunded liabilities. "Wisconsin, Florida, and North Carolina all had among the best-funded and most solvent public employee pension funds at the start of 2011, yet all three enacted dramatic cut-backs," according to the Economic Policy Institute.[23]

401(K) RETIREMENT SAVINGS PLANS, OTHER SAVINGS CANNOT DO THE JOB

So, Social Security benefits are being cut by about one-quarter, public pensions are under attack, and private employer–provided traditional pension plans are disappearing. When replaced at all, employers are generally substituting tax-favored 401(k) retirement savings vehicles.

But unlike defined benefit pensions, 401(k) plans are savings and not insurance. Consequently, employees bear the risk of sometimes volatile declines in the value of their savings, before and during retirement. Financial management fees and poor investment decisions can undermine growth of these assets. Employers often do not contribute to them at all. And, unlike defined benefit plans and Social Security, individuals can tap these savings, often without penalty, to fund educational, home-buying, and health care expenses—all potentially good uses of household wealth, but also undermining of retirement savings. They are portable from job to job, good for mobile workers, but are no substitute for Social Security.

Well, how much in the way of savings do today's workers have? As employers substituted 401(k) defined contribution plans for traditional defined benefit pensions, the proportion of households ages 26 to 61 having retirement savings not surprisingly increased to roughly one-half.[24] These arrangements have been spectacularly successful for the wealthiest few, but dismal failures for the vast majority of workers. During his run for the presidency in 2012, Mitt Romney disclosed that his individual retirement account (IRA), a 401(k)-type vehicle for those who do not have employer plans, had an account balance of between $20.7 million and $101.6 million.[25] More generally, in 2010, households with the highest earnings—those in the top quintile, or 20 percent—had 72 percent of their total savings in tax-favored retirement savings accounts.

Except for those at the top, though, even households with retirement savings often have far less than needed to maintain an adequate standard of living in their later years. The Economic Policy Institute reports that the "median retirement savings for households," ages 26 to 79 "in the top income fifth [was] $160,000" in 2010, "compared with $8,000–$36,000 for households in the bottom four-fifths."[26] Moreover, the National Institute on Retirement Security finds that the bottom half of all baby boomer households have only 4 percent of its generation's retirement savings, while the top quarter have 83 percent.[27] And looking at those close to retirement is not much more reassuring. The median savings of households ages 55 to 65 is just $100,000, a not inconsequential sum, but far less than needed to help middle-class households maintain their standard of living through twenty or more years of retirement.[28]

And those are the households with retirement savings accounts. As just mentioned, nearly half of all households have no retirement savings. When all households are taken into account, the median account balance was just $3,000 in 2010, and just $12,000 for households age 55 to 64![29]

And other trends are, if anything, worse. The near collapse of the economy in 2007 to 2009, the tepid recovery, and stagnating wages have fed into the retirement income crisis. Despite the stereotype that older people own their homes free and clear of mortgages, AARP's report "Nightmare on Main Street: Older Americans and the Mortgage Market Crisis" tells a different story:

> As of December 2011, approximately 3.5 million loans of people age 50+ were underwater—meaning homeowners owe more than their home is worth, so they have no equity; 600,000 loans of people age 50+ were in foreclosure, and another 625,000 loans were 90 or more days delinquent. From 2007 to 2011, more than 1.5 million older Americans lost their homes as a result of the mortgage crisis.[30]

More generally, with researchers at the Federal Reserve Bank of Dallas "conservatively [estimating] that 40 to 90 percent of one year's output ($6 trillion to $14 trillion, the equivalent of $50,000 to $120,000 for every U.S. household) was foregone due to the 2007–2009 recession," it is not surprising that the retirement income prospects of young and middle-aged workers suffered.[31] Household wealth dropped from a peak of $67.4 trillion before the Great Recession to $51.4 trillion in its depths in early 2009, before climbing slowly to $66.1 trillion at the end of 2012, 91 percent of the pre-crisis total wealth of households.

This sounds fairly good; some would even say we have repaired the damage done to households. But this is not so. Most of the recovery came from the rebound of stocks, much more beneficial to the very well-off than to middle- and low-income households, and this measure does not account for inflation and population growth.[32] When these are counted, the average American household lost 55 percent of its net worth between 2007 and the end of 2012.[33] Younger households, more modest-income households, and people of color suffered the largest losses, especially as housing prices tumbled, unemployment increased, and homes were lost to foreclosure. The retirement prospects of working Americans are further diminished by rising student debt; loans taken by parents to help their children through college; continuing high levels of unemployment; little wage growth, except at the top; and credit card debt.

MEDICAL AND LONG-TERM CARE COSTS THREATEN ALL BUT THE RICHEST

Making matters much worse, out-of-pocket expenditures for medical and long-term care costs pose major risks for all but the richest retirees, now and in the future. As discussed in chapter 3, Fidelity Investments estimates that a typical couple retiring at age 65 in 2013 will need $220,000 just to cover their out-of-pocket medical expenses—Medicare premiums, deductible, and co-payments; the same for supplemental health insurance; uncovered prescription drugs, hearing aids, eyeglasses, and the like.[34] Because the risk of such expenses is not distributed equally, the Employee Benefit Research Institute develops estimates of how much additional savings someone eligible for Medicare will need to pay for out-of-pocket health expenses, not including long-term care. In 2012, 65-year-old men and women needed an additional $70,000 and $93,000 in savings, respectively, to have a 50 percent chance of covering anticipated health expenses; $105,000 and $122,000 to have a 75 percent chance.[35] Even with such additional assets, some will succumb to catastrophic expenses. Neither of these estimates includes out-of-pocket costs for long-term care, always a major risk for the old, especially when the median annual cost of a room in a private nursing home is estimated by Genworth Financial Life Insurance to be $83,950.[36]

No question, absent major policy change, working Americans will be exposed to financial risks arising from medical and long-term care, likely significantly greater than those facing today's 65-year-olds. Remember again the 24 percent cut to Social Security for those born after 1959. Not included in that 24 percent cut is the anticipated increase in out-of-pocket costs under Medicare. Those receiving Medicare are generally also receiving Social Security—Medicare premiums are routinely deducted straight from Social Security checks. Consequently, an increase in Medicare costs is an indirect cut in Social Security income. When the rising cost of Medicare premiums is taken into account, Social Security's effective replacement rates are projected to go from 41 percent for workers with average earnings first accepting benefits at age 65 in 1986, to 39 percent for such workers in 2005, to just 32 percent in 2030.[37] When one accounts for taxation of Social Security benefits as well, that replacement rate in 2030 drops to 29 percent. And as we've discussed, nothing does it better than Social Security.

No surprise, then, that the large majority of working Americans worry about a retirement income crisis, their own and the nation's.

HARD-WORKING AMERICANS OF ALL AGES AT RISK

By virtually all measures, the harsh reality is that the majority of today's workforce—probably the large majority—are heading toward increasingly difficult and, in some cases, financially disastrous retirements.

The National Retirement Risk Index (NRRI), developed by the Center for Retirement Research at Boston College, reveals a large rise in the proportion of households with workers under age 65 on the road to a financially insecure retirement. In 1983, 31 percent were assessed as being at risk of not being able to maintain their standard of living in old age, rising to 44 percent in 2007 and 53 percent in 2010 (see figure 4.2).[38] The NRRI's estimate takes into account the various changes in the U.S. pension and Social Security systems, assumes that everyone works until age 65, and assumes that housing and other wealth are annuitized.

The outlook is even more dismal when anticipated health and long-term care expenditures are counted. The Center for Retirement Research estimated that in 2006 and 2007, just before the Great Recession, 44 percent of working-age households would be at risk of downward social mobility in retirement. But here's

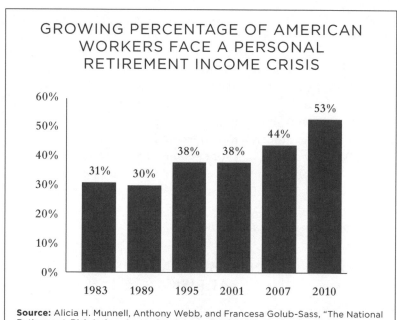

Source: Alicia H. Munnell, Anthony Webb, and Francesa Golub-Sass, "The National Retirement Risk Index: An Update," *Issue Brief* 12-20, Center for Retirement Research at Boston College, October 2012.

Figure 4.2

the scariest part: this percentage rose to 61 percent when health care costs were included.[39] And to 64 percent when long-term care costs were counted—an additional 21 percent.[40] The aggregate risks were estimated to be somewhat greater for Gen Xers than baby boomers. Still more frightening, consider that the Center's post-recession at-risk estimate jumped up from 44 percent in 2006 and 2007 to 53 percent in 2010 (see figure 4.2).[41] If health and long-term care expenses are counted, likely seven out of ten working households today would be at risk.[42] And this analysis is based on conservative assumptions that everyone will work until at least age 65 and takes out reverse mortgages on their homes!

Other analyses tell roughly the same story. Unlike the Boston College measure, which assesses whether households can maintain their standards of living, the Employee Benefit Research Institute (EBRI) produces a Retirement Readiness Rating that measures whether households will have enough resources to pay for "basic" retirement expenses—defined as "aggregate minimum retirement expenditures" and out-of-pocket health and long-term care costs. Using this more restrictive definition, EBRI estimates in 2010 that roughly 45 percent of people born from 1948 to 1974 are at risk.[43]

Noting the paucity of retirement savings—just $3,000 in the average working household—the National Institute on Retirement Security concludes that the "collective retirement savings gap among working households age 25–64 ranges from $6.8 to $14 trillion, depending on the financial measure." That is, the gap between what households will need and what they should have saved by now equals $6.8 trillion if you count the equity Americans have in their homes; $14 trillion if you only count retirement savings.[44]

While virtually every demographic group is at risk, some are more so—including African Americans, Latinos, American Indians, single women, people with disabilities or in poor health, the unemployed, those in the LGBT community, and low-wage workers.

With Social Security retirement benefits declining, with retirement savings schemes falling short for the vast majority of Americans, some are suggesting that working longer, much longer, is the solution to the retirement income crisis. If everyone could work until age 70, the Center for Retirement Research projects that roughly 85 percent of today's workers would be adequately prepared for retirement.[45] While there's nothing wrong with working to 70, 80, 90, or even 100 if you want and are able, beware of political, corporate, and opinion leaders who are selling "brave new world" visions of longer work lives and retirement age benefit cuts as a solution to the retirement crisis. Often unwilling to step outside their privileged social and economic position, they are blissfully unaware, or just do not care, that their "solution" would do great harm to many of those whose life experiences are very different from theirs. They may live in the same city as Joanne Femino Jacobsen, age 63, but they either do not see her or do not care how different her story is from theirs:

> I have worked in some form or fashion since I was 15. I saved money, supported my sons, and planned for my retirement. Yet when I reached what should have been my retirement age, the promise that I would receive health and pension benefits for the rest of my life was broken, and so were my hopes of retiring comfortably in Florida. Like many Baby Boomers battered by the Recession, I am still in the work force and will probably remain on the job for the foreseeable future. The older people like me you see working at places like Wal-Mart and Home Depot[—]a lot of us are not doing this because we're bored with retirement; we're doing it to survive.[46]

Even with the uptick in work among today's older workers, the vast majority of Social Security retirees—1.8 million out of 2.7 million in 2012—accept permanently reduced benefits before reaching the full retirement age.[47] Nearly two-fifths—675,160 in 2012—accept these benefits at age 62, when benefit reductions are largest.[48] The reality is that many of these early retirees have little or no alternative to claiming permanently reduced benefits. The Government Accountability Office found in 2010 that, from 1998 to 2008, 27.7 percent of all workers age 60 to 65 reported a work-limiting health condition, with higher percentages for African

Americans and Hispanics, 36.5 percent and 31.5 percent, respectively.[49] Moreover:

- The Social Security Administration estimates that more than one in four 20-year-olds will be disabled before age 67.[50]
- Twenty to 30 percent of workers in their 60s have work-limiting health conditions.
- One in five older Americans provides care to a family member, care that often compromises their ability to work or that would be compromised if they remained at work.
- Forty-five percent of today's older workers, ages 62 to 69, experience physically demanding or otherwise difficult work conditions.
- Two out of five of today's older workers end up retiring earlier than planned because of poor health, unemployment, caregiving, and the like.[51]

And this says nothing about employment discrimination, which though illegal, still occurs. Since the Great Recession, older workers have generally spent longer periods unemployed, and those lucky ones who found new jobs were on average employed at only 85 percent of what they made prior to losing their jobs.[52] Consider how Appleton, Wisconsin, resident Tonya Adams' story illustrates the problems older job seekers run into.[53]

Tonya Adams lost her job in 2009 at the age of 62. She told the *Wall Street Journal* that with experience as a freelance art director for advertising agencies and as a sales associate, "I never would have dreamed that I could not find a job, that I was unemployable." Unfortunately, like millions of other Americans (particularly older job seekers who can be the victims of age discrimination), she was still without work three years later. As a result, Adams was forced to claim Social Security benefits early, resulting in smaller Social Security checks for the rest of her life. The $1,280 provided by Social Security is not enough for Adams to cover all of her bills. To help bridge the gap, she utilizes food stamps and help from her elderly parents.

Not everyone can work into their 60s; not everyone wants to work into their 70s. Moreover, scheduled increases in the full retirement age to 67 will harm many, and additional increases would harm even more, especially those with health problems or who have worked for low and modest wages. And many working Americans, of all income classes, look forward to, and by the time they are in their 60s will have earned, the right to more choice in how they use their time—to give care, to work longer, to study, to be with grandchildren, to give back to their family and communities, to just plain play.

Providing greater opportunity for Americans to work longer is desirable, as long as the possibility of such work is not used to justify cuts in Social Security's modest benefits, and not used to impose a difficult and unfair set of expectations on older workers. Enforcement of age discrimination laws, flexible retirement, part-time work, retraining opportunities, second and third careers, small-business entrepreneurship, community service, and the like all have a place in our aging society. But the broad experiences of the American people need to be respected. While working longer may be a viable option for some, it is not for all. And even if many Americans worked longer, the crisis would not disappear.

Expanding Social Security remains the single most effective, and the only widespread, solution to the retirement income crisis. And it addresses other serious problems, as the next two chapters explain.

5

THE DEBT OWED TO THOSE WHO CARE

IMAGINE AGAIN THAT YOU HAVE JUST GIVEN BIRTH TO YOUR first child. Most likely everything went well. Your baby is healthy. It looks like you will only need to deal with the normal challenges of reviewing homework; hugging and bandaging your toddler when knees are scraped; attending plays, athletic events, and routine medical appointments; and worrying when your teen starts driving, dating, and making her or his way into the larger world. You give care every day, and while it is not without its challenges, problems, and sacrifices, it is pretty much what you signed up for.

Most likely, everything works out. But there is no guarantee. Your child could be among the one in thirty-three that the Centers for Disease Control and Prevention tells us will be born with a birth defect.[1] Or among the one in five—11.2 million—children under age 18 with special health care needs.[2] A severely disabling accident or illness could strike. No matter what, you'll do what you must because you could not do otherwise. You are just made that way. But the time, angst, and financial costs will be great, possibly so much so that there is little left over for more normal activities of life.

Another thought experiment: Your children are grown and doing well, but your mother, your father, your spouse, partner, or maybe a sibling just had a stroke and lost the ability to function without expensive in-home help. Again, as the 36 percent of adults who provide unpaid care to adults do, you'll do what you must, perhaps providing demanding personal care for many years.[3]

Care—*normal* and *extraordinary*—given by family and friends is the stuff of everyday life in America. It's what well-functioning, and even not-so-well-functioning, families do best. In its absence, children fail to thrive, community bonds fray, and generations— within families and society—cannot progress.

Across the political and cultural spectrum, politicians and other opinion leaders talk about the importance of the family, often praising those who give freely of themselves to care for others, those providing normal, everyday care to children, and those providing extraordinary unpaid care to family and friends with serious illnesses or disabilities. But when it comes to supporting the caregiving functions of families and friends, public deeds generally fall short of words. There are few supports that help share the burdens—emotional, physical, and financial—carried by those giving care, more often than not women. As a result:

- Too many parents of young children are in a proverbial pressure cooker as they juggle work in the home, paid employment, child care, children's schedules, and the rest of life.
- Parents caring for children with serious disabilities are often overwhelmed providing special physical care, supporting their child, accessing special services, and caring for their other children.
- Persons providing significant, ongoing care for family and friends experiencing major illness (e.g., HIV/AIDS, cancer) or whose disabilities severely limit their activities lose income, current and deferred, in the absence of paid leave.
- The health of very old caregivers is put at risk because of the absence of respite and other supports as they care for their spouses, siblings, and others.
- Older parents who have been caring many years for their developmentally disabled children, now middle-aged, often fear what will happen to their children once they themselves have died, because today it is not uncommon for such children to live into their 60s and 70s, or even longer.

THE NATION RELIES ON FAMILY CAREGIVERS

Family and friends regularly provide both normal and extraordinary care. Normal care is generally what is given to and what supports children every day as they grow into adulthood—time, meals, discipline, love, child care when parents need to work, and the like. It is also what is given to family members who are temporarily ill, to grandchildren needing a little supervision when a parent cannot be home, to adult children as they struggle with life choices, and to older relatives needing a little company. With the Census Bureau estimating there were roughly 74 million children (23.5 percent of the U.S. population) under age 18 in 2012, it is not surprising that the vast majority of normal care flows from parents and other adults downward to children.[4]

Estimates of how many people give extraordinary care vary, but are always large. The Pew Research Center reports that 36 percent of all adults provide unpaid care to an adult needing assistance with normal activities of life. Eight percent provide care to children with significant health problems or disabilities.[5] The National Alliance for Caregiving estimates that 65.7 million people provided unpaid care to functionally disabled children or adults in the course of 2009.[6] In any given week of 2009, AARP's Public Policy Institute reports that 42.1 million people age 18 or older provided an average of 18.4 hours of care to functionally disabled adults and that 61.6 million family caregivers provided such care at some point in 2009.[7]

Families, as a *Washington Post* article[8] highlights, are the heart and soul of the long-term services and support system (LTSS), with millions of caregivers echoing the type of sentiment expressed by Barbara Tucker Parker. She and her husband opened their home to care for her 87-year-old mother, Dorothy Tucker, whose dementia, brought on by a stroke in 2009, made independent living impossible. While her mother can still put on her own clothes when Barbara sets them out, she has lost the ability to read, to converse, to remember. What's been lost is "horrifyingly sad," according to Barbara, and the constant care requirements are stressful, but there's nothing else that she could do. Besides she says, "It's work, but there's also a lot of fun." "[I]t's my job . . .

she's my mother." "Who's going to take care of her better than me? Nobody."[9]

Parents and other family members participate in the care of our nation's wounded warriors, such as Sergeant Cory Remsburg, who received a long standing ovation when President Obama recognized him during the 2014 State of the Union address. Suffering devastating injuries from a 2009 roadside bomb in Afghanistan, slowly, and with numerous surgeries, resilience, and the continuing help of his parents, Annie and Craig Remsburg, he fought back, regaining his speech and ability to walk. His parents commuted for two years to be with him at a veterans' hospital in Tampa, his mother eventually leaving employment to help with his ongoing physical therapy. Still needing 24/7 assistance, he moved to his family home in 2013 and has since moved nearby to a specially equipped house with full-time support.[10]

Some estimates drill down to more specific types of extraordinary care. The Alzheimer's Association estimates that "nearly 15 million family and other unpaid caregivers provided an estimated 17 billion hours of care to people with Alzheimer's and other dementias."[11] A U.S. Department of Health and Human Services report identifies nearly one in four U.S. households (23 percent) as caring for one or more children with special needs; that's 11.2 million children, some of whom (27.1 percent) are greatly limited in their activities, while others (34.4 percent), despite having one or more special needs, can do everything other children do.[12] Many young and middle-aged parents invest countless hours and other resources as they care for, advocate for, and love their children with special needs. They are often the backbone, soul, and heart of their children's care team, as highlighted by the following story, written by a mother named Keisha whose son, Ibrahim, was diagnosed with autism at age 2½:

> My heart sunk. . . . I became a little depressed and unsure of myself as a mother, many questions raced through my head: what will become of him, what kind of life [will he] have, how will people treat him, etc.? My husband and I [had] a family meeting [about] . . .

how we could best help Ibrahim throughout his journey. I started looking for information about autism on the Internet since his doctor and daycare had no real information to share. Eventually, I became active and realized that I had to find the strength to advocate for him to ensure his access to the resources he needs. As . . . I help my son along this journey, I hope to help others by raising awareness in my community while steering parents away from cultural biases and the stigma associated with having a special needs child.[13]

We often think of extraordinary care as flowing, as in the story of Keisha and Ibrahim, from parents to children, but this is not always so. For example, the National Alliance for Caregiving reports that 1.3 to 1.4 million children, ages 8 to 18, take on significant caregiving responsibilities, often providing assistance with daily activities for functionally disabled grandparents, parents, siblings, and others.[14]

Similarly, other family members are engaged in the extraordinary commitment of family caregiving. Grandparents and other relatives may step in to care for young children when parents are not able. Nearly 7.8 million children under age 18 live in "grand-families," households headed by a grandparent or other relatives, sometimes with a parent present. More than one-third of these grandparents and other relatives, 2.5 million, are raising these children by themselves.[15] There are grandparents like Melanie, age 60 and rearing four grandchildren, ages 9, 10, and 11, and a 14-year-old who has Asperger's. Their resources are very limited, but the family gets by, she reports:

> I am raising these kids on state assistance, food stamps and death benefits from the 14-yr-old's father. There is absolutely nothing extra to do anything for the kids except things that are free. The same goes for me, so I do not take care of myself very well. . . . My health (arthritis & fibromyalgia) has definitely been affected by the stress. . . . Mom comes to visit every two weeks, so it's

like having 5 kids when she comes. She had been head injured in a car accident when she was young, so is cognitively and emotionally impaired. . . . [I]t is really hard at this age to be taking on the responsibility of these 4 kids, but I love them to pieces and wouldn't trade the experience for anything.[16]

The large majority of people needing long-term services and support live in the community, usually in their own or a family member's home. A small proportion live in residential communities (e.g., assisted living) that provide a range of supportive services. Others are in institutions like nursing homes, state hospitals for the developmentally disabled, and even the nation's prisons and jails, with an estimated 16.9 percent of prisoners experiencing severe mental illnesses.[17] A patchwork of informal and formal supports and services—private and public—provide assistance in people's homes. These include chore and personal care services (e.g., bathing), homemaker, home health, visiting nurse, and other medical and social services. But as the stories related above illustrate, families are the backbone of this system, providing the large majority of care to functionally disabled members—everything from financial management to very personal care, from household chores to monitoring medications, from caring for their loved ones in their homes to visiting them in institutional settings.

A FINANCIALLY VALUABLE NATIONAL RESOURCE

Taken together, informal care and support, normal and extraordinary, represents a huge contribution to the economy and society, not to mention to the well-being of many people.

The future of our economy and communities depends on how well we rear, invest, and educate our children, the next generation of workers, parents, and taxpayers. More than any other institution, the family is responsible for these critical tasks. The federal government estimates that the typical middle-class family will spend $241,080 (in 2012 dollars) rearing a child born in 2012 to age 18.[18]

Of course, many continue to provide much financial support to their young adult children—for education, housing, and the like.

What families spend in actual dollars is just part of the contribution that parents and other adults make rearing children, though. Arguably far more valuable for children is parents' investment of time. Ironically, as MacArthur fellow Nancy Folbre notes, the nation's most significant domestic investment—the care and time given to children—goes uncounted in the most important measure of productive output in the course of a year, the gross domestic product (GDP). That time simply is not factored in. If it were, our GDP would be much larger. Going back to 1979, economist James Morgan estimated the value to the economy of all informal care—normal care directed at maintaining family households (e.g., diapering, preparing meals for children, running errands for an older parent) and extraordinary care directed at sustaining functionally disabled family members. Assigning a value of $6 an hour in 1979 dollars (the rough equivalent of $19.40 in 2014 dollars) to informal caregiving, he estimated yearly transfers within families equivalent to 30 percent of the gross national product.[19]

Caregivers are demonstrably the most valuable economic component of the nation's long-term services and support system, serving roughly 12 million people with significant functional disabilities, 5 million of them under age 65.[20]

- The economic value of informal care to all adults, ages 18 and over, according to AARP's Public Policy Institute was $450 billion in 2009.[21]
- Using different methods and just focusing on the long-term services and supports of elderly persons, the Congressional Budget Office estimates that the economic value of informal unpaid care of family and friends amounted to $234 billion in 2011. In contrast, cash payments from all sources equaled about $192 billion, which included $39 billion in out-of-pocket payments.[22]
- The Alzheimer's Association values what they label the "17 billion hours of unpaid care" to persons with Alzheimer's and other dementias at more than $202 billion in 2010.[23]

- By keeping children out of foster care, "Grandfamilies save tax payers more than $6.5 billion each year," according to the organization Generations United.[24]

WHO GIVES CARE?

Virtually everyone gives and receives care over their lives, obviously some more than others. There's an ebb and flow of resources to individuals and cohorts over time. A one-dimensional, "time-freeze" approach provides an understanding of informal caregiving mainly as a transfer from parents to children, from the strong and healthy to the weak and ill, or from an adult child to a frail elder. Viewed over time, what some call a life-course perspective, it becomes clear that the young child who is being cared for later becomes the parent, the adult child who cares for a functionally disabled parent. The strong and the healthy who are giving care may later become the people who need care.

Individuals and cohorts are often positioned at one point in their development to primarily receive care, but over the course of their lives they are expected to, and nearly always do, provide care to others. Our investments of time, love, and support made to friends and family early in life have a way of coming back to us, not necessarily in equal amounts (whatever that might mean). Human society requires this reciprocity and interdependence, and shifting flows of giving and receiving.[25]

In terms of normal caregiving, there's been considerable convergence over the past fifty years in involvement of fathers and mothers—married and unmarried—in normal child-rearing and housework activities. But, no surprise, women generally still do the lioness's share. Including hours spent on unpaid work (housework and child care) and paid work (jobs), mothers with children in their homes devoted 83 percent of their time to unpaid work in the home in 1965 compared to 59 percent in 2011. Fathers devoted 14 percent of their time to unpaid work in the home in 1965 compared to 31 percent of their time in 2011. In terms of direct child care (e.g., bathing, homework, playing), in 2012 married mothers with children in their homes spent 14.3 hours a week in child care activities; married men, 7.2. Because of the generally greater financial pressures on single parents to work outside the home, the percentages spent by single parents is a bit less than married couples—11.3 hours for single mothers and about 8 hours for single fathers.[26]

As for those providing care to functionally disabled children and adults, there is much diversity with respect to age, gender, race, ethnicity, income status, employment, living arrangements, sexual orientation, and health among caregivers. A 2009 study by the National Alliance for Caregiving in collaboration with AARP provides a snapshot of those giving such care:

> Caregivers are predominantly female (66%). They are 48 years of age, on average. One-third take care of two or more people (34%). A large majority . . . provide care for a relative (86%), with over one-third taking care of a parent (36%). One in seven care for their own child (14%). Caregivers have been in their role for an average of 4.6 years, with three in ten having given care to their loved one for five years or more (31%). . . . Seven in ten caregivers take care of someone 50 years of age or older, 14% take care of an adult age 18 to 49, while 14% take care of a child under the age of 18.[27]

A few more generalizations about those providing extraordinary care:

- Nearly three-quarters (73 percent) had been employed, and one in five took leave from work at some point when giving care.[28]
- Most spend, on average, about twenty hours a week giving care and have been providing care for several years, 4.6 on average.[29]
- Almost half of those caring for functionally disabled relatives perform medical tasks, including wound care and administering medications.[30]
- Low-income families of children with special health care needs experience the greatest time demands, with 20 percent of poor families spending eleven hours or more each week providing care to their child compared to 6 percent

of the families with incomes in excess of 400 percent of poverty.[31]

THE COST OF CARING

"No good deed goes unpunished," as the saying goes. Informal caregiving is no exception.

The provision of informal care—normal and extraordinary—is costly to caregivers. There are the obvious financial costs: housing, health care, education, and recreation. Emotional costs may arise from having to be available 24/7, from tensions within the family, and sometimes from constant worry. There are opportunity costs. "Time devoted to the care of children," economist Nancy Folbre reminds us, "must be withdrawn from other activities, such as housework, paid work, sleep, and leisure."[32] The same applies for those giving informal care to family and friends with significant functional disabilities. Such opportunity costs, generally far less visible, are borne disproportionately by women—even as the benefits of their unremunerated labor protect families and potentially substitute for what might otherwise be costly public expenditures.

Because more than half (58 percent) of all caregivers are employed, they, women especially, have had to become masters at balancing their work, caregiving, and other family roles. It is no surprise, then, that seven out of ten caregivers (69 percent) report adjusting their work—reducing hours, taking time off, starting early or leaving late, or stopping work altogether.[33]

Giving care has its rewards, but financial security is not one of them, for women or men. A MetLife study based on a sample representative of 10 million daughters and sons over age 50 caring for parents in 2008 presents stunning information about the aggregate loss in wage and retirement benefits:

> Total wage, Social Security, and private pension losses due to caregiving could range from $283,716 for men to $324,044 for women, or $303,880 on average for a typical caregiver. When this $303,880 amount is multiplied

by the 9.7 million people age 50+ caring for their parents, the amount lost is $2,947,636,000,000, or nearly $3 trillion.[34]

For many, caregiving can be thought of as a lifelong career. Women especially often provide multiple sequences of care, beginning with their young children, then aging parents, perhaps followed by a very old functionally disabled spouse, sibling, or friend, possibly a grandchild. Although participating in the labor force at very high numbers, women are more likely than men to reduce or leave work at various points in the course of their lives caring for others.

Social Security benefits are based on a formula that essentially averages earnings over a worker's life. Unfortunately, women generally have lower wages and are also more likely than men to adjust their work lives to the demands of children, home, and older relatives needing care. As a result, women have more years of very low or no earnings, greatly reducing their potential Social Security benefits. Social Security does provide spousal benefits that may compensate for those who are married, or divorced after ten years, but it does not provide similar benefits for caregiving parents who do not meet these criteria.

We have failed as a nation to adequately recognize the cost of caring. It is time to begin addressing this shortcoming. Adding to the pressures on families and caregivers, the United States provides very limited support for those needing to leave work to care for a newly born or newly adopted child, for those leaving to care for children or adults needing extended support due to illness or functional disability, and for those needing time off to recover from their own health problems. The Family and Medical Leave Act of 1993, administered by the U.S. Department of Labor, was a step in the right direction, mandating that employers with fifty or more employees, as well as some smaller employers, provide up to twelve weeks of unpaid leave for eligible workers.[35] Some employers and a few states (e.g., California, New Jersey, and Rhode Island) have benefits that provide financial support for persons needing such leave.[36]

But unlike almost every other industrial democracy, the United

States federal government does not provide any protections against loss of income for those who must take leave. Among the thirty-four industrial democracies making up the Organisation for Economic Co-operation and Development, paid maternity leave averages about nineteen weeks; our federal government stands alone, providing none.[37] Responding to the value of family leave, to both the economy and to society, we advocate in chapter 7 a modest and affordable way of expanding Social Security to provide insurance against wages lost by such leave, and we also propose a small benefit at the birth or adoption of a child.

No matter how reciprocal or heartfelt, providing unpaid care to a family member is often exceptionally taxing. Public policies provide limited support for child care. Public long-term support and services are fragmented and often very limited—some funded by Medicaid, others through other government and private providers.

Politicians sometimes express concern that there is danger in doing too much for caregivers; that caregivers may take advantage of supportive public policy to shift more of the burden of care to the public sector. However, given demographic, labor force, and budgetary trends, and the emotional and physical toll on many caregivers, there is much evidence that the larger risk is that far too little is being done to support the caregiving of family and friends.[38] For example, one study suggests that 40 to 70 percent of those giving care to older adults exhibit symptoms of depression, a fourth to half showing signs of major depression.[39] Another study finds 17 percent of caregivers believe their health worsened by caregiving.[40]

Additionally, most caregivers are employed and so represent a significant financial risk for employers. With caregivers of seniors reporting more health problems, a 2010 MetLife study estimates that the employer health insurance costs for such people is 8 percent higher than for other employees, translating into $13.4 billion in additional employer health care costs in the private sector.[41] Caregiving by employees to adults ages 18 and over has been estimated to result in significant costs to employers from lost productivity—an estimated $33.6 billion in 2006.[42]

TENSION BETWEEN ANTICIPATED AVAILABILITY OF INFORMAL CAREGIVERS AND GROWING NEED

It's no secret that the number of Americans age 65 and over is projected to increase, from roughly 48 million in 2015 to 73 million in 2030, and to 92 million in 2060, when the last remaining baby boomers will be at least age 96.[43] Less well-known, the fastest growing age group is the very old, the one most at risk of needing informal and formal long-term support and services. Persons age 85 and over are projected to increase from roughly 6 million in 2015 to 9 million in 2030, and to 18 million by 2060, including 690,000 centenarians.[44]

The pool of potential informal caregivers is shrinking, largely because of the drop-off in birthrates following the large numbers of baby boomers born from 1946 through 1964. Assuming for the moment that the number of people aged 45 to 64 are the only people in the pool of potential caregivers for people 80 and over, AARP reports that where there were seven potential caregivers in 2010 for each person over age 80, this ratio will drop to four to one in 2030 and to less than three to one in 2050.[45] Of course, there are many complexities. There are many caregivers of all ages, and in today's world persons in their late 60s and 70s often find themselves caring for parents and others. And there are many other aspects of life in the twenty-first century that condition the potential size of the caregiver pool—for example, employment pressures and geographic mobility.

But the general point stands. The availability of informal caregivers will almost certainly shrink relative to growing demand. Plainly, this is a time to think carefully about how, as a nation, we can best harness and sustain this most human and critical service we provide for each other.

CONCLUSION

For too long, the financial and emotional pressures of the care family and friends give to each other have been viewed primarily as a private matter, what sociologist C. Wright Mills called "private troubles"—a problem that is not recognized as requiring a public response.[46] Normal risks, experienced over life by every family and every person, are not yet fully recognized as requiring greater public response. As families experience more constraints on their time, as the health care system shifts more costs and expectations onto caregivers, and as the nation ages, the pressures on families and informal caregivers will expand, and the expectation and demand for strengthening the family through support of its caregivers will grow.

We do not know which champions will move caregiving out of the home and into the "public square" in the way that Dorothea Dix, long ago, surfaced the treatment of the mentally ill, how Susan B. Anthony identified women's rights, how Martin Luther King spotlighted racial injustice, and how President Reagan's surgeon general, C. Everett Koop, focused attention on HIV/AIDS. It may be Ai-jen Poo, founding director of the National Domestic Workers Alliance, co-director of the Caring Across Generations Coalition, and author of the forthcoming book *The Age of Dignity*, who writes:

> We can view the Elder Boom as an opportunity to respond from the basis of something that all of us across the political spectrum hold dear: our right to live with dignity, independence, and self-determination. From that place, we can work together to reorganize society so that in all phases of life we can count on love, connection, and care. What could feel like the beginning of an epic national crisis in care, can in fact be one of our greatest opportunities for positive, transformative change at every level.[47]

No matter who the leaders are, it will be all of us working together to strengthen our families and the institutions that support caring across generations. The time is right for caregiving to burst forth as a policy issue requiring serious attention. And, as it does, we believe Social Security will play an important part in addressing the nation's emerging caregiving crisis, by adding financial supports for working families in ways that other nations do and by recognizing, supporting, and rewarding those who provide care—family, friends, domestic workers, and professionals—to the young, the old, and those in between.

6

THE NEW GILDED AGE

OCCUPY WALL STREET, A POPULIST MOVEMENT THAT STARTED in a park near Wall Street in New York City in the fall of 2011 and quickly spread across the country and around the world, transformed the nation's public conversation. The movement's simple slogan, "We are the 99 percent," focused political and media elites on rising income and wealth inequality—something everyone recognized viscerally.

Thanks to the Occupy movement, the issue of wealth and income inequality is now squarely on the national agenda. The issue has been propelled even more by the groundbreaking, surprise bestseller *Capital in the Twenty-First Century* by Thomas Piketty. His exhaustive research concludes that in the America of the 1950s and 1960s, the distribution of income and wealth grew more and more balanced among its people. Since the late 1970s, however—during the same period as the current decades-long campaign against Social Security—income and wealth in the United States have grown increasingly unequal, with greater and greater proportions going to those at the top.[1]

But what does all of this have to do with Social Security? Everything.

The connection was touched on in a major address that President Obama delivered on December 4, 2013. Calling income inequality "the defining challenge of our time," he explained government's important role:

> We've . . . seen how government action time and again can make an enormous difference in increasing opportunity and bolstering ladders into the middle class. Investments in education, laws establishing collective bargaining, and a minimum wage—these all contributed to rising standards of living for massive numbers of Americans. Likewise, *when previous generations declared that every citizen of this country deserved a basic measure of security—a floor through which they could not fall—we helped millions of Americans live in dignity, and gave millions more the confidence to aspire to something better, by taking a risk on a great idea.* Without Social Security, nearly half of seniors would be living in poverty—half. [Emphasis added.][2]

President Obama ended his speech by identifying a number of policy prescriptions to reduce inequality, including an increase in the minimum wage and universal prekindergarten education. Perhaps surprisingly, given the above quoted passage, he did not call for an increase in Social Security. We correct that defect while also making clear just how expanding Social Security accomplishes that goal. But first, some facts.

There has been a stunning increase in the share of all income going to the top 1 percent of America's households, rivaling the period of extraordinary inequality existing just before the Great Depression of the 1930s.[3] It is not simply that the rich are getting richer. It is that the rich are getting richer while everyone else is treading water or even losing ground. As figure 6.1 shows, from 1948 to 1979 two-thirds of aggregate income growth in the United States went to the bottom 90 percent. In stark contrast to the earlier period, all aggregate income growth from 1979 to 2012 has gone to the top 10 percent. And from 1993 to 2012, roughly two thirds of that growth went to the top 1 percent![4]

As a reflection of this income and wage distribution, the compensation of the CEOs of the 350 firms with the largest sales

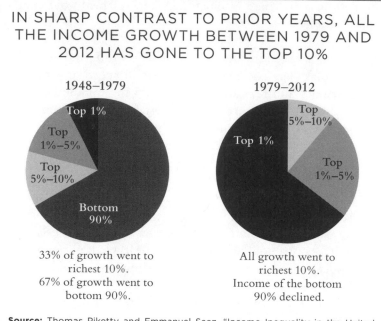

IN SHARP CONTRAST TO PRIOR YEARS, ALL THE INCOME GROWTH BETWEEN 1979 AND 2012 HAS GONE TO THE TOP 10%

1948–1979

Top 1%
Top 1%–5%
Top 5%–10%
Bottom 90%

33% of growth went to richest 10%.
67% of growth went to bottom 90%.

1979–2012

Top 5%–10%
Top 1%
Top 1%–5%

All growth went to richest 10%.
Income of the bottom 90% declined.

Source: Thomas Piketty and Emmanuel Saez, "Income Inequality in the United States, 1913–1998," *Quarterly Journal of Economics*, February 2003; updated to 2012 by Emmanuel Saez and available at http://elsa.berkeley.edu/users/saez.

Figure 6.1

rose from 20 times greater than their typical worker in 1965 to 273 times greater in 2012.[5] And along with those income gains is an increasing concentration of wealth. We are living in a time where wealth, especially financial wealth, has become increasingly concentrated. The richest 400 Americans have more wealth than the bottom 50 percent, which totals 155 million people.[6] In 2010, the top 1 percent controlled 42 percent of all the financial wealth in the United States; the bottom 80 percent controlled just 5 percent.[7]

DÉJÀ VU ALL OVER AGAIN

This enormous concentration of income and wealth didn't just happen by accident, or on its own. Nor is it a brand new phenomenon. The concentration of income and wealth and the economic and political power it generates in the hands of relatively few have all happened before. Mark Twain termed the late nineteenth century the Gilded Age, where on the surface the times looked golden, but where venality, exploitation, and hardship lurked just below. It had also happened during the Roaring Twenties, a time of excess memorialized by F. Scott Fitzgerald's *The Great Gatsby*. Both of these periods ended with economic breakdowns—the Panic of 1893 and the Great Depression of the 1930s—with businesses collapsing, banks closing, and widespread unemployment and poverty.

During both periods, those who benefited the most from the upward redistribution of wealth, and the political power that is a byproduct of that wealth, often justified their privileged positions with claims of social Darwinism—the wealthiest being, in their eyes, the fittest. For example, John D. Rockefeller—who captained Standard Oil so that, by the 1880s, it controlled the delivery of 90 percent of the nation's oil—justified monopolistic practices, telling students at Brown University in 1904: "The growth of large business is merely a survival of the fittest. . . . [T]he American Beauty rose can be produced in splendor and fragrance which brings cheer to its beholder only by sacrificing the early buds which grow up around it. This is not an evil tendency in business. It is merely the working out of the law of nature and the law of God."[8]

These early Masters of the Universe, as the novelist Thomas Wolfe labeled their spiritual descendants in his 1987 novel *Bonfire of the Vanities*, deified laissez-faire capitalism and "free" markets—though governments, of course, have always been involved in commerce and markets. Governments—federal, state, and local—build public roads that assist in getting goods to market, establish courts that adjudicate contract disputes, fund police and fire services to protect property, and play countless other roles.

Notwithstanding the reality, those titans of industry justified their business practices and the accumulation of great wealth as well as their disregard for the inequities and casualties of the system they profited from by claiming they were self-made and the font of economic progress. Seemingly without regard for human and moral consequences, many argued that there was nothing the federal government should do when the Great Depression crushed the economy, throwing one-third of workers out of work.

President Herbert Hoover's secretary of the treasury, Andrew Mellon, an industrialist, banker, and one of the richest men in the country, advised, "Liquidate labor, liquidate stocks, liquidate the farmers, liquidate real estate. . . . It will purge the rottenness out of the system. . . . People will work harder, live a more moral life. Values will be adjusted, and enterprising people will pick up from less competent people."[9]

LESSONS FROM THE GREAT DEPRESSION AND THE NEW DEAL

The Gilded Age and the Roaring Twenties ended in calamity. Both periods were followed by periods of social reforms: the Progressive Era and the New Deal. Concerned with the speculative, monopolistic, and labor practices, laws were written during both periods to regulate commerce, working conditions, and banking.

The Progressive Era witnessed a successful movement to enact state worker compensation laws, efforts to unionize as well as an unsuccessful push to enact government-provided health insurance. A number of states enacted minimum wage and maximum hour laws, only to have the Supreme Court rule the statutes unconstitutional on the grounds that they interfered with the right of employers and workers to enter into contracts freely.[10] Concerned with political corruption and the undemocratic concentration of wealth and political power, progressives successfully advanced constitutional amendments giving Congress the power to directly levy progressive income taxes (Sixteenth Amendment), requiring that United States senators be elected by popular vote not by state legislatures (Seventeenth Amendment), and empowering women to vote (Nineteenth Amendment).

The New Deal built on this legacy in its effort to build a fairer and more stable economy. The National Labor Relations Act of 1935 (also known as the Wagner Act) brought more balance to the worker-employer playing field, establishing ground rules enabling private sector employees to join unions and requiring employers to bargain collectively with their employees' representatives.[11] Designed to assure, as president Franklin Roosevelt put it, "all our able-bodied working men and women a fair day's pay for a fair day's work,"[12] the Fair Labor Standards Act of 1938 restricted child labor and established a minimum wage, maximum hours, and overtime pay rules for covered workers.[13]

About a month after the National Labor Relations Act was signed into law, Congress passed the Social Security Act of 1935. Even though Social Security addressed pressing needs and was overwhelmingly popular, social Darwinists nevertheless worried about its effect on what they deemed valuable in the struggle for survival. Senator Thomas P. Gore (D-OK), for example, showed his concern about this when he disapprovingly asked Secretary Perkins at the Senate Finance Committee hearing on the legislation, "Does the proposal involved in this legislation seek, in any sense, to substitute social security for the struggle for existence?"[14] The social Darwinists and glorifiers of laissez-faire capitalism were no match for the Great Depression and the New Deal, however. Nor, parenthetically, were they a match for Secretary Perkins, who calmly pointed out that, "cooperation between individuals has accounted for as much civilization as any personal struggle. Most of us have tried to give a certain security to those who are dependent upon us from the more serious aspect of the struggle for existence. . . . That is the purpose of civilization."[15]

These and other New Deal enactments laid the foundation for our modern economy, which has served the nation well for generations. They added more protections to the nation's markets and economic enterprises. They gave increased power to workers in an effort to allow them to bargain with their employers on more equal footing. They provided, in the form of Social Security and unemployment insurance, government-run mandatory wage insurance for workers, payable in the event that wages were lost as the result of unemployment, old age, or death. And they established an ongoing federal role in responding to the financial needs of poor families with children, poor elderly, poor blind people and, in time, poor people with disabilities more generally.

These various enactments paved the way for sustained prosperity and a strong belief in the value of government. The large industrial expansion during the World War II, together with these New Deal innovations and, later, the G.I. Bill of Rights and the growing size and influence of unions, sparked the twenty-five-year post-war economic expansion. Economic growth resulted in more opportunities for leisure (vacation, retirement, and education), higher standards of living, and strengthened health and employee pension protections, especially for unionized workers in both the private and public sectors. Not without its challenges, most significantly, racial oppression, gender inequality, the enforced closeting of those in the LGBT community, and the continuing threat of nuclear war, the American Dream was in reach of many and the "rules of the game" were clear for middle-class families: You worked hard and played by the rules. Others did, too. You could get ahead; if not you yourself, then your children.

The shared prosperity of much of the 1950s, 1960s, and early 1970s built a strong, robust middle class. Family incomes grew; home ownership became widespread. Unionized workers could, increasingly, count on defined pension benefits to supplement their Social Security benefits in retirement. Enactments of Medicare and Medicaid and expansions of Social Security provided growing protections against financial risks to workers and families, greater economic security, and the sense of personal security that one could weather difficult financial times if and when they struck. The highest marginal tax rates were thirty to fifty percentage points higher than today—ranging between 70 percent and 92 percent from 1946 to 1980, compared to 39.6 percent today (see figure 8.3).[16]

Though many Americans were strongly isolationist in the 1930s, most emerged from World War II believing that America's involvement in that war was right and just. The construction of the interstate highway system was again seen as government working for the benefit of all. And regular expansions of Social Security during the 1950s and 1960s were enacted by wide margins with broad bipartisan support.

Notwithstanding some strong political differences, these were not years in which most politicians sought to pull apart the understandings that emerged during the 1930s and 1940s. Writing to one of his brothers in 1956, president Dwight D. Eisenhower, a moderately conservative Republican, remarked on the strength of these understandings: "Should any political party attempt to abolish social security, unemployment insurance and eliminate labor laws and farm programs you would not hear of that party again in our political history. There is a tiny splinter group, of course, that believes you can do these things. . . . Their number is negligible and they are stupid."[17]

GOVERNMENT'S NEW ROLE IN THE UPWARD REDISTRIBUTION OF WEALTH

The first rumblings of tectonic changes to come could be heard by the 1960s. The consensus supporting government action was fraying. Tensions generated by just demands for civil rights, women's rights, and gay rights; an unpopular war; assassinations that shook the nation; urban riots; a president resigning from office in disgrace; and an economy simultaneously experiencing high unemployment and even higher inflation all contributed to unrest and a questioning of whether government played a positive or negative role in its citizens' lives.

This shift was felt powerfully with the election of Ronald Reagan. On January 20, 1981, in his first inaugural address, the newly elected Reagan asserted that "government is not the solution to our problem; government is the problem."[18] With that simple declaration, the so-called Reagan Revolution began, setting in motion an upward redistribution of income and wealth. Transforming his words into actions, his administration pursued policies that tilted power in favor of the most advantaged among us.

HELPING THE RICH BY DRASTICALLY CUTTING THEIR TAXES

Since government is the problem, according to Reagan, "starving the beast" became a major strategic goal.[19] The beast, of course, is the federal government, and what supports it are taxes, so starving it means cutting taxes. To assist in pressuring politicians to adopt this help-the-richest-among-us approach, Grover Norquist, a young conservative acolyte, formed Americans for Tax Reform at Reagan's request and in 1986 instituted the Taxpayer Protection Pledge, which sought to pressure politicians to pledge in writing never to vote to raise a penny in taxes.[20]

The anti-tax approach gained steam in 1984, when Democratic

presidential nominee Walter Mondale lost in a landslide, after asserting, in his speech accepting his party's nomination, that raising taxes was inevitable.[21] It gained even more steam when vice president George H.W. Bush emphatically declared, in his Republican presidential nomination acceptance speech in 1988, "Read my lips: No new taxes."[22] When Bush signed a budget compromise as president, which did include taxes, Democratic presidential candidate Bill Clinton pointed out the flip-flop in several ads, and Bush lost, many pundits attributing the cause to the breach of his pledge.

The 1990s were a predictably strong economic time, because the baby boom generation was at its most productive, peak earning years. As the National Commission on Social Security Reform planned, Social Security built up large reserves in anticipation of the coming retirement of baby boomers. With the slogan "Save Social Security First,"[23] Clinton resisted pressure to cut taxes, and indeed produced a small surplus. The surplus resulted by adding Social Security's growing surplus to the smaller general fund surplus. It was projected to grow over the subsequent ten years to $5.6 trillion.[24] But president George W. Bush secured two rounds of new tax cuts, again primarily benefiting the well-off. As of this writing, no prominent Republican endorses any new taxes whatsoever.

All of those tax cuts have had their predictable result. In 2010, the top 0.1 percent of earners—those making more than $3 million—received the benefit of the bulk of the Bush tax cuts. Their average tax cut of around $520,000 is more than 450 times larger than the one enjoyed by the average middle-class family. Indeed, more than half of these tax benefits went to those earning more than $170,000.[25]

Here's another illustration of the impact of the Bush tax cuts: twenty-five of the nation's hundred highest-paid U.S. chief executives earned more in 2010 than the companies they headed paid in federal income tax. These companies averaged $1.9 billion in global profits; twenty spent more on lobbying politicians than they paid in taxes.[26] The effective federal income tax rate—the rate paid on all taxable income—on the top four hundred taxpayers, whose incomes averaged $270 million, was 18.1 percent in 2008, smaller than the rate paid by some single workers with incomes less than $90,000.[27]

Though Social Security has its own dedicated income, it has not been immune from the starve-the-beast mania. As explained in chapter 2 and discussed in more detail in chapter 8, Social Security contributions are assessed on incomes only up to a maximum amount—$117,000 in 2014. In 1977, when Congress enacted annual automatic adjustments to the maximum amount, it intended that the maximum should capture 90 percent of all wages earned nationwide.[28] (That is, most people would have all of their wages covered; Social Security would cover 90 percent of everyone's combined wages; the only wages not covered would be the highest 10 percent of wages that are earned in this country.)

However, the automatic adjustment has not worked as planned because the earnings of high-income workers have increased much more rapidly than the average in the last several decades. Congress intended that the 90 percent remain constant by adjusting the maximum annually by the percentage growth in average wages. And it would remain constant if wage growth were distributed evenly across all workers, but as figure 6.1 shows, income gains have all gone to those at the top. Social Security now covers only about 82.5 percent of all wages.[29]

That seemingly small slippage, from 90 percent to 82.5 percent, translates into tens of billions of dollars each and every year. For example, in 2014 alone it's a roughly $60 billion loss.[30] Those are billions of dollars that should have gone to Social Security but instead stayed in the pockets of the wealthiest among us. It is just one indication that the richest are not paying their fair share into Social Security.

HELPING THE RICH BY CUTTING DOMESTIC AND INCREASING MILITARY SPENDING

In addition to starving the beast by cutting taxes, Reagan sought to cut spending—but not all spending. By the time Reagan left office, he had expanded military spending a whopping 43 percent over what it had been at the height of the Vietnam War.

A favorite target for cuts was means-tested welfare. Often drawing on pernicious gender and racial stereotypes, such as the so-called Welfare Queen, Reagan routinely vilified those who were dependent on those programs, implying that they were undeserving and lazy or, worse, outright crooks.[31]

Other domestic spending was cut as well. In 1981, Congress repealed Social Security benefits for children ages 18 to 22 in college or vocational school whose parent had lost wages as the result of death, disability, or old age, and cut the program other ways. Further cuts were enacted in 1983.

Reagan's successors did little to change the overall narrative that government is the problem, nor the shift from domestic to military spending. It was Democrat Bill Clinton who signed legislation in 1996 ending Aid to Families with Dependent Children, which had been enacted as part of the Social Security Act of 1935, substituting the much less adequate Temporary Assistance for Needy Families. Poor children would no longer have a right to a federally supported welfare benefit. And president George W. Bush dramatically increased military spending in the wake of the 9/11 terrorist attacks.

Social welfare spending helps middle- and lower-income Americans; military spending primarily benefits the defense industry. For the most part, those who serve or have served our nation in uniform have not been the beneficiaries of this new military spending, but, unfortunately, have been harmed by the domestic spending cuts.

HELPING THE RICH AND HURTING EVERYONE ELSE BY PRIVATIZING GOVERNMENT FUNCTIONS

The deification of the market system and the vilification of government have led conservative activists to call for, and in many cases successfully advance, policies that redistribute wealth upward through the privatization of government functions and jobs.[32] Even in as essential a part of government as national defense, this has happened, and resulted in enriching corporations to the detriment of most Americans and our values. This privatization is perhaps most visibly and starkly epitomized by Blackwater, Halliburton, and all the other private contractors employed to help with the Iraq and Afghanistan wars.[33]

Given the privatization in an enterprise as important and life threatening as war, it should not be a surprise that conservatives would seek to dismantle Social Security by privatizing the goal of achieving retirement security, despite Social Security's proven superiority to all private-sector counterparts. While the Bush privatization plan was defeated, a number of well-meaning but misguided politicians seek what some call the back-door privatization of Social Security.[34] They propose to cut Social Security while expanding private retirement savings vehicles—accomplishing in two steps essentially what President Bush sought to accomplish in one.[35]

Although unsuccessful in privatizing Social Security, President Bush was successful in partially privatizing Medicare. He signed the 2003 Medicare Modernization Act, which added prescription drug benefits to Medicare and moved incrementally in the direction of privatizing Medicare.[36] The drug benefit opened up new markets for insurance companies and HMOs, the vehicles designated for contracting with beneficiaries to administer these new benefits. The new law also created greater opportunity for beneficiaries to select a private plan, Medicare Advantage, as an alternative to the traditional public Medicare plan, providing, as enacted, significantly larger per capita reimbursement for those covered by private plans.[37]

The privatization of government functions enriches some corporations often while costing taxpayers.[38] It has resulted in the upward redistribution of wealth indirectly as well by trading good-paying public sector jobs, protected by strong unions, for generally nonunionized jobs with fewer protections and less security.[39] Cutting or, more radically, privatizing Social Security, would, like other efforts to shift functions from the public sector to the private, benefit powerful interests while drastically reducing the economic security of America's families and intensifying the dangerously skewed distribution of income and wealth.

HELPING CORPORATIONS AND HURTING TYPICAL AMERICANS BY FAILING TO PROTECT WORKERS WHO ORGANIZE

Privatizing government functions sometimes serves, intended or not, to redistribute wealth upward by weakening unions. Collective bargaining, and unions generally, have been essential in building a strong middle class.

Early on in 1981, Reagan signaled his disregard for the role unions played in building a strong middle class. Firing thirteen thousand striking air traffic controllers, he destroyed their union and, with anti-union appointments to agencies created to protect workers, including the National Labor Relations Board and the Department of Labor, he sent a message that union-busting would be tolerated, and even actively encouraged.[40]

These attacks are with us still—and they have had their impact. In 1983, 21.6 percent of workers were members of unions. Today, it is only 12.4 percent—and half of those work in the public sector. Only 6.7 percent of today's private sector workers are unionized.[41] This has indirect but serious consequences for Social Security. Union support for Social Security has been essential in both protecting it from cuts and successfully pushing for its expansion.

HELPING THE RICH AND HURTING EVERYONE ELSE BY DEREGULATING

The attacks on unions were just one aspect of weakening protections of workers and promoting the upward redistribution of income and wealth. Eroding the minimum wage was another. Using July 2013 dollars, the real value of the minimum wage declined from $9.67 in 1979 to $7.25 in November 2013.[42] (The minimum wage did not increase by even a penny during the Reagan presidency. Its increase in 2007 was the first in ten years.[43]) The failure to increase the minimum wage not only affected workers, it robbed Social Security of revenue, since its premiums are assessed against wages.[44]

The Reagan years also saw a reduction in the enforcement of occupational safety and other safeguards.[45] These policies were part of a larger redistribution of wealth upward through the reduction of so-called anti-business regulations. Indeed, Nobel Prize winner and newspaper columnist Paul Krugman blames Reagan's deregulation efforts for turning the savings and loan collapse of the 1980s and 1990s from "modest-sized troubles" into "an utter catastrophe." And he says this deregulation made the recent Great Recession "inevitable."[46] One of the side effects of these economic downturns was to reduce Social Security's income and increase its costs. In fairness, the focus on deregulation started with presidents Richard Nixon and Jimmy Carter, but it accelerated under Reagan, and continued under his successors. Perhaps most visibly, in 1999, the New Deal Glass-Steagall legislation, which had protected us against irresponsible action by banks, was repealed, arguably one of the most important causes of the Great Recession.

The response to the banking crisis and the Great Recession it sparked was necessarily swift. To stabilize the economy, the banks defined as "too big to fail" were bailed out by the public through the Troubled Assets Relief Program. But not so for the many middle-class workers and families straining under the press of declining housing prices, foreclosures, job loss, and credit card and student debt.

The economic lessons of the past were largely ignored: that active and large federal government investments are needed to jump-start a depressed economy, not laissez-faire economics and budget balancing. To help citizens help themselves when so many workers and families are negotiating the shoals of job loss and home foreclosures, large-scale government action is needed, not callous disregard and domestic budget cuts.

THE HIGH COST OF INEQUALITY

The result of these policies, which all flow from the idea that government harms us rather than helps us and evens the playing field, has resulted in the startling and rising income and wealth inequality that the nation continues to experience. We have experienced an upward redistribution of wealth in a game that is rigged for the very rich and against everyone else.

Where the 1950s and 1960s were a time when the middle class swelled, the current one is a time of a disappearing middle class.[47]

Throughout history, middle-aged adults have been squeezed between their aging parents and dependent children. Social Security alleviated that squeeze, but the pressure on these families is once again increasing. When once a single paycheck could support a family, now it generally takes two.[48] When once young adults could emerge from college with manageable debt and bright prospects, now they are often greeted with enormous debt and, all too frequently, few job opportunities.[49] And the trajectory of student debt is upward, increasing fourfold in just ten years, from $253 billion in 2003 to $1.1 trillion in 2013. Moreover, despite the stereotype of Europe as a rigid, class-based, "old world," today we have less upward mobility than much of Europe.[50]

And these conditions have a serious and corrosive impact on our society at large. Rising inequality and declining upward mobility harm our economy. They have been linked to more frequent recessions.[51] They also harm our stability and cohesion as a nation. And, perhaps most seriously, those twin conditions harm our very democracy.

The increasing concentration of income and wealth and decline in unionization are intertwined with the dependence of politicians on large donors from the business world. Ignoring the lessons of the past, some people with extraordinary economic power (e.g., the Koch Brothers, Peter G. Peterson, discussed in chapter 9) have been using their money to bend the nation's politics, democracy, and economy in ways that hemorrhage income, wealth, and political power to the most well-off.

But there is hope. Our nation still adheres to the principle of one person, one vote—despite the efforts of some to suppress the votes of others. All of us together can reinstate the rules that led to decades of prosperity. One important place to start—one where the American people are overwhelmingly united—is in the expansion of Social Security.

EXPANDING SOCIAL SECURITY
REDUCES INEQUALITY

The politics and economics of inequality are closely connected to that of Social Security. The various efforts to cut Social Security are part of the larger attacks on social spending, government regulation, progressive taxation, unions, and fair labor standards—all feeding the nation's increased income and wealth inequality. Cutting, privatizing, or otherwise radically undermining Social Security makes perfect sense from the point of view of those favoring minimal government, a cornerstone of laissez-faire ideology. And it would result in greater inequality.

Moreover, the income inequality of recent decades has undermined Social Security's revenue stream. Congress did not anticipate that wage growth over the last three decades would go primarily to higher income workers, a reality responsible for more than one-fourth of the program's projected long-term shortfall (which is discussed at length in chapter 8).[52]

Nor did Congress anticipate the unexpected consequence to benefits of increases in wage inequality; that the relatively flat (and for some declining) growth in wages means that the Social Security benefits Americans are earning are less than they would have been if wage growth had been distributed more evenly across income groups as they were from roughly 1950 to 1979.[53]

Because Social Security and those earning its benefits have been hurt by income inequality, an expanded Social Security is a solution, helping to lessen that very inequality. Social Security does more to offset lost wages, income inequalities, and poverty than any other institution, public or private. Because Social Security's benefit formula provides, as chapter 2 explains, a proportionally larger benefit to low- and moderate-income workers and to workers who have had years of unemployment, it corrects for some of the rampant income inequalities that exist today. Funding these expanded benefits by requiring the wealthiest among us to contribute more is a further solution to that income and wealth inequality.

Expanding Social Security moves the nation in the direction of building an economy that works for all Americans, one in which the rules of the game are less malleable to the benefit of the most well-off.

Expanding benefit protections is not a panacea, but it is a critical start for addressing the problems facing those receiving today's modest Social Security benefits, those working today with little prospect of economic security during their retirement years, those who have shortchanged their income security in retirement by giving care to others, parents needing to leave work to care for a newborn, or college students facing crushing debt. Nor is it a panacea for the nation's unacceptable level of inequality. But it is an important step in moving the nation forward in the right direction.

These last four chapters have explained why Social Security should be expanded. The next two chapters explain how.

PART THREE

THE SOLUTION

7

EXPAND SOCIAL SECURITY FOR ALL GENERATIONS

AN EXPANDED SOCIAL SECURITY SYSTEM IS A SOLUTION TO the challenges highlighted in the last four chapters: the income insufficiency of today's seniors; the retirement income crisis confronting today's middle-aged and young workers; insufficient recognition of and public support for the caregiving functions of the family; and increased inequality, now hollowing out the middle class. While not a total solution, Social Security has a key role to play.

This chapter and the next demonstrate that key role, by presenting our plan, the Social Security Works All Generations Plan—a comprehensive package of benefit and revenue changes that expands Social Security's protections in important ways.[1] Our plan is but one among a number of excellent plans. A growing number of United States senators, members of the House of Representatives, academics, and leading organizations representing, among others, women, seniors, people with disabilities, low-income Americans, and people of color, have put forward Social Security expansion plans.

All of the plans present solutions to pressing challenges. All pay for the improvements. All truly strengthen, rather than cut, our Social Security system. Combined, these proposals and plans illustrate that there are many paths to building on our existing Social Security system to provide stronger, affordable protection for America's families, while reducing income inequality.

In this chapter and the next, we discuss the various elements of our plan, as well as other proposals, some of which appear in other plans. This chapter describes benefit improvements and how they strengthen retirement security for today's retirees and workers, and how they strengthen protections across all generations in the family, including those giving care to others. The next chapter explains why and how the richest nation in the world can pay for these benefit improvements. How doing so can slow the rapid growth of income inequality, while correcting the damage to Social Security's financing that income inequality has wrought.

Toward the end of chapter 8, we provide a summary of our plan. Greater detail about all of the proposals in the two chapters, including their costs and potential revenue sources as well as a chart showing costs and revenues of the All Generations Plan can be found in appendix B. A chart summarizing other major expansion plans that have been put forward at the time of this writing can be found in appendix C.

INCREASING THE ECONOMIC SECURITY OF CURRENT AND FUTURE SENIORS

As we discuss in chapters 1 and 2, prior to the enactment of Social Security, the large majority of workers were unable to retire with enough income to live with independence and dignity. Social Security changed that. But, as chapters 3 and 4 explain, we may be returning to a time where a growing number of seniors who want to live independently without burdening their children will lack the financial resources to do so. As chapter 3 discusses, the majority of today's seniors are at significant economic risk—some living in or close to poverty, and many others just one economic shock away from trouble meeting basic needs. And, as chapter 4 makes clear, tomorrow's seniors are likely to be in worse financial shape.

Social Security currently provides a strong foundation, but its benefits are far from adequate by themselves. Indeed, they are modest by virtually any measure. Social Security's retirement benefits average just $15,571 a year.[2] They do not come close to replacing a large enough percentage of wages to allow workers to maintain their standards of living once wages are gone. Moreover, these already minimal replacement rates will be lower in the future, as the result of the already enacted cuts, now being phased in, described in chapter 4. As another measure, Social Security's benefits are extremely low by international standards, ranking near the bottom when measured against the old-age benefits provided by other developed countries.[3]

In light of Social Security's near universality, efficiency, fairness in its benefit distribution, portability from job to job, and security, the obvious solution to the nation's looming retirement income crisis is to increase Social Security's modest benefits. Recognizing the retirement income crisis, a number of policymakers have proposed additional savings vehicles and incentives to save. Some have proposed building on tax-favored IRAs and 401(k)s. But savings will not be effective for the vast majority of workers; what will unquestionably be effective is insurance, in the form of time-tested Social Security, as chapter 2 explains.

Increasing Social Security's benefits can be done simply and quickly, with no start-up costs, no additional regulation, and virtually no additional administrative costs. It is very important to recognize that benefit improvements will, over time, be conveyed to all generations in the family and those to come. In fact, younger generations will reap greater benefits from an across-the-board increase than today's old. That's because, in raising the benefits of current beneficiaries, we also raise the benefits of those who will receive them in the future, and because today's old will receive this benefit improvement for fewer years than tomorrow's old. It will also lessen the squeeze on those who feel responsible to supplement the incomes of their aging parents while also assisting their own children and grandchildren.

Moreover, increasing Social Security benefits will increase the benefits not just of retired workers but also of disabled workers, their families, and the families of deceased workers. This increase would occur automatically, without reference to specific groups, because Social Security's benefits are primarily generated from the same formula (which is described in appendix A).

INCREASE BENEFITS FOR ALL CURRENT AND FUTURE BENEFICIARIES

In light of the looming retirement income crisis, which will affect most workers, Social Security's modest benefits should be increased for everyone. There are many ways to design this increase. The increase can be structured so that lower-wage workers and their families receive benefits that are a larger percentage of their pre-retirement wages as some proposals do, or proportionately, as the All Generations Plan does. Increasing everyone's benefits fits with the spirit of Social Security and ensures that all workers and their families have a somewhat stronger and larger foundation when wages are gone.

And so the All Generations Plan proposes an across-the-board 10 percent increase in benefits for everyone who receives Social Security benefits now, or will in the future. Just as Social Security has a minimum benefit and a maximum family benefit, we limit our plan's maximum benefit increase to $150 a month.

ADOPT A MORE ACCURATE COST OF LIVING ADJUSTMENT

Virtually every expansion plan proposes the adoption of a more accurate measure of the cost of living experienced by Social Security beneficiaries, and the All Generations Plan does so as well. This change is not really an increase in benefits; it is designed to ensure that benefits do not erode.

The automatic annual cost of living adjustment (COLA) is one of the most important features of our Social Security system. It is intended to assure that benefits, once received, maintain their purchasing power no matter how long someone lives. That's why Social Security benefits are adjusted automatically every January to prevent their erosion if and when there has been inflation. Without accurate and timely inflation adjustments, retirees, people with serious and permanent disabilities and other beneficiaries would see their Social Security lose value as they age. The current inflation index under-measures how inflation eats away at the purchasing power of benefits. That's because it is calculated for workers and the general public. But seniors and people with disabilities spend more on health care—where prices rise faster—and less on clothing, recreation, and other items—where prices tend to rise more slowly—than younger, healthier Americans.[4]

Figure 7.1 tells the story of three inflation measures—what we deem the good, the bad, and the ugly. Experts generally call them by the following warm and fuzzy names—Consumer Price Index for the Elderly (CPI-E), Consumer Price Index for Urban Wage Earners (CPI-W), and Chained Consumer Price Index (Chained-CPI). The CPI-E generally does the best job of reflecting the spending habits of seniors and people with disabilities. The CPI-W is currently used to calculate the cost of living adjustment of Social Security beneficiaries. The Chained-CPI is a stingier measure, proposed by some as a benefit cut.[5]

As figure 7.1 illustrates:

- If the "good" Consumer Price Index for the Elderly were used as the basis of the annual cost of living adjustment, the purchasing power of an average earner who started Social Security benefits at age 65 in 2012 would remain the same, no matter how long he or she lives;
- Under the current measure, the "bad" Consumer Price Index for Urban Wage Earners, an individual's annual benefit in 2012 dollars declines over time. That same individual's benefit will be $440 lower at age 75, $771 lower at age 85, and $1,096 lower at age 95. Cumulatively, the individual will lose $18,834 over thirty years compared to what he or she would have received if the individual's benefit kept pace with inflation experienced by seniors (i.e., were adjusted with the CPI-E);
- Under the "ugly" Chained Consumer Price Index, the individual's annual benefit in 2012 dollars would decline even more sharply. It would be $1,081 lower at age 75, $1,868 lower at age 85, and, if he or she has the good fortune of living to age 95, the individual's benefit in that year would be $2,617 lower—a whopping cumulative loss of $45,667.[6]

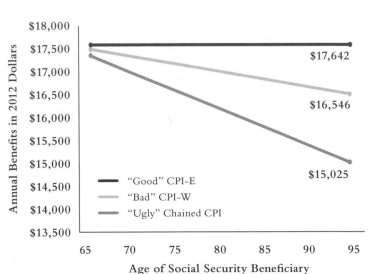

ANNUAL SOCIAL SECURITY BENEFITS UNDER THE "GOOD" CPI-E, THE "BAD" CURRENT LAW, AND THE "UGLY" CHAINED CPI

For Average Earner Retiring at Age 65

Note: Because cost-of-living adjustments are applied from age 62 onward (regardless of one's age of retirement), benefits under the three CPIs already diverge by age 65.

Source: Social Security Works' calculations based on Social Security Office of the Chief Actuary, Memorandum to Rep. Becerra, June 21, 2011; Social Security Administration, Annual Statistical Supplement, 2012, Table 2.A26, 2012.

Figure 7.1

Because the erosion of the benefits compounds over time, the largest impact falls on the oldest old and those disabled for the longest time. Distressingly, this occurs as other resources are exhausted and health costs are increasing on average.

The intent of the cost of living adjustment is to allow beneficiaries to tread water; instead, they are slowly sinking. That is why it is so important to adopt the Consumer Price Index for the Elderly as the basis of the annual cost of living adjustment.

INCREASE BENEFITS TARGETED TO ALLEVIATING POVERTY

In addition to a better Consumer Price Index and an across-the-board benefit increase, the All Generations Plan calls for targeted benefit increases to alleviate poverty. As chapter 4 explains, poverty among seniors has declined sharply over the last half century. Nevertheless, some serious pockets of poverty remain. Frequently, people who were poor at younger ages remain poor in retirement. Low-wage workers, as well as workers who were disadvantaged during their working years—disproportionately, people of color, women, and members of the LGBT community—are likely to have disproportionately high rates of poverty in old age. Indeed, many women who were secure at younger ages find themselves financially strapped as they grow older.[7] Women live longer on average than men, are less likely to have supplemental pensions, and, as chapter 5 details, often are the ones to take time out from the workforce for the essential but uncompensated job of caring for family members.[8]

Social Security is by no means a total solution. People should have a living wage when they work full-time. No one in this country should be penalized in the workplace for his or her race, gender, sexual orientation, religion, or ethnicity. Caregivers should receive the economic and emotional support they deserve. But Social Security, because of its ingenious structure, helps those workers and their families when they reach old age. It could easily do even more.

One of the values underlying Social Security is that workers who retire after a lifetime of work should not retire into poverty. Moreover, the architects of Social Security believed that workers who contributed to Social Security should receive benefits larger than they could receive simply by applying for means-tested welfare. Social Security provides benefits that, as chapter 2 explains, are disproportionately larger for those who have experienced lower wages over their careers. As a consequence, even an across-the-board percentage increase, as the All Generations Plan provides, helps these workers disproportionately.

In addition, Social Security has included a minimum benefit since 1939. Because the minimum originally did not differentiate between high-paid workers who had only a few years of work and low-paid workers with long work histories, Congress in 1972 introduced the so-called special minimum for low-income workers with many years of work. Because the special minimum is only indexed to the rise in prices, not wages, it has not kept pace with the nation's rising standard of living. Consequently, it covers fewer and fewer workers each year.

It is time to update the special minimum benefit so that when fully implemented, those working for at least thirty years and retiring at their full retirement age will receive a benefit equal to 125 percent of the federal poverty line. The All Generations Plan proposes to do just that.

As chapter 3 explains, another area of disproportionate poverty occurs among the very old, who likely have exhausted other resources. Those disproportionately poor at very old ages are more likely to be women, who may be widowed, divorced, or never married, and who may never have earned much during their younger years. To address this issue, some have proposed increasing benefits at an advanced age, such as 85. Some colloquially refer to these proposed increases as birthday bumps. In fairness to those who have experienced serious and permanent disabilities at young ages and who have been receiving benefits for many years and, like the very old, may have exhausted other resources, these proposals sometimes simply raise benefits after a certain amount of time—for example, for those who have been receiving benefits for twenty years. Another proposal is to increase benefits for widows, who have disproportionately high rates of poverty. Others have proposed so-called earnings sharing between spouses, whether still married or divorced. Although the All Generations Plan does not include these specific, targeted reforms, we applaud them. We think they would help many who are disadvantaged, while remaining consistent with Social Security's overall structure and conceptual underpinning.

A SERIOUS CAUTION ABOUT THE GOAL OF ANTI-POVERTY AND SOCIAL SECURITY

While targeted increases (like the ones just highlighted and discussed in more detail in appendix B) are valuable and relatively inexpensive, they should not be done while scaling back, or worse, eliminating benefits for others. Some who don't like Social Security, or simply don't understand it, have proposed enacting these targeted expansions while scaling back on benefits for what they call higher-income workers.

Although it is a clever sound bite to ask why billionaires should get Social Security, there are practical as well as conceptual reasons why everyone should receive the benefits they have earned.

Scaling back or eliminating the benefits of millionaires and billionaires would produce relatively minute savings, since there are so few of them and their benefit levels are low already in relation to their contributions, as a result of Social Security's progressive benefit formula. That is why, when one examines the details of the proposals that have been put forward to scale back benefits for "higher income" individuals, those proposals invariably cut the benefits of middle-class workers and their families. Those putting forth these proposals rarely, if ever, define what they mean by higher income, but "higher income" is simply used as a relative term, since, as we discuss in chapter 3, most seniors have modest incomes. Every proposal that has any noticeable cost savings involves reducing the benefits of solidly middle-class Americans, sometimes those with annual incomes as low as $25,000.[9] If the proposals did not do that, they would show virtually no savings on official projections.

While eliminating the benefits of millionaires and billionaires does not produce much in the way of savings, that action would have detrimental shortcomings, which, it is not too hyperbolic to say, are potential poison pills to our Social Security system. First, affluence-testing Social Security would create enormous administrative problems and costs. No matter where the limit was put, it would mean that every one of us would then have to prove to the Social Security Administration, through income tax returns, house valuations, and other evidence, that we are not too rich to receive Social Security.

Perhaps most importantly, taking away benefits from the wealthiest, who have nonetheless earned those benefits, would subtly but fundamentally undermine a widely popular program that has done more to eradicate poverty in this country than any other program. Our Social Security system is the nation's most effective anti-poverty program. It lifts 22 million people—including more than 1 million children—out of poverty each year.[10] But that is a byproduct of its central mission, which is to provide universal insurance against the loss of wages.

No proposal should be enacted if it transforms Social Security from an insurance program into a welfare program. Though the distinction between government-sponsored insurance and welfare is not well understood, it is crucial in evaluating proposed changes to Social Security.

Insurance programs involve arrangements among equals who are pooling their risks. Eligibility for insurance is based on achieving insured status, not on need. Benefits result from experiencing the event covered by the insurance. They are paid irrespective of need. Beneficiaries of Social Security must prove something positive— that they have worked and contributed long enough to qualify for benefits.

Welfare programs are an important part of our nation's income protection system and, indeed, are essential as long as there is poverty, but they have inescapable, inherent weaknesses not found in insurance arrangements. Eligibility is based on need, which is determined by an examination of the potential recipient's income and assets to ensure that he or she is really in need. Welfare benefits are generally very low, designed simply to provide enough, in the community's estimation, to get by, to subsist. Because welfare involves the community providing help to those less fortunate, the arrangement is unfortunately often seen by the providers as an unequal arrangement—those materially better off providing assistance to those less advantaged.[11]

A few examples of the differences between Social Security and the means-tested Supplemental Security Income program (SSI) illuminate the stark differences between government-provided insurance and welfare. Both programs provide benefits to people who are old and to people with disabilities, but there are important differences. Eligibility for Social Security results from workers having worked and contributed to Social Security long enough to become insured. Designed as wage insurance, the higher one's earnings that are insured, and the longer one works and pays premiums, the larger the dollar amount of the Social Security benefit received. Savings and other assets have no impact on Social Security benefits.

In stark contrast, SSI benefit amounts are determined exclusively by an examination of need and are very low in amount, designed simply to allow bare subsistence, if that.[12] Both earned and unearned income reduce a person's SSI benefit.[13] Those individuals must have extremely limited assets in order to qualify for any benefit at all. In order to ensure that the income and assets limitations are not exceeded, those receiving SSI are required to regularly report many intrusive details about their lives. Every month, for example, they must take or mail all pay stubs to the Social Security Administration.[14] In contrast, Social Security retirees are not required to file any burdensome and intrusive reports about the details of their lives. The different ways that assets and income are treated in the determination of benefits is a direct result of inherent difference between welfare programs such as SSI and insurance programs like Social Security.

Expensive to administer and all too often seen by society as a sign of individual failing, as opposed to the product of unfortunate circumstance, receipt of SSI and other forms of welfare can feel demeaning, often stabbing at the dignity of those who are often the most vulnerable among us. To reiterate, welfare is necessary as long as there is poverty. But supporters of Social Security, which prevents poverty in the first place, should be alert to changes that would transform Social Security from insurance into welfare.

TO FURTHER ALLEVIATE POVERTY, IMPROVE THE SUPPLEMENTAL SECURITY INCOME PROGRAM

SSI, which currently serves more than 8.3 million low-income aged and disabled Americans,[15] is an important complement to Social Security but its extremely modest benefits and very restrictive eligibility criteria are in desperate need of updating.

That's why in addition to expanding Social Security, it is time to increase SSI's meager benefits as well as its income and assets limitations.[16] At a minimum, the SSI benefit should be set at the official poverty level (inadequate as that is, as we discuss in chapter 3).

If that were done, the federal benefit,[17] in 2014, would have been a still meager $973 a month rather than the actual level of $721 a month for individuals, and $1,311 a month rather than the actual $1,082 a month for couples. The assets limit, which is $2,000 for individuals and $3,000 for couples, has only been updated once, in 1989. It should be updated and then increased automatically each year to offset changes in the cost of living. Same for the earnings limitations, which have not been increased since the program's enactment in 1972![18]

What should not be done, though, is to transform Social Security into SSI in the name of targeting its benefits toward the poor. Certain targeted increases, like increasing benefits for the very old or increasing the minimum benefit, can be enacted within the insurance framework of Social Security, but a means test or affluence test transforms Social Security into welfare and should not be enacted. We also should not scale back middle-class benefits, so that workers no longer get a fair deal on the premiums that are paid. Bill Gates and other billionaires should still receive Social Security, but we should require them to pay more, as described in the next chapter.

STRENGTHENING FAMILY PROTECTIONS AND REINFORCING CAREGIVING

Although Social Security is often thought of as a program for the old, it is more accurately a family protection program. Nearly three out of ten beneficiaries receive disability or survivor benefits.[19] As described above, increasing benefits across the board will increase benefits for tens of millions of younger Americans.

Moreover, increasing the benefits of Social Security beneficiaries reduces the burden on adult children to care for aged parents and expands the income of extended families. Throughout history, adult children have cared for aging parents. One way to think about Social Security is as an institution that routinizes and streamlines that age-old transfer, in recognition that some people have many children who can share the costs, while others have few or none at all. Social Security allows this transfer to be made while allowing seniors to have the dignity that comes with having earned the support, and the autonomy provided by an independent source of income—all while alleviating the pressure on younger family members.

But expanding Social Security beyond a simple increase in benefits can help families even more directly.

SUPPORT CARE GIVEN TO OTHERS

In addition to death, disability, and old age, other times that wages may disappear are when a child is born, when a worker becomes sick, or when a worker leaves paid employment to care for a sick or functionally disabled relative. Federal law already mandates that workers may take up to twelve weeks of leave without losing employment.[20] It is a simple step to say that the wages lost during those weeks should be insured and replaced through Social Security. The All Generations Plan takes that simple step and adds these circumstances as insurable events that Social Security covers.

We base our proposal on the Family and Medical Insurance Leave (FAMILY) Act, which representative Rosa DeLauro (D-CT) has introduced, with eighty-two co-sponsors at the time of this writing, in the House of Representatives,[21] and which senator Kirsten Gillibrand (D-NY) has introduced, with four co-sponsors, in the Senate.[22] Our proposal is nearly identical to theirs, but simply adds these circumstances as insurable events under Social Security, while the FAMILY Act designates its own earmarked contribution, separate and apart from what is now paid for Social Security's old age, survivors, and disability insurance.[23]

In addition to the income lost when a child is born or adopted, which the paid family leave proposal addresses, expenses increase. Many other industrialized countries provide not only paid family leave, but also children's allowances.[24] The All Generations Plan proposes a $1,000 allowance at the birth or adoption of a child.

When workers take time out from the workforce to care for family members, they not only lose wages, but also fail to earn credit toward their own Social Security benefits in the event of old age, disability, or premature death. Yet, as we explain in chapter 5, many people, disproportionately women, withdraw from paid work to undertake this enormously important unpaid work.

Indeed, anyone who has cared for children or sick or functionally disabled relatives, or witnessed another who has done so, understands how important and how hard that work is, yet it is unremunerated. In order to increase the economic security of those who engage in this invaluable labor, the All Generations Plan provides credit toward Social Security benefits when parents leave work to care for young children—a first step on which to expand further in years to come.

RESTORE STUDENT BENEFITS FOR CHILDREN OF DECEASED OR DISABLED WORKERS

Many younger Americans are finding advanced education either out of their financial reach or are taking on huge amounts of debt to continue to attend school. While the major solution to this challenge lies outside of Social Security, the program can do its part.

As chapter 2 has described, Social Security provides benefits to minor children whose parents have died or become disabled.[25] The concept is that if those tragedies had not occurred, those workers' wages would have provided their support. At one time, those children's benefits continued until age 22 for those who attended post-secondary colleges, universities, or vocational schools. But at the beginning of the Reagan administration—when the current campaign against Social Security was just getting underway—those benefits were repealed.[26] At that time, the cost of that education was more affordable, and government-provided student loans and grants were more readily available. The All Generations Plan restores student benefits for children of disabled or deceased workers.

Most parents, if they are financially able to do so, contribute to the costs of their children's post-secondary education. All of us, through Social Security, should provide that support when workers have lost wages as the result of death or disability. Children's benefits, received when a worker has died or become disabled, should continue beyond high school—as they did for many years—if those children attend college or vocational school. Though these benefits should be provided to any working family that has earned them, these beneficiaries tend to be lower income. Consequently, children receiving Social Security disproportionately live in families with lower incomes and disproportionately are racial and ethnic minorities. So, for example, in 2010, almost one out of four children—23 percent—receiving Social Security survivor benefits were African American, even though African Americans constituted only 12.6 percent of the population.[27] More generally, the median family income of all children in the United States was $54,366 in 2009. For children receiving Social Security, the median family income was just $48,751—almost $6,000 less.[28]

ENHANCE PROTECTIONS FOR DISABLED ADULT CHILDREN AND DISABLED WIDOW(ER)S

Disabled adult children are adults who became disabled before age 22 and who, as a result of a parent's eligibility for Social Security benefits, can, as adults, receive Social Security children's benefits, even though they haven't qualified based on their own contributions.[29]

Parents generally worry especially about children with disabilities and want to make sure that they are cared for after the parents have died. Parents also want those children to have as independent and productive lives as possible. Social Security addresses the first concern: it provides benefits for the life of the child.[30] With respect to the second, though, Social Security could be improved.

Social Security has a family maximum, which limits the amount that can be paid based on a worker's earnings record. This may apply even if the disabled adult child is able to live independently. This can have the unfortunate side effect of reducing monthly benefits for the family unit. While this limitation may make sense when a disabled-adult-child beneficiary lives in the family home and shares household expenses, it makes no sense for those beneficiaries who do not live with their parents. Although the number is small, the limitation poses a significant barrier for disabled-adult-child beneficiaries who wish to live more independently. The All Generations Plan addresses this shortcoming.

Social Security also recognizes the special hardship faced by people with disabilities who are widowed. While widow(er)s cannot receive survivor benefits until age 60 at the earliest (unless they are caring for dependent children), widow(er)s who are disabled can receive benefits at younger ages, in recognition of their inability to work. But there is an arbitrary age, 50, for the start of these benefits and a requirement not applied to other persons with disabilities about how recent the onset of the disability must be. Moreover, unlike disabled workers, their benefits are reduced substantially, to 71.5 percent of a full benefit, when they are received at age 50. The All Generations Plan proposes to drop these arbitrary restrictions and harsh reductions. Like the disabled–adult–child proposal, relatively few people are affected and so the cost is relatively low, but the importance to those who would benefit is substantial.

NOW IS THE TIME TO EXPAND SOCIAL SECURITY

All of the expansions highlighted in this chapter and discussed in appendix B fit within the solid structure of Social Security, the cornerstone of which was laid more than three-quarters of a century ago. We are the wealthiest nation in the world, much wealthier than we were when Social Security was created, and much wealthier than when it was expanded in the past.

The last major legislative expansion occurred almost a half century ago, in 1972.[31] It is time to expand it again. Expanding Social Security, where the benefits go largely to low- and middle-class families, and paying for those expansions by requiring the wealthiest among us to pay their fair share, will reduce the growing income inequality discussed in chapter 6. The next chapter and appendix B explain just how affordable these expansions are. But we believe the right question to ask is not can we afford these expansions. Rather, the question we should ask is, how can we afford not to expand Social Security in these ways. The results will be greater economic security for America's working families and a fairer distribution of the nation's bounty.

8

PAYING THE BILL

THE UNITED STATES IS THE WEALTHIEST NATION IN THE
world.[1] It may not feel that way, because, as we discussed in chapter 6,
most of the recent gains in income have gone to those at the very top
of the economic ladder. Nevertheless, together all of us who are part
of the United States are wealthy enough to afford the modest wage
insurance that Social Security provides. We are wealthy enough to
afford a much more robust, expanded Social Security system.

Before demonstrating that this is so, let's start with an important point. Understanding is sharper and deeper if, instead of using
large, unwieldy numbers, with which none of us have real-world
experience, we work with numbers that are more human in scale.
Astronomers do not describe most astronomical distances in miles
or kilometers, but rather in terms of the distance light travels in a
year, or light-years. It is much easier to understand the relative distances from the Earth to, for example, the stars Sirius and Polaris
by comparing 8.6 light-years and 323 light-years, as opposed
to approximately 50,600,000.000,000 miles to approximately
1,890,000,000.000,000 miles. The use of the more human-scale
numbers allows easier and clearer understanding of the magnitude
of the relative distances.

Similarly, rather than talking about the cost of Social Security
or our nation's economy or other large monetary amounts in terms
of hundreds of billions and trillions of dollars, a more comprehen-
sible measure is in terms of percentages of gross domestic product,

which is the total value of all goods the nation produces and all paid services it provides in a single year.[2]

To add to the problem of comparing large dollar amounts, it is even more difficult when comparing those large dollar amounts over many decades, because the face amount changes over time. For example, in 1935, when Social Security was enacted, gasoline cost 19¢ a gallon, a loaf of bread was 8¢, the average home price was $6,300, and the average salary was $1,500.[3] Today's prices and salaries would have sounded astronomically large back then. And future prices sound astronomically large to us. Seventy years from now, a loaf of bread is projected to cost around $35, average homes, $12 million, and the lowest paying jobs will pay hundreds of thousands of dollars a year.[4]

How do those prices compare? Would you rather earn $1,500 in 1935 dollars, $24,000 in today's dollars, or $50,000 in 2085 dollars? One must get out one's calculator, check past inflation rates, and project those rates forward to know. (If you want to earn more, you should choose the 1935 dollars, because inflation has caused $1,500 in 1935 to have inflated to more than $25,000 in today's dollars![5] And you certainly don't want 2085's $50,000. Assuming the average annual rate of inflation is a low 2.8 percent—it was 3.9 percent over the last seventy years—then in today's dollars that $50,000 is worth only $7,038![6] If the inflation rate turns out to be closer to the historical average, the dollar amount would be worth less. For example, if the rate were to be 3.5 percent, that $50,000 in today's dollars is worth only $4,500![7])

Opponents of Social Security often express its long-range cost in trillions of dollars, because those numbers sound scarily large and unaffordable. But talking about trillions of dollars over decades is largely meaningless, because there is no perspective or frame of reference. In contrast, talking in terms of percent of GDP is much more understandable and meaningful. Percent of GDP provides not only a frame of reference, but human-scale numbers.

We all know how much 1 percent, 10 percent, and 100 percent are, and can easily distinguish between them. Looking at the percent of GDP that something costs may take a bit of practice, just as budding astronomers have to learn to be comfortable with light-years, but the good news is that it gives us the ability to judge affordability and make comparisons much more easily and accurately than raw dollar amounts thrown around without any context. Just as 1 percent, 10 percent, and 100 percent of one year's pay provides a frame of reference, so do 1 percent, 10 percent, and 100 percent of our combined earnings, or GDP. The percentages are meaningful because they show costs in relation to how wealthy we are.

SOCIAL SECURITY IS FULLY AFFORDABLE

So what will Social Security cost in the future? As figure 8.1 shows, the cost of Social Security as a percentage of GDP is close to a flat line for the next three-quarters of a century and beyond. Social Security currently accounts for a bit less than 5 percent of GDP. That percentage is projected to peak at 6.16 percent in 2035, when the youngest baby boomers, those born in 1964, reach their 71st birthdays, and then drop slightly, remaining below that peak of 6.16 percent for the the next fifty years and beyond.[8]

To put those percentages into perspective, in 2009, as figure 8.2 highlights, a number of other industrialized countries spent considerably higher percentages of their GDP on the part of their

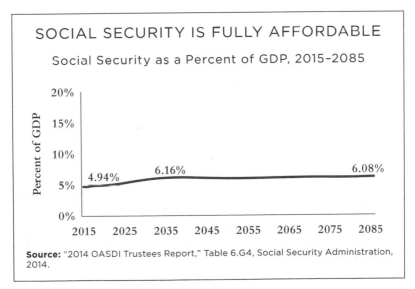

SOCIAL SECURITY IS FULLY AFFORDABLE

Social Security as a Percent of GDP, 2015-2085

Source: "2014 OASDI Trustees Report," Table 6.G4, Social Security Administration, 2014.

Figure 8.1

social security systems that provides old-age, disability, and survivor benefits.[9] Moreover, they spend more today, as a percentage of GDP, than we will spend in 2035, when the entire baby boom will be over age 70. Indeed, we will even spend less at the end of the century than those nations spend today![10]

And our nation will be much wealthier then, just as we are wealthier now than we were seventy-five years ago, before computers, smartphones, and other technological advances. Economists project that our GDP will be 430 percent larger in seventy-five years than it is today, just as today it is 1,364 percent larger than it was seventy-five years ago—and that is using inflation-adjusted numbers, so the growth is real growth.[11] That means that the 6.16 percent of GDP will be easier to afford in the future, just as 10 percent is a larger amount, but more easily afforded, if you are earning $100,000 than if you are earning $10,000. In one case, you have $90,000 remaining; in the other, just $9,000.

Nor should the increase from 4.94 percent to 6.16 percent of GDP over the next few decades produce an impact that anyone is likely to notice. Just between 2006 and today, we have experienced almost a one percentage point of GDP increase in the cost of Social Security, from 4.01 to 4.94 percent of GDP. But did you notice?[12]

To put that projected increase between now and 2035 of 1.22 percent of GDP in perspective, military spending after the 9/11 terrorist attack increased 1.1 percent of GDP, as a result of the Iraq and Afghanistan wars—and that increase was the result of a surprise attack, with no advance warning.[13] As another example, spending on public education nationwide went up 2.8 percent of GDP between 1950 and 1975, when the baby boom generation showed up as schoolchildren, without much advance warning.[14]

In contrast to the wars that followed the surprise 9/11 attack and the increased numbers of kindergartners who started showing up in 1950, Social Security's actuaries and policymakers knew, shortly after the baby boomers were born, that they would someday retire and claim benefits. The actuaries knew that life expectancies would increase. They have been preparing for the eventuality of larger numbers of retirees, living longer, for at least a half century. And they are good at their projections.

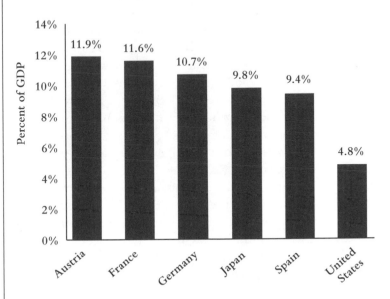

MANY NATIONS SPEND MUCH MORE THAN THE UNITED STATES ON RETIREMENT, DISABILITY, AND SURVIVOR PROTECTION

Note: All data are for 2009 (most recent comparative data available). All countries compared have similar, defined-benefit pension systems. Private systems are excluded, as are targeted social assistance programs. To increase data comparability, only half of spending was counted for program components in other countries that cover all government employees (and only a quarter of spending on those that cover a combination of government employees and members of the military/veterans), as only roughly half (a quarter) of such spending in United States is Social Security spending.

Source: Analysis by Benjamin W. Veghte of OECD Social Expenditure Database.

Figure 8.2

From the beginning, the actuaries working on Social Security have made careful, educated projections. In 1934, the actuaries working on President Roosevelt's Committee on Economic Security, the group that devised the Social Security program, made projections about what the world would look like in the year 2000, sixty-six years into the future. In 1934, they projected that the percentage of the population that would be 65 or older in 2000 would be 12.7 percent.[15] How accurate were they? Extremely accurate.

According to census figures from year 2000, the actual percentage was 12.4 percent.[16]

So it is unlikely that today's actuaries are wildly off, despite all the hype that Social Security is unaffordable. Not only can we afford a larger Social Security program, it is completely appropriate. Today, about 13 percent of our nation consists of people 65 and older.[17] By 2050, that percentage is projected to rise to about 20 percent.[18] It is only reasonable that a somewhat greater percentage of the nation's goods and services should be consumed by seniors as their numbers increase. (In chapter 10, we will explain why this increased spending does not hurt young people, despite claims of intergenerational unfairness.)

Spending through the Internal Revenue Code—giving tax breaks for inducing action (as opposed to simply spending in a more direct, straightforward, and often more efficient way)—is known, oxymoronically, as tax "spending" or tax "expenditures." The preferential treatment given to 401(k) plans and other retirement plans as a way of inducing savings for retirement is among the nation's largest tax expenditures. The nonpartisan Congressional Budget Office has estimated that the cost of tax-favored, employer-provided, and individual retirement vehicles, for just the ten years from 2015 to 2024, is $2.1 trillion, which translates to 0.93 percent of GDP.[19]

Many politicians treat these arrangements as free to the public, but, of course, they are not. Moreover, the distribution of these retirement tax benefits is highly skewed to the wealthiest among us, one of the many policies discussed in chapter 6 that contributes to the upward redistribution of wealth.[20]

If we can afford to spend 0.93 percent of our GDP on these tax-favored arrangements, surely we can also afford to expand our Social Security system, which is more universal, secure, efficient, and fair than the plans on which those tax expenditures are being spent.

FAIRLY SHARING COSTS OF AN EXPANDED SOCIAL SECURITY

The question is, how should the costs of an expanded Social Security be shared without unduly burdening anyone? There are numerous options, all quite affordable, reasonable, good policy, and fair. As we highlighted at the beginning of chapter 7 and explain in this chapter, the All Generations Plan builds on the existing financing of Social Security in a manner that is not only fair, but will slow the perilously rising upward redistribution of wealth.

Before getting into that, though, we have to make a brief digression. If you have even been casually following the Social Security debate, you have probably heard that Social Security is going bankrupt. It's not. Nor can it. We will address that in detail in chapter 10. But where does the claim come from?

Opponents have latched onto an unremarkable fact about pensions as part of their effort to undermine confidence in Social Security. As explained in chapter 2, the annuities provided by Social Security are insurance, as are the annuities provided by traditional, defined benefit pension plans. Because insurers often face a substantial time lag between the receipt of premiums and the expenditure of benefits, they must, to be prudent, project their annual income and outgo over a substantial period of time into the future. As a prudent insurer, the Social Security Administration employs more than forty actuaries whose job it is to make those projections. Moreover, Social Security is so conservatively managed that it makes those projections out for three-quarters of a century. This is a longer valuation period than that used by private pension plans or by the Social Security programs of nearly all other countries. The projections appear in an annual trustees report to the Congress.

Whenever projections are made over such a long time horizon, they will rarely show perfect balance.[21] Rather, they may show a surplus, or they may show a deficit. That is unremarkable. The question is, how large is the shortfall and how imminent? Out of concern about the financial well-being of private sector pension plans, known as multiemployer plans, Congress enacted the Pension Protection Act of 2006, which established three categories of plans, based on the strength of their funding and ability to pay promised benefits. Plans that are deemed in critical condition are said to be in the red zone; plans that are "endangered," in the yellow zone; and healthy plans, in the green zone. The law requires that each plan announce its status within the first ninety days of each plan year.[22]

If Social Security had the same reporting requirement as those private sector multiemployer plans, it would announce that it is in the green zone. It is projecting a deficit, but that deficit is manageable in size and still 15 to 20 years away. The good news is that Social Security not only has substantial revenue coming in now, but will in the future, even without Congress doing anything whatsoever.

These projections should provide Americans with a sense of confidence, because Social Security is being so carefully monitored and managed. Instead, the annual trustees reports have been turned on their heads, creating hysterical cries of bankruptcy every time a distant shortfall is projected.

The remainder of this chapter describes the wide range of options available, not only to eliminate the projected shortfall that recent reports have forecast, but also to pay for all expansions. It identifies those revenue sources proposed as part of the All Generations Plan, as well as some other reasonable funding sources. At the conclusion of the chapter, we summarize the All Generations Plan, including all the expansions and all the revenue sources. Appendix B includes the cost and revenues of the individual elements in the plan. Spoiler alert: Under the All Generations Plan, Social Security will be in surplus for the next seventy-five years and beyond!

All options discussed in this chapter, and further detailed in appendix B, build on the three existing sources of Social Security revenue—premiums, investments, and taxation of benefits. All of the options bring in substantial revenue. None of them impose unfair burdens on anyone.

INCREASE PREMIUMS

As chapter 2 explains, Social Security's wage insurance has been financed, from the beginning, primarily from premiums split evenly between employees and employers. Those premiums today are 12.4 percent of wages, equally divided between employer and employee, up to a maximum salary amount. The 12.4 percent rate has not increased since 1990.[23]

It is instructive to note that a number of policymakers have proposed something called auto-IRAs. For employees who are not participating in other private retirement arrangements, employers would be required to automatically enroll them in retirement savings accounts and deduct contributions, generally 3 percent of their pay.[24] (Employees would have the ability to opt out or change the percentage, but 3 percent is most commonly the default option.) No one has proposed it (including the authors), but if that 3 percent were instead directed to Social Security and, even more, matched by employer contributions, the money would be much more efficiently invested, would include disability and survivor protection (as well as all of the other benefits highlighted in chapter 2), would result in an immediate increase in benefits (as opposed to waiting decades, as the auto-IRA proposals would require), and, most importantly, would provide insurance protection, not just savings, which could be lost if invested in stocks. And that revenue would be so significant that it would permit Social Security benefits to be substantially increased. We are not advocating such a large increase.

If the rate were to be gradually increased by 1 percent on employers and employees each, over a two-decade period, as some have recommended and the All Generations Plan proposes, that would translate to an average increase of about 50¢ a week each year.[25] Just that gradual increase would bring in substantial revenue, as appendix B details.[26]

Social Security premiums are assessed against covered compensation. A larger and larger proportion of compensation is paid not as cash but as deferred or noncash compensation, such as health insurance and so-called flexible spending accounts for such items as medical expenses, dependent care, and commuting costs. This compensation is generally not treated as compensation covered by Social Security.[27] The failure of this compensation to be counted for Social Security purposes means that those noncash wages are not insured against loss in the event of death, disability, or old age. Moreover, that failure may encourage employers and employees to set up deferred or noncash compensation plans for the express purpose of avoiding part of the cost of the mandatory Social Security premiums. If just payments to flexible spending accounts were considered wages for Social Security purposes—as contributions to 401(k) plans already are, and as the All Generations Plan advocates—the change alone would generate meaningful new revenue.[28] The revenue produced would be even more if combined with increases in both the Social Security contribution rate and the maximum dollar amount on which that rate is assessed—a possibility that is described next.

The maximum amount of wages on which Social Security contributions are made—$117,000 in 2014—increases every year by the percentage that average wages nationwide increase.[29] However, because wages at the top have gone up rapidly over the last thirty years, while nearly everyone else's have stagnated, the impact is that more and more wages at the top escape from being assessed for Social Security.[30] Some have argued that instead of just restoring the maximum to where Congress intended—which should have been done years ago—it should be scrapped altogether, or at least with respect to the employer match. This would result in workers all paying the same rate on all their wages whether they earn the minimum wage or are CEO of a Fortune 500 company. It also would mean that all wages would be insured against loss in the event of death, disability, or old age.

Only 6 percent of the workforce earns in excess of the maximum.[31] The All Generations Plan gradually phases out the maximum, so that all workers would contribute to Social Security at the same rate on all their cash compensation. (It is instructive to note that Congress eliminated the maximum with respect to the hospital insurance part of Medicare in 1994.)[32] Those 6 percent, who would under the proposal make larger contributions, would also receive somewhat higher benefits. Nevertheless, the net revenue produced would be substantial.[33]

There is no reason that employers and employees have to pay the same rate, or cover the same wages. Employers could pay premiums on their entire payroll, while employees could continue to pay only up to a maximum wage amount. Employees earning at the top 1 percent of the wage scale and their employers could pay premiums on their highest earnings at a higher rate. There are a multitude of ways that the increased premiums could be allocated. Although the All Generations Plan does not include these types of proposals, they are all reasonable and would produce substantial revenues to pay for expanded benefits.

DIVERSIFY SOCIAL SECURITY'S INVESTMENT PORTFOLIO

In addition to premiums, Social Security has other sources of income. In any year that Social Security has more income than outgo, the surplus is held in trust and invested in interest-bearing treasury bonds backed by the full faith and credit of the United States.[34] These are the safest investment on the planet. (If you have heard that the trust funds aren't real and the bonds are worthless IOUs, you will learn the truth in chapter 10.)

Thanks to past surpluses, the Social Security trust funds have accumulated reserves of $2.8 trillion.[35] The interest from the investments of these funds accounted for about 12 percent of Social Security's total income in 2013, or $103 billion in that one year alone.[36] By law, these funds can only be invested in interest-bearing United States' obligations or in entities whose principal and interest are guaranteed by the United States.[37] While Social Security's principal is secure and its income is fixed, bonds tend to produce less income over time than investment in stocks. To get a higher return, Social Security could diversify its portfolio by investing a portion of its assets in broad-based stock funds. Virtually all other pension funds have this kind of diversified investment portfolio, including most public pensions. Assets of the Railroad Retirement Plan, the Federal Reserve Board Plan, the Tennessee Valley Authority Plan, many state plans, and Canada's Social Security system are invested in equities. That's because higher market returns could be realized simultaneously with achieving the paramount goal of advancing the economic security of workers and their families.

For all these reasons, the All Generations Plan advocates diversifying Social Security's portfolio by investment in broad-based equity funds, with appropriate safeguards to ensure no improper interference in the governing of the businesses or markets. It is important to understand that this is a very different proposal from simply placing contributions in individual retirement accounts, which subject individuals to the vagaries of the stock market. Regardless of whether the stock market went up or down, Social Security benefits would remain guaranteed. Retirement income would continue to be based on earnings records, not stock market fluctuations. Unlike investments by individuals, investment by Social Security spreads the risk across the entire population over an unlimited time horizon. Diversifying Social Security's portfolio would permit the benefit of higher market returns without individual risk.

INCREASE PROGRESSIVE REVENUES

Social Security has only one source of revenue that is progressive —where those with higher incomes pay proportionally larger amounts. That source is the dedicated revenue from the taxation of benefits. As explained in chapter 2, if your income is high enough, a portion of your Social Security benefits is treated as income when determining how much you must pay in taxes on April 15 each year.

As we all know, the amount of federal income taxes you pay is determined by a set of progressive income tax rates. The higher your income, the higher the percentage you pay in income taxes. The revenue collected from the taxation of a portion of Social Security benefits is dedicated to Social Security and Medicare.[38]

This one progressive source of Social Security revenue constitutes only 2.5 percent of Social Security's total annual income.[39] In contrast, premium income and investment earnings, which make up virtually all of the rest of Social Security's annual revenue,[40] do not require the wealthy—no matter how many hundreds of millions of dollars they earn each year—to pay a larger percentage of their income or wealth. And none of the new revenue for Social Security proposed by the All Generations Plan and discussed so far in this chapter would require them to pay a larger percentage of their vast wealth. But we believe that it is just and fair that they do.

Requiring the wealthiest among us to pay more, while still retaining the great bulk of their fortunes, has precedent. In fact, it was the norm for most of the past one hundred years. The top marginal income tax rates were 70 percent or higher each and every year between 1936 and 1980, before dropping to today's low rates.[41] Indeed, even during the relatively conservative administration of President Eisenhower from 1953 to 1961, marginal tax rates exceeded 90 percent. Today, the top rate is only 39.6 percent.[42] As figure 8.3 shows, a top marginal rate ten percentage points higher would still be well below what it was in the 1950s and 1960s, when the nation had a thriving middle class and much greater income and wealth equality.

Having the wealthiest bear a greater burden of expenses for the common good is as American as apple pie, and for good reason. All of us benefit from public expenditures, but the wealthy benefit the most. Since they have the most property, they are arguably disproportionately advantaged by having police, military, court systems, fire departments, and other public services designed to protect us and our property. The accumulation of large estates is dependent,

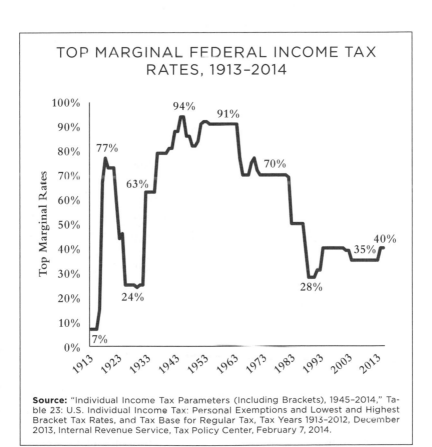

TOP MARGINAL FEDERAL INCOME TAX RATES, 1913–2014

Source: "Individual Income Tax Parameters (Including Brackets), 1945–2014," Table 23: U.S. Individual Income Tax: Personal Exemptions and Lowest and Highest Bracket Tax Rates, and Tax Base for Regular Tax, Tax Years 1913–2012, December 2013, Internal Revenue Service, Tax Policy Center, February 7, 2014.

Figure 8.3

in part, on the general productivity of the American economy and its infrastructure—including, for example, roads, police, and education. Also, the very well-off benefited far more than others from large tax cuts, initiated during Ronald Reagan's and George W. Bush's presidencies. Further, as chapter 6 highlights, since the mid-1970s a dramatic increase has taken place in the share of income going to the top 1 percent of American households, and there has been an enormous concentration of wealth. It is reasonable to ask of those who have benefited so greatly from the commonwealth (i.e., common wealth) to contribute more to the common good, specifically more to Social Security.[43]

A new stream of progressive revenues for Social Security could fund significant benefit expansions such as those proposed in chapter 7. It would also ameliorate excessive income and wealth inequalities. Accordingly, the All Generations Plan proposes a millionaire's tax; that is, a new marginal income tax rate, ten percentage points higher than the current top rate (now 39.6 percent) on incomes of more than $1 million, with the new revenue dedicated to Social Security.[44] Under this proposal, millionaires and billionaires would pay no more on their first million dollars. For every dollar earned in excess of $1 million, they would pay 10 percent. In other words, on the million-and-first dollar, just 10¢ would go to Social Security. The All Generations Plan imposes only a 10 percent tax. If, for example, a 20 percent rate were levied on annual incomes of more than $20 million, that, of course, would bring in considerably more revenue.

An even more progressive tax could be used. The federal estate tax is the nation's most progressive tax. Estates left to spouses are not subject to tax. More than $5 million of wealth can be left tax-free to other heirs, meaning couples can bequeath more than $10 million tax-free. Not surprisingly, the top 5 percent of estates paid 97.5 percent of the estate tax collected in 2011. In fact, more than half of it was collected from the top 0.1 percent.[45]

The estate tax should be preserved as a matter of principle. Inherited wealth undercuts the democratic ideal of a meritocracy. Imposition of a tax upon the transfer of huge estates from one generation to another is consistent with basic democratic principles, as was recognized by, among others, Thomas Paine, one of the leading intellectuals behind the American Revolution and an advocate of an inheritance tax.[46]

An estate tax implicitly recognizes that it is impossible to build a sizable estate solely on one's own efforts, without roads, bridges, the protection of police and the military, and other goods and services provided by government. Requiring the very wealthiest Americans to contribute a portion of their fortune—on a one-time basis, only after death—to the common good, while still transferring more than half of their assets to heirs, seems a reasonable minimum to ask of those who have benefited so greatly from living in the United States.[47] And dedicating those funds to Social Security makes perfect sense.

Another progressive tax, also with a good policy impact, is a financial speculation tax, again dedicated to Social Security. Speculation in stocks, derivatives, and other financial instruments has no economic benefit. Indeed, irresponsible speculation and defaults on exotic financial instruments are what nearly brought our economy to its knees in 2008. A tax on Wall Street speculation, a so-called financial transactions tax, imposed at a very low rate and primarily levied on large banks, would, if its proceeds were dedicated to Social Security, allow benefits to be expanded substantially. Many industrialized countries have had such a tax for many decades. The tax would help cut down on wasteful, unproductive Wall Street speculation.

England has had such a tax since 1694. The United Kingdom imposes a modest tax of 0.5 percent on stock transfers—0.25 percent on the purchaser and 0.25 percent on the seller.[48] Although most Americans are unaware of it, the United States currently imposes a very small assessment on stock transfers as well, its revenues dedicated to funding the Securities and Exchange Commission.[49] Generally passed along to investors, it amounted in 2013 to just $0.0042 for each transaction—$0.0021 on the purchaser and $0.0021 on the seller, when a contract of sale is entered into.[50]

If the United States increased the amount of the tax to equal what the United Kingdom assesses—just 0.5 percent on stock transfers—and imposed it on the sale and purchase of stocks, credit swaps, and other exotic financial instruments, it would fall mainly on large banks that engage in proprietary, speculative trading, and serve the public goal of reducing stock market speculation by large Wall Street banks. If the proceeds of the tax were dedicated to Social Security, the program would be so flush that not only would it be in surplus for the next seventy-five years and beyond, but benefits could be raised by about 5 percent across the board. Although the All Generations Plan does not propose an increase in the estate tax or a new financial transactions tax—sometimes referred to as a Robin Hood tax—these and other progressive taxes have substantial merit and they could be used to greatly increase the economic security of all Americans by financing the expansion of Social Security.

SUMMARY OF THE SOCIAL SECURITY WORKS ALL GENERATIONS PLAN

To strengthen retirement security and address the retirement income crisis, the All Generations Plan would:

- Increase benefits for all current and future beneficiaries by 10 percent, up to a maximum increase of $150 a month.
- Ensure that benefits do not erode over time by enacting the more accurate Consumer Price Index for the Elderly (CPI-E).
- Provide a minimum benefit of 125 percent of poverty at full retirement age with thirty years of work.

To strengthen family protections for all generations and to reinforce the caregiving functions of the family, the plan would:

- Provide up to twelve weeks of paid family leave upon the birth or adoption of a child or illness of a covered worker or family member.
- Provide up to five years of Social Security benefit credits for caring for one or more children under age 6.
- Facilitate higher education by restoring student benefits for children up to age 22 in case of the death or disability of covered parents.

- Provide a new child benefit of $1,000 upon the birth or adoption of a child.
- Enhance protections for the category of beneficiaries known as disabled adult children and for disabled widow(er)s.

To secure Social Security's financing for generations to come, the plan would:

- Gradually eliminate the maximum taxable wage base, giving credit for these contributions.
- Introduce a dedicated 10 percent marginal income tax on income more than $1 million.
- Gradually, over twenty years, increase the Social Security contribution rate by 1 percent on employees, matched by their employers.
- Diversify Social Security's portfolio by investing 40 percent of its reserve in broad-based equity funds (phased in over fifteen years).
- Treat all salary reduction plans the same as 401(k) plans with respect to the definition of wages under Social Security.
- Combine the OASI Trust Fund with the DI Trust Fund. (See chapter 11 and appendix B for additional information about these two trust funds.)

For readers interested in a more detailed discussion of the All Generations Plan, including estimates of the costs of benefit expansion and financing proposals, please see appendix B. Taken together, the increased revenues from our expansion plan fully pay for the benefit improvements and leave Social Security in long-range actuarial balance for the next three-quarters of a century and beyond.

CONCLUSION

The revenue sources described in this chapter are just some of the dozens of revenue sources and variations that exist. With the exception of increasing the Social Security premium rate, which would cause virtually all workers to pay a modest amount more, these revenue sources would have no impact on the vast majority of

American workers. None of them would impose an undue burden on anyone. Moreover, the existing refundable Earned Income Tax Credit, enacted in 1975, in part to offset the cost of Social Security contributions to low-income workers, could be expanded to soften or even eliminate the impact of those increased contributions on lower income workers.

The various revenue sources can be mixed and matched depending on how substantially the nation wants to expand Social Security. They could be phased in gradually to blunt the impact on individuals. Most importantly, they would build on Social Security's existing financing and retain premiums as the primary source of income, consistent with the earned-benefit nature of Social Security.

If we want to expand our Social Security system, we can afford to do it. Unfortunately, it is not as simple as that last sentence sounds. Standing in the way are determined, powerful, and well-financed foes. The next chapter reveals who they are.

PART FOUR

THE THREATS

9

THE BILLIONAIRES' WAR AGAINST
SOCIAL SECURITY

OUT OF SIGHT FROM MOST AMERICANS, POWERFUL, ORGA-
nized, and determined moneyed interests have waged a more than
three-decade-long, billionaire-funded campaign to dismantle Social Security, brick by brick. That campaign has enjoyed some success. And it is with us still.

It is not hard to see the successes of that campaign. Many have
been persuaded that Social Security is unaffordable, perhaps in crisis, and must, at the very least, be scaled back. Prominent leaders
and major media outlets asked not whether Social Security should
be cut, but rather whether the changes should be at the edges or
more radical. The media asked whether politicians were acting re-
sponsibly, and supporting cuts—or cowardly, and opposing them—
in the face of overwhelming opposition to Social Security cuts by
the American people. And all the supposedly serious people fretted
for years over how to force action, in light of that opposition.

So, in the October 7, 2008, presidential debate between Barack
Obama and John McCain, moderator and highly respected (but
in this case misinformed) journalist Tom Brokaw asked: "Would
you give Congress a date certain to reform Social Security and
Medicare within two years after you take office? Because *in a bipartisan way, everyone agrees, that's a big ticking time bomb that will eat us up
maybe even more than the mortgage crisis.*"[1] [Emphasis added.]

An October 27, 2011, front-page *Washington Post* news story declared: "But while talk about fixing the nation's finances has grown more urgent, fixing Social Security has largely vanished from the conversation. *Lawmakers in both parties are ducking the issue,* wary of agitating older voters and their advocates in Washington."[2] [Emphasis added.]

The fiscal year 2013 budget resolution passed the House of Representatives on March 29, 2012.[3] Nine days earlier, chairman of the House Budget Committee and soon-to-be vice presidential candidate Paul Ryan (R-WI) released *The Path to Prosperity: A Blueprint for American Renewal*, which described the Republican budget that formed the resolution. The Blueprint used alarmist language: "The risk to Social Security, driven by demographic changes, is nearer at hand than most acknowledge. *This budget heads off a crisis* by calling on the President *and* both chambers of Congress to ensure the solvency of this critical program."[4] [Emphasis added.]

Later that year, during the October 11, 2012, vice presidential debate, Martha Raddatz, the distinguished ABC News chief global affairs correspondent, framed the Social Security policy exchange for candidates Joe Biden and Paul Ryan by first asserting, "*Both Medicare and Social Security are going broke* and taking a larger share of the budget in the process." [Emphasis added.] She then asked Candidate Ryan, "Will benefits for Americans under these programs have to change for the programs to survive?" Not surprisingly, Ryan quickly responded, "Absolutely. *Medicare and Social Security are going bankrupt. These are indisputable facts.*"[5] [Emphasis added.]

During a roundtable discussion on the October 27, 2013, episode of *Meet the Press*, Alex Castellanos, a political consultant and frequent guest on political talk shows, blithely commented, in a discussion about the implementation of the Affordable Care Act (often called Obamacare): "And if Obamacare was an anomaly, that would be one thing. But tell me something that Washington is doing a good job at. Education? A disaster. *Social Security? It's bankrupt, a Ponzi scheme.* Name something Washington is doing well."[6] [Emphasis added.]

In her germinal article, "How the Media Has Shaped the Social Security Debate," Trudy Lieberman—a highly regarded, award-winning journalist of more than four decades—makes clear that the false characterizations you just read are only a few examples of the distortions that have characterized the mainstream-media reporting on Social Security: "For nearly three years CJR [the *Columbia Journalism Review*, where Lieberman is a contributing editor] has observed that much of the press has reported only one side of this story using 'facts' that are misleading or flat-out wrong while ignoring others."[7]

It is no accident that the discussions have had this flavor. This has resulted from a deliberate campaign, backed by hundreds of millions of dollars and a cottage industry of academics who have built their careers on criticizing Social Security. Together, those forces have brought a veneer of respectability to claims that Social Security is unsustainable, in crisis, and spawning competition and conflict between generations.

Abetting the effort have been journalists and politicians who have either willingly advanced an anti–Social Security agenda or fallen prey to myths, misunderstandings, half-truths, and a few outright lies that have been masquerading as incontrovertible facts. Perhaps unwittingly, they have advanced policy changes that would render Social Security unrecognizable and undermine the economic security of the American people. Only recently have some prominent, well-informed voices challenged this orthodoxy by asserting that Social Security should be expanded, not cut.

The next chapter will explode the pervasive myths, half-truths, opinions, and mischaracterizations that have been put forward by this well-financed campaign and that have gained such traction in the public discourse. But first, in this chapter, we pull back the curtain and reveal the campaign itself.

The three-decade-long period is bookended by two commissions, whose differing approaches and recommendations reveal just how successful the campaign has been in shaping the contemporary debate.[8] A third commission, about halfway through the period, provides an informative and inside look at one of the least well-known, but most influential, billionaires driving the campaign.

A TALE OF THREE COMMISSIONS

The first commission was the National Commission on Social Security Reform (often referred to as the Greenspan Commission in reference to the economist, Alan Greenspan, who chaired it. (Both authors of this book served as staff to the commission.) The Greenspan Commission has been touted as an enormous success and a shining example of bipartisanship at its best.[9] What is largely forgotten is that it was born out of a failed attempt in 1981 to undermine the program by determined opponents.

As explained in the previous chapter, Social Security is extremely conservatively managed. Unsurprisingly, as good as actuaries are, and as hard as they work, projections are just that: projections, not crystal balls. Consequently, they may not be right on target, and, indeed, may be way off the mark on occasion. This is why projections are made every year. In response to a projected shortfall, Congress took action in 1977,[10] and the subsequent Trustees Report showed that the legislative changes had accomplished their intended purpose.[11] Accordingly, Social Security's 1979 Trustees Report projected that the program could pay all benefits through 2032.[12] But the very next year, thanks to a continued bad economy and a technical problem with the 1977 legislation, the 1980 Trustees Report was now projecting a shortfall just three years away, in 1983.[13]

Despite claims after the 1977 amendments that Social Security had been restored to balance, it was once again projecting an immediate deficit. In addition, much like today, there was concern in Washington about federal deficits in the nation's general operating fund. In those twin deficits—one in the government's operating budget, the other in Social Security—opponents saw an opportunity.

One of those opponents was David Stockman, who was appointed budget director by the newly elected president, Ronald Reagan. In his memoir, written a few years later, after leaving government, Stockman admitted that he considered Social Security "closet socialism."[14] He had earlier confided in an interview with journalist Bill Greider that Social Security's projected deficit would "permit the politicians to make it look like they're doing something *for* the beneficiary population when they are doing something *to* it, which they normally wouldn't have the courage to undertake."[15] [Emphasis added.] But Stockman was too clever for his own good.

Congress was well on its way to passing legislation in 1981 to eliminate the new projected shortfall, when Stockman inadvertently derailed the process. In the midst of congressional deliberations, the Reagan administration, at Stockman's urging, unveiled a Social Security package that called for draconian benefit reductions.[16] One reduction would have fallen very heavily on workers reaching retirement age the very next year, workers who were counting on that income to be able to retire.[17]

Not surprisingly, the proposal set off a political firestorm. Stockman had seriously miscalculated. The proposal, and, indeed, the entire package, had little to do with good Social Security policy and everything to do with diminishing the size of the program. It is that episode that gave rise to the now-famous expression that Social Security is the third rail of politics.[18] The strong, negative public outcry forced the administration to withdraw the not-yet-submitted package, but that was not enough.

The outcry was so great that President Reagan, in a face-saving move, announced that he, together with the leaders in Congress, would appoint a bipartisan commission. The ensuing Greenspan Commission was hastily conceived to quench the political firestorm.[19]

Fast forward to today: the commission that enters the story more recently is President Obama's National Commission on Fiscal Responsibility and Reform. Like the Greenspan Commission, it is best known by the name of its chairs. As a sign of the times, President Obama selected not one, but two chairs, one from each political party: a center-right Democrat and a Republican, both of whom have long sought to cut Social Security.[20] They are Erskine Bowles, businessman and former chief of staff to President Clinton, and former Republican senator Alan Simpson.

The executive orders establishing these two commissions reveal how attitudes have changed, thanks to the campaign, in the nearly thirty years that have intervened. President Reagan's December 16, 1981, Executive Order 12335 defined the Greenspan Commission's task as recommending solutions "that will both assure the financial integrity of the Social Security System and the provision of appropriate benefits."[21] President Obama's February 18, 2010, Executive Order 13531 defined the task as proposing recommendations that "balance the budget, excluding interest payments on the debt, by

2015," and "that meaningfully improve the long-run fiscal outlook, *including changes to address the growth of entitlement spending* and
the gap between the projected revenues and expenditures of the
Federal Government."[22] [Emphasis added.]

Note the difference in substance and language. By the very terms
of the Reagan executive order, the commission was required to focus on Social Security on its own, apart from general budgetary
concerns. And Reagan's order instructed the commission to focus
not just on solvency, but also on the provision of adequate benefits.

The Greenspan Commission itself limited its focus even more.
Early on, the commission members agreed to exclude Medicare
from consideration.[23] They recognized that Medicare was a very
different program from Social Security's cash benefits, and required
different expertise and different solutions. They also understood
that incorporating Medicare into the commission's deliberations
would make political resolution of the Social Security financing
issue far more complex than it needed to be.

Also ruled off the table were proposals to means-test, privatize,
or otherwise fundamentally change Social Security.[24] Indeed, the
Greenspan Commission's very first recommendation stated that
Congress "should not alter the fundamental structure of the Social
Security program or undermine its fundamental principles."[25]

The 1982 commission and its staff functioned within the framework of serious knowledge and support for Social Security. Alan
Greenspan's appointment, as executive director, of Robert J. Myers,
chief actuary of Social Security from 1947 to 1970, and Speaker
Tip O'Neill's appointment, as a member of the commission, of
Robert M. Ball, Social Security commissioner from 1962 to 1973,
epitomized Republican and Democratic commitment to the institution of Social Security. Its voting membership included senators
and representatives, and public representatives from business and
labor, from both parties, the majority of whom had significant expertise in Social Security. Thus it is not surprising that substantial
analytic attention was given to the consequences of reform options
on workers and future Social Security beneficiaries, including implications across income classes. In other words, both taxpayer and
beneficiary costs were fully assessed.[26]

In contrast to the limited scope of Reagan's executive order,

President Obama's executive order was expansive, covering all of the federal government's expenditures—other than interest on the debt—and all of its revenue. Unlike the Greenspan Commission, which explicitly separated the discussion of Social Security's cash benefit programs from Medicare, the Obama order lumped together Social Security, Medicare, and Medicaid under the rubric "entitlement spending." Moreover, there were few members and staff with in-depth understanding of Social Security. And while some members sought to include information about the distributional impact of various policy options or of what the benefit reductions might mean to individuals and their families, for the commission as a whole, such information appeared to be little more than an afterthought.[27]

Let's pause for a moment on the language of the Reagan and Obama executive orders. They offer an important insight into a crucial tactic of the thirty-year campaign against Social Security.

President Reagan's executive order refers straightforwardly to "the Social Security System." In stark contrast, President Obama's executive order refers opaquely to "entitlement spending," a budgetary term that could include numerous mandatory spending programs, as well as provisions in the Internal Revenue Code, sometimes referred to as tax entitlements. But the reference is well understood as Washington-speak referring to Social Security, Medicare, and Medicaid—three extremely different programs with different structures, goals, budgetary impacts, and financial outlooks.

Indeed, the change in terminology—the fact that many policymakers now call Social Security an entitlement—is part of the story. The popularization and promulgation of the terms "entitlement" and "entitlement crisis" as political tools to strengthen the hand of those wanting to cut Social Security was the handiwork of yet another commission, this one established by President Clinton's November 9, 1993, executive order—the Bipartisan Commission on Entitlement and Tax Reform.[28] (Co-author Eric R. Kingson was on staff to this commission.)

This commission never produced recommendations that garnered even a majority of votes.[29] While never achieving consensus, the commission, by lumping Social Security, Medicare, and

Medicaid together as part of a unified entitlement crisis, helped set the terms of the Social Security debates that would follow.

Pity the poor word "entitlement." In less than a year, this eleven-letter term migrated from being perfectly respectable budget jargon—though boring, wonky, and technical—into the proverbial four-letter word, used to suggest that the benefits Americans had and were earning were less than deserved, and to obfuscate the goals of those who sought to radically diminish social protections.

Focus groups indicate that most people equate the word "entitlement" with a government handout—receiving something for nothing. But here's the catch that pollster Celinda Lake uncovered: when told that the term "entitlement" includes Social Security, they vigorously disagree. Social Security can't be an entitlement, focus group members say, since they have earned their benefits, just as they earn their other compensation for work performed.[30] When they are told that, in Washington, entitlement does indeed refer to Social Security, as well as to Medicare and Medicaid, they are often angry and insulted.[31]

The American people do not like the change in language, but the media loved the storyline that entitlement spending on the old was crowding out spending on the young and ruining the country. When the Entitlement Commission released an interim report identifying the size of the so-called problem,[32] front-page newspaper stories appeared and network news shows ran major segments on the problems caused by out-of-control entitlement spending.[33] A headline in the *Los Angeles Times* alarmingly trumpeted, for example, "Entitlements Seen Taking Up Nearly All Taxes by 2012."[34]

But the reach of some of the commission's members was greater than simply the commission's legacy of transforming a technical eleven-letter term—"entitlement"—into a proverbial four-letter word.[35] Alan Simpson, the co-chair of Obama's commission, was a member of the Entitlement Commission. The final report[36] was released two months after Erskine Bowles, Obama's other co-chair, became President Clinton's deputy chief of staff.[37] Presumably, Bowles read it, and, based on his subsequent actions, it seems likely that he was influenced by it.

President Obama gave both men considerable prominence by naming them as co-chairs to his commission, notwithstanding the hostility that both had displayed to Social Security in the past. Indeed, as chapter 3 relates, the outspoken Simpson has helped popularize the phrase "greedy geezers,"[38] and once referred crudely to Social Security as "a milk cow with 310 million tits!"[39] Not surprisingly, the cuts proposed for Social Security by Bowles and Simpson were not only deep, but would radically transform the program, gradually but inexorably, from wage insurance—where benefits are designed to replace a set percentage of wages—to a program where all beneficiaries receive about the same subsistence-level benefit amount, largely unrelated to wages.

The overall Bowles-Simpson deficit reduction proposal has been widely lauded in the mainstream media, but has thankfully faded from view, at least at the time of this writing. But there was another member of the Entitlement Commission whose name is not well-known by the general public, but whose money and activities are largely responsible for the change over the last thirty years so well exemplified by the Greenspan and Bowles-Simpson commissions.

MONEY, MONEY, MONEY

He is Peter G. Peterson. Ranked in 2008 as the 147th richest American on the Forbes 400: The Richest People in America list, with a reported net worth of $2.8 billion, he is the money behind the campaign.[40] In the same year he ranked 147th, he created the Peter G. Peterson Foundation and endowed it with $1 billion.[41]

The Peterson Foundation describes its mission as working "to increase public awareness of the nature and urgency of key fiscal challenges threatening America's future and to accelerate action on them."[42] It has been a major player in recent efforts to cut Social Security. But Peterson himself has been spending time and money on this crusade for more than thirty years.

In 1982, Peterson—then the chairman and CEO of Lehman Brothers, and former secretary of commerce in the cabinet of president Richard Nixon—wrote two articles for the *New York Review of Books*, both published shortly before the Greenspan Commission issued its report. The first appeared on December 2, 1982, and was titled "Social Security: The Coming Crash." It began: "Social Security's troubles are fundamental. Its financial problems are not minor and temporary, as most politicians, at least in election years, feel compelled to insist. Unless the system is reorganized, these problems will become overwhelming. To put the matter bluntly, Social Security is heading for a crash."[43]

The second article, titled "The Salvation of Social Security," appeared two weeks later, and asserted:

> Social Security . . . threatens the entire economy. In the recent election campaign, practically all the candidates promised to "preserve Social Security," to "resist any cuts in benefits," and to "protect the elderly poor." No one dared to say that without major reforms—including "cuts"—the Social Security system will run huge deficits, that these deficits will push our children into a situation of economic stagnation and social conflict and create a potentially disastrous situation for the elderly of the future.[44]

This might have been the first time anyone claimed that Social Security is hurting young people.[45] Ironically, Peterson's own children (and the authors themselves) were young adults when he first began making the intergenerational theft claims.[46] Now, all of us are approaching or have reached old age—and are the ones supposedly threatening the well-being of today's children and young adults. Fast forward twenty-five years from now. No doubt Peterson's ideological progeny will be claiming that Gen Xers, persons born from 1965 to 1984, are stealing from Millennials and those who follow! (For more on the campaign's efforts to ignite intergenerational warfare and why seniors are not robbing children, see the next chapter.)

In yet another *New York Review of Books* article that appeared shortly after the Greenspan Commission had reported in 1983, but before Congress had taken action, Peterson wrote, "if, as with past reforms, we pretend that the report has restored long-term solvency to the system, we will find that it has become simply another example of unjustified optimism."[47] Peterson was dismayed that the Greenspan Commission's recommendations, which were largely enacted as the Social Security Amendments of 1983, did not fundamentally restructure Social Security. Despite Peterson's alarmist warnings, all benefits have been paid in full and on time to this day.[48]

Peterson did more than just write and found the Peterson Foundation in order to get his point of view across. Over the years, he has funded numerous nonprofit organizations, all working to convince politicians and the mainstream media that the federal deficit must be tamed by cutting entitlements. In 1981, for example, he helped to form the Committee for a Responsible Federal Budget, which has been a major player in arguing for the need to cut Social Security, and on whose board he currently serves. In 1992, he was the founding president of the Concord Coalition,[49] whose mission, according to its website, includes "educating the public about . . . the long-term challenges facing America's unsustainable entitlement programs."[50] More recently, he funded the development, by Columbia Teachers College, of a high school curriculum on fiscal issues, which was distributed free of charge to high schools around the country.[51]

His Peterson Foundation promoted a movie, called *I.O.U.S.A.*, which opened in four hundred theaters[52] and was broadcast on CNN.[53] The movie starred David Walker, the then-president and CEO of the Peterson Foundation, and Robert Bixby, the executive director of the Concord Coalition.[54] The foundation also gave out a number of grants to produce guides and other teaching tools to accompany the movie.[55]

Walker left the Peterson Foundation in 2010 to head his own organization, Comeback America, which received a $3.1 million grant from the Peterson Foundation,[56] and, for three years, supported an agenda closely aligned with the Peterson Foundation's. (Comeback America ceased operations in September 2013.)[57]

Peterson has been a key player and is omnipresent in the deficit debates that have consumed much of the Obama presidency. During that period, his foundation has hosted annual high-profile fiscal summits, where former president Clinton and other luminaries have spoken.[58] Prior to the 2008 election, he bought two full pages in the *New York Times* urging the creation of a "bipartisan fiscal responsibility commission" by whoever was elected.[59] His son, Michael, who is president of his foundation,[60] is on the board of directors, together with Alan Simpson and Erskine Bowles,[61] of an organization called Fix the Debt—many of whose leaders have close ties to big corporations and the financial industry.

The hypocrisy of Fix the Debt is remarkable. Fix the Debt claims to want to reduce the federal deficit, but nearly half of its board and steering committee members have ties to companies that lobby hard to preserve corporate tax breaks.[62] Among its leadership are seventy-one CEOs heading publicly held companies. Fifty-four of them, according to a 2012 report, had personal savings in their firms' retirement plans totaling $649 million, or an average of $12 million each—enough, if annuitized at age 65, to provide each of these CEOs with an average of $66,000 a month in retirement benefits.[63] With $78 million in retirement savings, David Cote, the CEO of Honeywell and a member of the Bowles-Simpson fiscal commission, heads the list, as figure 9.1 reveals. (His little Honeywell "nest egg" has been reported more recently to be $134.5 million.)[64] Cote is on the front lines of those calling for fiscal austerity and cuts to Social Security, Medicare, and Medicaid. Yet Honeywell's own employee pension plan, the funding of which is presumably part of Cote's responsibility, was running a $2.8 billion unfunded liability in 2012 while Cote was busy railing against the federal deficit. Indeed, twelve Fix the Debt CEOs with personal pension savings worth in excess of $20 million manage companies that collectively have $63 billion in unfunded pension liabilities.[65]

Fix the Debt has a track record of misleading the public. On November 14, 2013, for example, the Center for Media and Democracy's *PR Watch* reported, under the headline "Astroturf 'Fix the Debt' Caught Ghostwriting for College Students,"

> Our friend Jon Romano, press secretary for the inside-the-beltway PR campaign "Fix the Debt" and its pet youth group, The Can Kicks Back, have been caught writing op-eds for college students and placing the identical op-eds in papers across the country.
>
> This is the latest slip-up in Fix the Debt's efforts

THE RETIREMENT SAVINGS OF SOME FIX-THE-DEBT CEOS WHO WANT TO CUT YOUR SOCIAL SECURITY

CEO (Company)	Total CEO retirement assets	Estimated CEO monthly pension	Employee pension fund deficit
David Cote (Honeywell)	$78,084,717	$428,092	$2,764,000,000
Jeffrey Immelt (General Electric)	$53,301,387	$292,220	$21,756,000,000
Randall Stephenson (AT&T)	$47,001,565	$257,681	$10,203,000,000
W. James McNerney (Boeing)	$39,089,893	$214,306	$16,598,000,000
Michael Ward (CSX)	$32,292,517	$177,040	$818,000,000
Steven Roth (Vornado Realty Trust)	$26,636,463	$146,032	(not available)
John McGlade (Air Products and Chemicals)	$24,513,351	$134,392	$762,000,000
Andrew Liveris (Dow Chemical)	$23,726,536	$130,078	$7,010,000,00
Wendell Weeks (Corning)	$21,229,195	$116,387	$454,000,000
Alesander Cutler (Eaton)	$21,055,632	$115,435	$1,235,000,000
James Tisch (CEO) (Loews)	$21,028,506	$115,287	$958,000,000
Andrew Tisch (co-chair of the board) (Loews)	$20,677,631	$113,363	$958,000,000

Source: Sarah Anderson and Scott Klinger, "A Pension Deficit Disorder: The Massive CEO Retirement Funds and Underfunded Worker Pensions at Firms Pushing Social Security Cuts," Institute for Policy Studies, November 27, 2012, www.ips-dc.org/reports/pension-deficit-disorder. Monthly pension derived from www.immediateannuitites.com annuity calculator, using total retirement assets, and assuming payments would start at age 65. Based on rates available in New York and assume payments to one individual with no benefits.

Figure 9.1

to portray itself as representing America's youth. Previously, they were caught paying dancers to participate in a pro-austerity flash mob and paying Change.org to gather online petition signers for them.

The newspapers involved in the scam were not amused.[66]

MORE MONEY

Although Peterson is the primary money player, he and his Fix the Debt comrades-in-austerity are not the only tycoons involved in this debate. One of the conservative Koch brothers, Charles Koch, for example, used a drop of his vast fortune to found the Cato Institute, a libertarian think tank. (It was founded in 1974 as the Charles Koch Foundation but changed its name to the Cato Foundation in 1976.)[67] The financial troubles of Social Security then making headlines were just too inviting a target.

In 1980, Cato published *Social Security: The Inherent Contradiction*, which argues that Social Security should be replaced with a system of private accounts.[68] The author, Peter Ferrara, then just out of law school, has made a career out of pushing his Social Security views. He is currently a senior fellow for entitlement and budget policy at the Heartland Institute and a senior fellow at the Social Security Institute.[69] In the more than thirty years since the publication of his book, Ferrara has, among other things, been a senior fellow at the Cato Institute, directed the Social Security Project of the Free Enterprise Fund, and has served as senior policy advisor on Social Security and Medicare for the Institute for Policy Innovation and as senior policy advisor on Social Security for Americans for Tax Reform.[70]

Ferrara has also spent time at the Heritage Foundation, another conservative think tank. The Heritage Foundation was started in 1973 by another tycoon, beer magnate Joseph Coors, together with two young congressional aides.[71]

The determined foes of Social Security redoubled their efforts in the wake of their disappointment that their hero, Ronald Reagan, had not dismantled Social Security, the crown jewel of the New Deal. Just a few months after the enactment of the recommendations of the Greenspan Commission, the Koch-funded Cato Institute devoted its entire fall journal to criticizing Social Security and plotting its demise through the substitution of private accounts.[72]

Two employees of the Heritage Foundation co-authored one of the articles, provocatively titled "Achieving Social Security Reform: A 'Leninist' Strategy." The authors chose that title because, they explained, they advocated adopting Lenin's insight: "that fundamental change is contingent both upon a movement's ability to create a focused political coalition and upon its success in isolating and weakening its opponents."[73] The authors encouraged their comrades to prepare for the long haul, concluding, "as Lenin well knew, to be a successful revolutionary, one must also be patient and consistently plan for real reform."[74]

The last thirty years have played out much as the revolutionaries envisioned it might. It has been aided by academics, some of whom were just starting out in the 1970s, when Social Security was first trumpeted in newspaper headlines as going bankrupt. Laurence J. Kotlikoff, professor of economics at Boston University, for example, published his very first professional article, titled "Social Security: Time for Reform," in June 1978.[75] It was published by the Institute for Contemporary Studies, a think tank established in 1974 by associates of then-governor Ronald Reagan.[76] Since the publication of that first article, Kotlikoff has spent the last thirty-five years or so arguing that Social Security is unfair to younger generations. His recent writings, for example, include two co-authored books: *The Coming Generational Storm*,[77] written in 2004, and *The Clash of Generations: Saving Ourselves, Our Kids, and Our Economy*, written in 2012.[78]

Journalist Trudy Lieberman illuminates the access to media and the interlocking strategies employed by those dedicated to pulling Social Security apart brick by brick. Commenting on a lengthy *Esquire* piece titled "The War Against Youth," and subtitled "The recession didn't gut the prospects of American young people. The Baby Boomers took care of that," she observes:

> The argument that fat-cat elders are shafting young people follows from [the title and subtitle]. The author, Stephen Marche, writes: "The biggest boondoggle of all is Social Security," and he goes on to explain that the Baby Boomers are to blame.
>
> What readers of *Esquire* may not know is that, two years ago, the magazine assembled a bipartisan commission, similar to Obama's Simpson-Bowles Commission, that—in three days' time—came up with a plan to balance the federal budget. The *Esquire* group's recommendations were similar to those made by Simpson-Bowles.

At the end of its report, the *Esquire* panel thanked the Committee for a Responsible Federal Budget and its president, Maya MacGuineas, "for their invaluable assistance in providing the commission with accurate data and budget options." That committee has received support from Peter G. Peterson, an arch-foe of Social Security who has tried to get the media to see things his way. The media consensus continues to build.[79]

Thanks to all of these forces, political and media elites have lost an understanding of the conceptual underpinnings that have led to Social Security's popularity, and have been convinced to see Social Security as a problem rather than the solution that it is. They have caused questionable assertions, half-truths, and even outright lies to become part of conventional "wisdom," something everyone knows, like the sun rising in the east (which, of course, it doesn't really). Ideas that have only become mainstream in the last thirty years are, in many minds, simple facts. The next chapter will explain how flawed and wrong all of that conventional thinking and all of those so-called facts are.

10

THE CONVENTIONAL "WISDOM" IS JUST PLAIN WRONG

If you've followed the public debate about Social Security even casually, you've likely heard one or more of the following comments asserted as incontrovertible fact:

- Social Security is going bankrupt, going broke, in crisis; young people will never see a penny in benefits.[1]
- Social Security spends more money than it takes in. In technical terms, it is cash negative and is projected to remain so.[2]
- Social Security's trust funds are not real, but simply an accounting gimmick. The $2.8 trillion in bonds that Social Security holds are just a bunch of paper, worthless IOUs. The federal government has already spent the money, so it will have to raise everyone's taxes to pay promised benefits.[3]
- Spending on entitlements—Social Security, Medicare, and Medicaid—is by far the major cause of federal deficits and debt. Left unchecked, this spending will bankrupt the nation.[4]
- Social Security is unsustainable. Just look at the numbers. With ten thousand baby boomers turning 65 every day from 2011 to 2029, there just will not be enough working-age people to support them.[5]
- A demographic tsunami is on its way, threatening to drown

our children and grandchildren. It's not just the growing cost of Social Security we have to worry about, it's all those programs directed at supporting a largely unproductive group—today's old and the roughly ten thousand baby boomers who will turn 65 every day through 2029.[6]

- Everyone's living longer; it only makes sense to raise the retirement age.[7]
- Social Security is unfair to younger Americans. Too much is going to seniors, and not enough to children. And when children grow up, they will be burdened with crushing levels of national debt.[8]
- Social Security is unfair to African Americans, because on average they have shorter life expectancies.[9]
- You could do better investing on your own.[10]
- Social Security worked for the twentieth century, but now we have to target benefits to those who truly need them. Rich people should not get Social Security.[11]

There are other claims, which sometimes appear in one's email inbox, and only occasionally make their way into the mainstream discussion. They include:

- Social Security is a Ponzi scheme.[12]
- Senators and members of Congress make us pay into Social Security, but they don't. They should be forced to participate in Social Security, like everyone else.[13]
- Illegal aliens get benefits without paying in. They should not get Social Security.[14]

This chapter first offers a point-by-point refutation of each of these assertions. We then step back and put each point/counterpoint into perspective, showing how these claims undermine confidence in the future of Social Security and distract attention from what is really going on. But first, the facts:

CHARGE: *Social Security is going bankrupt, going broke, in crisis; young people will never see a penny in benefits.*

TRUTH: As long as there are Americans who work, there is simply no way that Social Security can run out of money. Social Security has a dedicated revenue stream that is not going away. As discussed in chapters 2 and 8, its major source of income comes from the contributions of workers and employers. Consequently, as long as there are workers, Social Security will continue to collect billions of dollars in income, week in and week out, for the next seventy-five years and beyond.

Starting back in 1941, the year after monthly benefits began, Social Security's board of trustees has reported to Congress each and every year, in wartime and in peace, through good economic times and bad, about the long-range financial health of the program. The Trustees Report projects Social Security's annual income and outgo not just for five years, ten years, or even twenty years; the report projects out its income and outgo for seventy-five years, each and every year.

The report comes out every year, usually in April, and projects out seventy-five years, so that Congress always has plenty of time to act whenever there is a projected imbalance, to ensure that promised benefits can be met.[15] This careful monitoring should provide the American people with a sense of confidence that this vital program will always be adjusted to ensure that all benefits will always be paid.

Instead, the annual reports have been the occasion for scare stories every time there is a projection of a deficit, no matter how manageable in size or how far out in the future. Ironically, opponents of Social Security are able to spin the reports that way for the press because of Social Security's conservative fiscal structure. Social Security cannot pay benefits unless it has the income to cover the costs. It has no borrowing authority.

This prohibition against deficit spending is what allows cries of bankruptcy to be made. The reality is that bankruptcy is a meaningless concept when applied to the federal government or any of its programs. No one says that the Pentagon is going bankrupt, or the Department of Agriculture, yet unlike Social Security, they have no dedicated revenue stream and estimates of those costs are generally not projected out more than five or ten years.

Unlike private employers who sponsor pension plans and can go out of business, Social Security's plan sponsor is the federal government, which is permanent. Moreover, unlike private employers, the federal government is in charge of its own currency and has the power to tax. The only way that Social Security could cease to pay benefits is if Congress passed legislation repealing Social Security and the president signed it into law.

Even if Congress were to take no action for a decade, Social Security is projected to have sufficient dedicated revenue to pay 100 percent of promised benefits for the next 15 to 20 years. After that, it is projected to have enough income to pay about 75¢ on the dollar for the foreseeable future. Obviously, in addition to expanding benefits, enough revenue should be brought in to cover that manageable shortfall, as the All Generations Plan does.

Americans should be confident about Social Security: Congress has never failed to act to secure its funding. As chapter 8 explains, we are wealthy enough to afford Social Security. The issue is one of political will, not economics, demographics, or mathematics.

CHARGE: *Social Security spends more money than it takes in. In technical terms, it is cash negative and is projected to remain so.*

TRUTH: This is a particularly slippery charge. Social Security has three sources of income, as explained in chapters 2 and 8: insurance contributions or premiums (today, generally called payroll taxes), investment income, and revenue from taxation of benefits. This charge ignores Social Security's investment income (and sometimes its revenue from taxation of benefits).

When you count all of Social Security's income, including its investment income, Social Security ran a $32 billion surplus in 2013, according to the 2014 Trustees Report (the most recent one at the time of this writing).[16] In fact, as mentioned above, Social Security cannot pay benefits if it has insufficient cash to cover the costs. That has never happened in the history of the program. If it were to happen, benefits would automatically be reduced to match its income. And, no doubt, members of Congress could count on their constituents to send them on a very long, unpaid vacation!

CHARGE: *Social Security's trust funds are not real, but simply an accounting gimmick. The $2.8 trillion in bonds that Social Security holds are just a bunch of paper, worthless IOUs. The federal government has already spent the money, so it will have to raise everyone's taxes to pay promised benefits.*

TRUTH: Social Security's trust funds are as real as any private pension trust fund. They are governed by a board of trustees, who have the same legal obligations that trustees of other trusts have. From the beginning, Congress has wanted the moneys that workers and their employers have entrusted to Social Security to be invested prudently and conservatively. Consequently, the trustees are required to invest Social Security's trust funds in interest-bearing treasury obligations or in entities whose principal and interest are guaranteed by the United States.

These are not casual promises to pay. These are legal instruments backed by the full faith and credit of the United States, just like those green paper things you have in your wallet. Those green paper dollars have value because they too are backed by the full faith and credit of the United States. The treasury bonds held by Social Security have the same legal status as bonds bought by you, a bank, a foreign government, or any other person or entity that invests in U.S. treasuries.

Sometimes, opponents of Social Security make the arcane point that the trust fund bonds aren't real, because they are "special issue." Sometimes, the claim is that, real or not, the money has already been spent.

The special-issue charge is particularly deceptive. The claim relies on the use of technical language to deceive. The bonds do indeed tend to be special issue, though they are not required to be.[17] That is up to the trustees. But, as just stated, the bonds have the same priority as treasury bonds issued to the public. Indeed, they are more valuable, because unlike other bonds, which can only be redeemed at full value at their maturity date, the special issue bonds can be redeemed at any time for full value—one reason the trustees choose to purchase them.

Similarly, the charge that the money has already been spent indicates either a misunderstanding of bonds or a desire to deceive. All those who issue bonds, whether they are corporations or government entities, do so to raise funds to be spent. One hopes that the bond issuer uses the funds in ways that are productive and will make repayment easier. But the fact that the funds are spent, and what they are spent on, does not alter the legal obligation to repay.

Those who say that the money has been spent and will require the federal government to raise taxes, cut benefits, or borrow in order to repay are implying, perhaps inadvertently, the possibility of default. If our United States is to default, why shouldn't the very last place be the moneys held in trust for America's workers? Why shouldn't those obligations be honored before those held by China, Iran, Russia, or private pension funds? But, more fundamentally, why should the wealthiest nation in the world default on any of its obligations? And why would anyone claim that our nation would ever do so?

None of these charges about the trust funds and the money they hold are new. Indeed, they are zombie charges. They just won't die. They have been around since the 1936 presidential election, just one year after Social Security was enacted, when they were leveled by Republican presidential standard-bearer Alf Landon and his allies.[18]

To combat these unsettling charges, a bipartisan panel of experts issued a statement on April 29, 1938, in order "to allay unwarranted fears." They declared that the purchase of special issue bonds and the use of the moneys the United States realized on the sale of the bonds to Social Security "do not involve any misuse of these moneys or endanger the safety of these funds."[19]

This is as true today as it was more than three-quarters of a century ago. Social Security has an accumulated surplus of more than $2.8 trillion. Those bonds have been invested according to law, and they have not been raided. They have real value and are rock-solid safe. The Social Security trust funds earned interest from these bonds of $102.8 billion in 2013 alone.[20]

The talk about the trust funds not being real, the money already having been spent, and the rest of the charges undermine confidence. But left unanswered, they could lay the groundwork for a back-door raid on the trust funds. If the earned benefits of the American people were cut deeply enough, the moneys already collected would not be needed, and the bonds would never have to be redeemed and repaid.

It is important to realize that the $2.8 trillion surplus, coming primarily from premiums paid by America's workers, belongs to those workers and their families. It is not government largesse. It is our money. The government is simply holding it in trust for all of us.

CHARGE: *Spending on entitlements—Social Security, Medicare, and Medicaid—is by far the major cause of federal deficits and debt. Left unchecked, this spending will bankrupt the nation.*

TRUTH: Social Security, Medicare, and Medicaid are very different programs, with different structures and purposes. Lumping them together confuses clear analysis. Moreover, as discussed in chapter 9, "entitlement" sounds to typical Americans like a government handout. Social Security and Medicare are earned through hard work, deductions from pay, and premiums. Medicaid ensures that the very sick and poorest among us can obtain medical care, sometimes lifesaving medical care.

When one treats these three programs as distinct, several points become clear. First, Social Security does not add a penny to the public debt. By law, it cannot pay benefits without sufficient income to cover the costs, and it has no borrowing authority.[21]

Moreover, the drivers of our current, short-term budget deficits were two wars fought on a credit card, tax cuts for the wealthy, the Great Recession, and the spending required to bail out the banks that crashed the economy and begin to restore the economy more generally.[22]

In the long term, our projected deficits are caused by unsustainable health care costs, private as well as public. In chapter 8, figure 8.1 shows that Social Security's costs are essentially a flat line, at around 6 percent of GDP. In contrast, figure 10.1, produced in 2007 by the nonpartisan Congressional Budget Office, illustrates that, if health care costs—private and public—were to continue to rise as they did from 1975 through 2005, these costs would consume a whopping 99 percent of GDP in seventy-five years.

Obviously, not even a country as wealthy as ours can spend

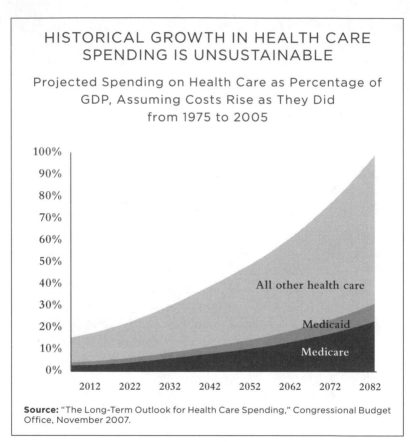

HISTORICAL GROWTH IN HEALTH CARE SPENDING IS UNSUSTAINABLE

Projected Spending on Health Care as Percentage of GDP, Assuming Costs Rise as They Did from 1975 to 2005

Source: "The Long-Term Outlook for Health Care Spending," Congressional Budget Office, November 2007.

Figure 10.1

99 percent of its GDP on health care. Figure 10.2 uses more recent data, including a recent slowdown in health care costs and the projected impact of the Affordable Care Act.[23] It also projects out just a few years.[24] Still, the basic trend is the same.

What figures 10.1 and 10.2 reveal is that the rising costs of Medicare and Medicaid are symptoms of our inefficient and overly expensive health care system, not causes. Indeed, Medicare's per capita administrative costs are lower than those in the private sector—around 2 percent of program expenditures[25] versus 11 to 17 percent in private plans[26]—despite covering seniors and people with disabilities, groups that, on average, need more medical care.

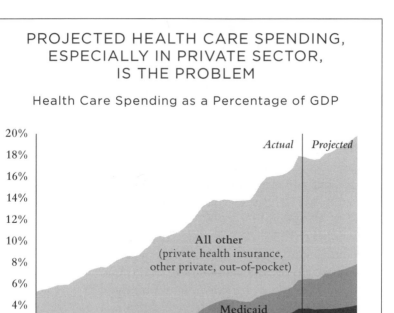

PROJECTED HEALTH CARE SPENDING,
ESPECIALLY IN PRIVATE SECTOR,
IS THE PROBLEM

Health Care Spending as a Percentage of GDP

Actual | *Projected*

All other
(private health insurance,
other private, out-of-pocket)

Medicaid

Medicare

Source: "The Financial Outlook for Medicare, Medicaid, and Total National Health Expenditures," Testimony before House Budget Committee by Richard Foster, Chief Actuary, Center for Medicare and Medicaid Services, February 28, 2012.

Figure 10.2

Even more striking, Medicaid, which has the complicated administrative burden of means-testing those it covers, also has much lower administrative costs than private insurance—just 4.52 percent in 2012.[27]

If the United States had the same per capita health care cost as any other industrialized country, our nation would project long-term federal budget surpluses for the next seventy-five years and beyond. (The highly respected Center for Economic Policy Research has an online calculator that allows you to pick any of those other countries and see the effect on the U.S. budget.)[28]

When one stops looking simplistically at "entitlements," but instead analyzes with greater sophistication the three programs separately, the blinders come off, and what is affordable and what is not comes sharply into focus.

CHARGE: *Social Security is unsustainable. Just look at the numbers. With ten thousand baby boomers turning 65 every day from 2011 to 2029, there just will not be enough working-age people to support them.*

TRUTH: Our population is indeed aging, and many Americans understandably but mistakenly believe that Social Security will be unaffordable in the future as a result. Many, including the Peter G. Peterson Foundation,[29] as well as Erskine Bowles and Alan Simpson, President Obama's fiscal commission co-chairs, have contributed to this mistaken view.[30] Perhaps the single person who has contributed most to this mistaken view is former president George W. Bush. In his 2005 State of the Union address, he said the following, points he subsequently repeated in virtually every speech as he toured the country to promote his Social Security privatization plan:

> Social Security was created decades ago, for a very different era. . . . [A] half century ago, about 16 workers paid into the system for each person drawing benefits. . . . And instead of 16 workers paying in for every beneficiary, right now it's only about three workers. And over the next few decades, that number will fall to just two workers per beneficiary. . . . With each passing year, fewer workers are paying ever-higher benefits to an ever-larger number of retirees.

This is a scary claim, but it falls apart with a little analysis. The sixteen-to-one ratio is a meaningless factoid, plucked from 1950, when Social Security was expanded to cover millions of new workers in agriculture and other parts of the economy. All of these new workers were paying into Social Security, but none of them had worked long enough to become insured and start collecting benefits. This is the kind of ratio experienced by all pension plans, public and private, at the start, when few workers have yet qualified for benefits. Only five years later, in 1955, the worker-to-beneficiary ratio was just about halved, from 16.5-to-1 in 1950, to 8.6-to-1 in 1955, and by 1975 it was down to about 3-to-1, which is what it is today.[31]

The worker-to-beneficiary ratio, which compares the number of workers contributing to Social Security to the number of people drawing Social Security benefits, reveals virtually nothing about the affordability of Social Security, because it sheds no light on how productive those workers are, on whether other burdens on those workers are increasing or decreasing, or on how the 50 percent increase in real compensation that Social Security's trustees project over the next thirty years will be distributed.[32] The worker-to-beneficiary ratio does not reveal the burdens imposed on workers from support of all dependents, just of those receiving Social Security benefits. All of these points are elaborated in response to the next, related charge.

CHARGE: *A demographic tsunami is on its way, threatening to drown our children and grandchildren. It's not just the growing cost of Social Security we have to worry about; it's all those programs directed at supporting a largely unproductive group—today's old and the roughly ten thousand baby boomers who will turn 65 every day through 2029.[33]*

TRUTH: This is another iteration of scare tactics, based on half-truths, misinformation, and harmful stereotypes used to create a sense of crisis where none exists, and to pave the way for cuts that will fall most heavily on today's young. We should not turn one of the great successes of our nation, our people living longer and better, into a failure. And harmful stereotypes of the old, today's and tomorrow's, should not go unchallenged.

Yes, more people are reaching old age, and once getting there are, on average, living somewhat longer than in the past, though the gains have been exaggerated and not equally distributed. More about that in the response to the next charge.

The quality of life of the old, while still problematic for many, is much better than it was before Social Security, Medicare, and Medicaid, and a whole host of other investments made, some early in the twentieth century—in sanitation, improved public health, control of life-threatening diseases, education, the economy, and the like.

Consequently, the United States, like virtually every other advanced industrial society, has reached a point in its social development where there is far less infant and childhood mortality than in the past and a growing older population relative to its younger populations. Of course, there are challenges that come with this, including questions of how to engage the productive capacity of older people, how we should make meaning of the gift of longer lives, and how to approach the frailties and significant disabilities that often accompany old age, especially advanced old age. But paying for Social Security's modest benefits is not one of those challenges.

We have become accustomed to hearing that with the aging of baby boomers, the burden of Social Security on the young will be crushing. That working-age persons have never experienced anything like what's coming. But that conventional "wisdom" is wrong.

Opponents of Social Security focus attention on the number of people between ages 20 and 64 as compared to the retiree population. Referencing the so-called old-age dependency ratio, they like to argue that a growing aged population cannot be supported by tomorrow's workforce. No question, the estimates of the old-age dependency ratio show an increasing number of persons age 65 and over (assumed to be financially dependent) to every hundred persons age 20 to 64 (assumed to be productive workers). For example, it grows from twenty-three per hundred in 2012 to forty-one per hundred in 2065 when all surviving baby boomers will be at least 100 years old.[34]

Putting aside the question of whether everyone 65 and over is financially dependent and whether everyone 20 to 64 is a productive worker, the old-age dependency ratio presents a one-sided, distorted picture of the "dependency" equation. It leaves out children under age 20, the vast majority of whom (no surprise!) do not work.

A very different story emerges when children are counted as part of the dependent population, that is when the overall dependency ratio is used that includes children under 20 and seniors 65 and over. As figure 10.3 plainly shows, the ratio of the number of children and seniors to every hundred persons ages 20 to 64 will not be greater even in 2065 than it was in 1965.[35] That is, in the foreseeable future, it will never be greater than when baby boomers were children, not even when all surviving baby boomers are age 65 and over.[36]

But this figure tells only part of the story. It does not show that many people age 65 and older work and that more may do so in the future. Or that some adults ages 20 to 64 do not work and that some children under age 20 do work. Most fundamentally, it does not reflect the productivity of the economy or of how the benefits of this productivity will be distributed across various groups. It does not show how immigration may change the equation, how

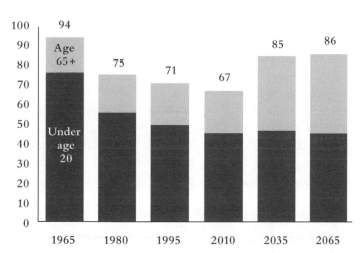

MORE THAN ENOUGH FUTURE WORKERS TO SUPPORT YOUNG AND OLD

Persons Under Age 20 and Over 65 per 100 Persons Aged 20–64

Note: Historical data are provided for 1965, 1980, 1995, and 2010. Data for 2035 and 2065 are projections based on Social Securit Administration Office of the Actuary's intermediate assumptions.

Source: "2013 OASDI Trustees Report," Table 5.A2, Social Security Administration, May 31, 2013.

Figure 10.3

investments in education may result in a more productive work-force, how political decisions to promote—or not promote—investment in green energy, environmental protection, and the nation's infrastructure may alter the equation. In other words, the ability of our nation to support people of all ages is not a simple matter of demographics.

Neither do dependency ratio charts reflect potential implications of the increasing diversity of older and younger populations, or of differing investments made by local, state, and federal government in advancing the well-being of various age groups. Nor do the various support ratios account for how much more time and energy is expended in family care to children, or of the care that flows in all directions when providing extraordinary care to functionally disabled or severely ill family members of all ages. In other words, not only is demography not destiny, but reality is also far more complex than the generational warriors would have us believe.

CHARGE: *Everyone's living longer; it only makes sense to raise the retirement age.*

TRUTH: According to Alan Simpson, who as Obama's fiscal commission co-chair championed a proposal to raise the Social Security retirement age, "[Social Security] was never intended as a retirement program. . . . The [life expectancy] was 63. That's why they set retirement age at 65."[37]

Aside from the fact that Social Security was indeed set up as a retirement program—and it is both a disservice to Americans and an outrageous slander of President Roosevelt to insinuate that he and the others who created Social Security were taking workers' money while setting eligibility for benefits out of reach for more than half of them—Simpson's figures are highly misleading. His figures are an average of life expectancies from birth before medicine had conquered many of the diseases that killed many infants and children. Back in 1935, when Social Security was enacted, 55.7 of every thousand children died, and in 1940, the year that Simpson plucked his misleading statistic, child mortality rates were 47.0 per thousand.[38] In contrast, in 2010, the child mortality rate was 6.2 per thousand.[39] The age 63 that Simpson refers to is an average that includes all of those people who died in childhood. (To be precise, the average life expectancy for men at birth was 61.4; for females, 65.7.)[40] Those who survived childhood and made it to age 21 generally made it to age 65.[41]

In the very same table in the Social Security Trustees Report, indeed in the adjoining columns where you find Simpson's data, you also find life expectancies for those who made it to age 65. According to that very same table, men who made it to age 65 in 1940 lived, on average, an additional 11.9 years, to age 76.9, and women lived on average an additional 13.4 years, to age 78.4. How does that compare to today? In 2013, men are living, on average, 6.1 years longer than they were in 1940; women, on average, 7.1 years longer.[42]

Moreover, these are average increases across the population. Women in the bottom half of the income scale have actually seen their average life expectancy at age 65 decline over the last 25 years.[43] But facts such as these do not slow down the rhetoric of people like Senator Simpson or Peter Peterson.

Indeed, the emphasis on changing life expectancies by Social Security's most vociferous opponents is simply their rationalization for cutting benefits. As chapter 4 explains, raising Social Security's defined "retirement age" by a year is mathematically indistinguishable from about a 6 to 7 percent benefit cut in retirement benefits, whether one retires at age 62, 67, 70, or any age in between. It is easy to think that if the retirement age is increased and you work longer, you will catch up—and that sounds reasonable, but it is wrong. To really, deeply understand why, one must be thoroughly immersed in how benefits are calculated. Figure 10.4 presents a picture that is better, we hope, than the proverbial thousand words. As that figure shows, if the retirement age is increased, you always get less than you would have without the change.

Cutting benefits when the nation confronts a retirement income crisis takes us in the wrong direction. We should be expanding benefits. Moreover, this manner of cutting benefits—by raising the statutory retirement age—is especially hard on low-wage workers—disproportionately, people of color—who are more likely to work in physically demanding jobs, as well as caregivers—disproportionately, women—who must retire early to

INCREASING "FULL RETIREMENT AGE" BY TWO YEARS CUTS RETIREE BENEFITS BY ROUGHLY 13%

Monthly benefit a worker would get, claiming benefits at different ages, the only difference in the amount for each age being different "Full Retirement Age" in the law

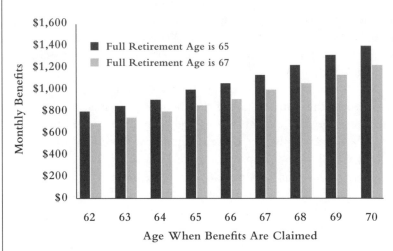

■ Full Retirement Age is 65
▨ Full Retirement Age is 67

Monthly Benefits (y-axis)
Age When Benefits Are Claimed (x-axis)

Note: The Full Retirement Age is currently rising from 65 for those born before 1938 to 67 for those born in 1960 or later. Monthly benefits reflect 8 percent delayed retirement credit after Full Retirement Age.

Source: Virginia P. Reno and Elisa A. Walker, "Social Security Benefits, Finances, and Policy Options: A Primer," National Academy of Social Insurance, April 2012.

Figure 10.4

care for aged parents or other family members, as we discuss in chapter 5. Finally, despite the existence of the Age Discrimination in Employment Act, older workers have a much harder time finding new work after being laid off. With no job prospects, they may find themselves with no choice but to claim permanently reduced early retirement benefits at age 62.

We are right now in the middle of seeing the full retirement age rise to 67—a 13 percent across-the-board benefit cut. We think the current increase is poor policy which may produce unanticipated hardship. Let's, at the very least, allow the change to be fully phased in and assess carefully its impact on low-income workers, women, minorities, and everyone else before contemplating more changes in the same direction.

CHARGE: *Social Security is unfair to younger Americans. Too much is going to seniors, and not enough to children. And when children grow up, they will be burdened with crushing levels of national debt.*

TRUTH: The claim is that federal spending on seniors, primarily through spending on Social Security, Medicare, and Medicaid, is crowding out spending on young people and children. Let's start with Social Security. This charge has a veneer of reasonableness and even some academic respectability. It has been repeated approvingly by David Brooks of the *New York Times*, Robert Samuelson of the *Washington Post*, and other prominent journalists. It has been repeated by Democrats as well as Republicans. This concern has even found its way into bipartisan and bicameral legislation—the so-called Inform Act which, if enacted, would require analyzing the federal budget in terms of intergenerational spending.

The veneer of reasonableness is just a veneer, however. Old versus young is catchy, and it may sell newspapers, but it makes no sense as a way to frame policy discussions. The federal government spends money on many important concerns, including the military, the environment, agriculture, and much more. This spending involves money that goes to defense contractors, regulators, farmers, and many other parts of the population. It makes no sense to pit just two subgroups of this spending against each other.

Well, that's not quite true. It makes sense if your goal is to strip away public support for Social Security.

Those making claims of unfairness between generations fail to acknowledge that Social Security is our largest children's program, providing benefits directly or indirectly to about 11 percent of America's children.[44] It lifts more than a million children out of poverty each year.[45] Moreover, it is the most important, and often the only, source of life insurance and disability insurance that young people have, as chapter 2 describes.

They also fail to mention that young workers and their families are also accruing valuable retirement benefits and that the children of today will be the seniors of tomorrow. They, like today's old, will need these supports when they age. In this regard, it is noteworthy that spending on Alzheimer's research sounds like spending on the old. Yet it is not today's old, but today's children who will benefit most. Taking a snapshot in time fails to depict public spending that occurs over a lifetime. Moreover, it obfuscates an inescapable and inconvenient fact for those wanting to dismantle Social Security. It is today's young workers and today's children who will experience the largest cuts if the "generational equity" crowd has their way.

It is instructive to note that, rather than the old and young competing for scarce resources, spending on both tends to go together internationally, rising and falling in tandem. Those countries that spend more on seniors also spend more on children; those countries that spend less on seniors spend less on children as well.[46]

Moreover, framing the policy discussion in terms of competition and fairness between generations distracts attention away from hugely important inequities of income, wealth, race, class, and gender. There is much more inequality within any given age group than there is between age groups. The real equity questions concern how best to secure a middle-class lifestyle for all cohorts and how to eliminate the poverty and difficult circumstances that scars people at all ages. There is little "inequality" between rich old people and rich children. But there is much inequality and much to be concerned about when it comes to poverty and inequality that spans generations.[47]

And there are other problems with this framing. It promotes the kinds of harmful stereotypes about the old that we mention at the start of chapter 3—greedy geezers and the like. It ignores the projected growth in our nation's wealth and future standards of living. And it is based on a very narrow measure of what's fair, one that implicitly raises a virtually unmeasurable notion of fairness between generations over more measurable and visible matters of fairness, for example, between the top 1 percent and the 99 percent.

We should, as a society, spend more on children, especially those at greatest risk. And more on seniors and other groups as well. As the wealthiest nation in the world, we can certainly do so, if we so choose.

CHARGE: *Social Security is unfair to African Americans, because on average they have shorter life expectancies.*

TRUTH: This is a particularly despicable charge. It is true that African Americans have shorter life expectancies, on average, than European Americans. Although, upon reaching 65, the life expectancies of white and black Americans are much closer than at younger ages.[48] According to 2012 data from the Social Security Administration, a 65-year-old African American woman has a life expectancy of 83, compared to 85 for all women, and a 65-year-old African American man has a life expectancy of 79, compared to 82 for all men.[49] Nevertheless, because of the average shorter life expectancies, African Americans collect Social Security's retirement benefits, on average, for a shorter period of time than their white counterparts.

We all look forward to the day when these disparities are behind us. We believe that the government should be investing aggressively to eliminate the causes of the disparities. But Social Security is neither the cause, nor is it unfair to African Americans. In addition to retirement benefits, the program also provides benefits in the event of disability or death. Because of their poorer health status, African Americans are more likely to become disabled or die prematurely than their white counterparts. While approximately 13 percent of the population is black, African American children constitute 23 percent of the children receiving Social Security survivor benefits,[50] and African Americans represent 19 percent of those receiving disability insurance benefits.[51] Moreover, Social Security's benefits are progressively structured. Due to lower median earnings than the population as a whole, and higher rates of unemployment, on average, African Americans receive benefits that are proportionately higher, as a percentage of wages, than those with higher wages and fewer years of unemployment.

More fundamentally the charge fails to acknowledge Social

Security's vital importance to African Americans. It is virtually the only source of retirement income for almost four out of ten African Americans age 65 and over.[52] Without Social Security, the poverty rate among African American seniors would have increased from 17 to 50 percent.[53]

But again, the explanation so far doesn't really get to the heart of the matter. At base, those making this charge are doing so in a particularly cold-blooded and calculated way. They rarely, if ever, focus on the root causes of these disparities or propose to address the factors that lead to the shorter average life expectancy, including disproportionately high rates of poverty, and other conditions such as unaffordability of health care, that cause the discrepancy in the first place. Asserting the claim that Social Security is unfair to African Americans in order to undermine support for a program which is a lifeline for so many African American families, is simply adding insult to a terribly unjust injury.

CHARGE: *You could do better investing on your own.*

TRUTH: As chapter 2 explains, Social Security is insurance, not savings. It provides joint and survivor old-age annuities, life insurance, and disability insurance. Plus it provides inflation protection and protection in the case of divorce. Everyone should save, but for secure, guaranteed income to replace wages lost in the event of death, disability, and old age, what is needed is wage insurance. Everyone who has a home should have fire insurance, not just savings. Everyone who has a car should have car insurance, not just savings. And everyone who works must—and should—have wage insurance in the form of Social Security. Savings on that valuable foundation of insurance are to be applauded, but savings are not a replacement for Social Security. It is time to expand that foundation.

CHARGE: *Social Security worked for the twentieth century, but now we have to target benefits to those who truly need them. Rich people should not get Social Security.*

TRUTH: As chapter 2 explains, Social Security works for the twenty-first century as well. Chapter 7 explains in more detail why everyone, including the wealthiest among us, should receive the benefits they have earned. In addition to that basic point of fairness, a very small portion of Social Security benefits go to the wealthy, and so taking away their benefits would save relatively nothing. It is unlikely to change a single number in the annual Trustees Report. It would, though—again, as chapter 7 explains—fundamentally change the nature of Social Security and cause the administrative costs to skyrocket. (Of every dollar spent, the Social Security Administration spends less than a penny on administrative costs.)[54] Right now, workers applying for Social Security have to present only their Social Security numbers, proof of age, their most recent W-2, and if not born in this country, proof of legal status. If there were a means test, even one set at $10 million, everyone applying for benefits would likely have to disclose tax returns, bank accounts, valuations on homes, and other personal information to prove that they were poor enough to qualify. Social Security is insurance, not welfare. Benefits are not based on need, only on working long enough to be insured. That is a design the American people like. And it is a design that works well. And here's the kicker. Means testing would penalize those who save!

CHARGE: *Social Security is a Ponzi scheme.*

TRUTH: A Ponzi scheme is a criminal endeavor, a deceptive promise, made by a swindler, that investors will reap huge returns. Like a chain letter, it collapses, usually after a short period of time, leaving many investors holding the bag. Social Security has been around for more than three-quarters of a century, and there is absolutely no reason that it can't continue as long as the United States is here. It is completely transparent and aboveboard: the polar opposite of a Ponzi scheme.

Social Security is, in pension jargon, primarily current-funded. That means that most of current benefits are paid out of current premiums from today's workers. Private pensions are required to be advance-funded, because employers can go out of business and so they might not be around to pay future pensions. Because the government is permanent, that safeguard is unnecessary.

To call Social Security a Ponzi scheme is a slur on every president and every Congress since its creation, as well as every contributor and every beneficiary. The future of Social Security is too important to the well-being of future generations of workers to be shaped by such slanderous comparisons and name calling.

CHARGE: *Senators and members of Congress make us pay into Social Security, but they don't. They should be forced to participate in Social Security, like everyone else.*

TRUTH: They already do. All federal employees, including senators, members of Congress, and the president of the United States have been covered by Social Security since January 1, 1984.[55]

CHARGE: *Illegal aliens get benefits without paying in. They should not get Social Security.*

TRUTH: They don't. Illegal aliens (undocumented workers) are prohibited by law from receiving Social Security benefits.[56] As an aside, Social Security's financing is strengthened by the contributions of immigrants and new Americans because they tend to be younger and also have more children.

PULLING BACK THE CURTAIN AND REVEALING THE TRICK

In taking on the conventional wisdom, this chapter corrects myths, misunderstandings, misinformation, and, in some cases, outright lies.

Now let's again pull back the curtain and see what's really going on. All of the charges, when analyzed, look like solutions in search of a problem. The solution is to cut Social Security or even dismantle it completely. The problem changes. Sometimes the problem is young people not getting their fair share. Sometimes, it's that African Americans don't live as long as whites. Sometimes, it's the cost of an aging population. Sometimes, it's that seniors have lower poverty rates than children.

The problem changes, but the solution is always the same: cut or dismantle Social Security and related institutions. The intergenerational theft charge—that spending on seniors is crowding out spending on children—is particularly deplorable. It is targeted at young people and designed not just to get them to oppose Social Security, but to be angry at seniors who are, supposedly, acting selfishly by opposing benefit cuts. Deplorable as the charge is, it is also, perhaps, the most revealing.

One giveaway that this is a solution in search of a problem is that the solution doesn't fit. The solutions proposed to address this concern would fall most heavily, or even entirely, on the supposed victims—today's young people and children. Indeed, most politicians proclaim that the benefits of those 55 or older won't be touched, perhaps unwittingly taking a play from the Leninist strategy playbook. So what gives?

In magic acts, this is called misdirection—focusing attention on one thing over here in order to distract from the real action over there. Linking the fact that the federal government should do more for children and young adults to the fact that seniors are benefited by Social Security is classic misdirection. The problem is not intergenerational; the problem is income and wealth inequality—which exists within every generation and, as chapter 6 details, is growing.

All of the charges discussed in this chapter are efforts of misdirection. Every one takes attention away from the fact that the wealthy are not being required to contribute their fair share toward the common good. Franklin Roosevelt understood this tactic extremely well. He laid it bare when he addressed the dirty pay-envelope trick on the eve of the 1936 election.

Roosevelt called the misdirection for what it was, famously charging, "It is an old strategy of tyrants to delude their victims into fighting their battles for them."[57] That is what is going on today. The tyrant is the same. Moneyed interests behind the Peterson Foundation, Fix the Debt, The Can Kicks Back (the supposed millennial group), and other groups seeking to undermine confidence, undermine support, and get natural allies to fight with one another. These are zombie charges. We have been responding to them over and over again since the late 1970s, and those who came before us did the same. But the charges never die; they always come back, because they are not really about seeking truth.

Everyone who wants an expanded Social Security and a more just society must be vigilant against these charges. The opponents of Social Security are clever and well-funded. And, as the next chapter explains, they are with us still.

PART FIVE

NEXT STEPS

11

THERE THEY GO AGAIN: WHY SUPPORTERS OF SOCIAL SECURITY MUST REMAIN VIGILANT

UNRELENTING FOES OF SOCIAL SECURITY HAVE ALWAYS been, in the words of President Eisenhower, "a tiny splinter group" whose "number is negligible."[1] They have never been a match for the American people whose support for Social Security has been nearly universal. But the thirty-year campaign, still with us, has almost allowed that small splinter group to achieve what their grandfathers tried but failed to do.

In most cases, today's opponents are the heirs of spiritual grandparents, but in a few cases, the line is an actual genetic one. Harry Koch was the grandfather of today's Koch brothers, whose vast fortune has helped fund today's campaign against Social Security. An implacable opponent of Social Security, as well as other New Deal programs, Harry Koch was a Texas newspaper baron who used his newspaper platform to relentlessly attack Social Security and the rest of the New Deal.[2]

Similarly, Prescott Bush was the grandfather of president George W. Bush, whose 2005 privatization proposal represented the first and only time that a sitting president publicly fought for a proposal that would have slowly but inexorably dismantled our Social Security system. Prescott Bush, like Harry Koch, hated Social Security. After President Roosevelt's death and burial in Hyde Park, New York, Prescott Bush remarked, "The only man I truly hated lies buried in Hyde Park."[3]

In contrast to past efforts, the organizational infrastructure and hundreds of millions of dollars behind the current, small splinter group of Social Security haters makes today's threat rival all the past efforts. Today, thanks to those efforts, a dwindling number of younger Americans believe that Social Security will even be there for them. And the anti–Social Security campaign has convinced many influential people. Many among the mainstream media and centrist politicians believe it their moral duty, for the good of future generations, to chip away at the foundations of our Social Security system. Some among the Democratic leadership, including President Obama, have actively advocated giving away a piece of the American people's Social Security to secure the smallest of concessions from Republicans. Indeed, Obama has referred to serious cuts in the cost of living adjustment as a "tweak,"[4] but they are not.

No cut to Social Security should be viewed as trivial for the following reasons. Most seniors and people with disabilities live on fixed budgets, many with little or no discretionary income. What may appear to be just a tweak to those who are affluent is a serious blow to the standard of living for those who are not. Moreover, once a Social Security cut is enacted against the will of the American people, more closed-door cuts could follow.

The campaign against Social Security remains well-funded and well-organized. Because of its efforts many policymakers and opinion leaders have been persuaded that Social Security is unsustainable. Some of these leaders, now actively favor well-intentioned but destructive changes such as dramatically cutting benefits for the middle class, means-testing Social Security or converting Social Security away from an insurance model toward a private savings model.

The American people, for the most part, have no idea how influential the anti–Social Security campaign has been. Most do not realize just how close it came to succeeding over the last decade.

THE MOST RECENT EFFORTS TO CUT SOCIAL SECURITY

Soon after he was returned to office in the 2004 election, President Bush put the power of his presidency behind privatizing Social Security. He failed, because Democratic politicians united and alerted the American people to the implications of what was being proposed—the dismantling of Social Security.

The resounding defeat of the Bush effort to privatize Social Security held the wolves at bay for a while. But the Wall Street–caused crash of the economy in 2008 and the election of Barack Obama, a man who values compromise with those who disagree with him, brought those forces new life.[5]

One of the impediments to dismantling Social Security is the overwhelming unpopularity of the idea. It has long been the goal of the small splinter group to set up a process that would allow politicians to avoid political accountability for doing so. Their strategy has been to convince politicians and the media that "hard choices" (i.e., unpopular ones) had to be made, and that the system was "broke." Accordingly, those pushing President Bill Clinton to establish the Entitlement Commission, discussed in chapter 9, wanted its recommendations subject to a speedy up-or-down vote, without amendment, in Congress. They were able to get the commission, but not the fast track. Unfortunately for supporters of Social Security, President Obama embraced the fast-track idea.

The most serious and immediate problem facing the nation as Obama prepared to take office was the Great Recession, which had caused many Americans to lose their jobs and homes. Progressives believed that increased government spending was necessary to get the economy moving. Upon taking office, President Obama proposed a stimulus package, which became law on February 17, 2009, less than a month after his inauguration.

Conservatives, on the other hand, argued that government spending was the problem, not the cure. They believed that deficit reduction was the key to solving our economic woes. Along with the need for short-term spending, Obama expressed the need for long-range deficit measures, including reform of entitlements. That was the opening those who were itching to undo Social Security needed.

By focusing simultaneously on increased spending in the short term and long-term deficit reduction, President Obama may have been seeking to appease both sides. Instead, he delivered a muddy message and put cutting Social Security squarely on the agenda.

Five days before Obama was inaugurated as the forty-fourth president of the United States, he gave an interview to the *Washington*

Post, which reported: "President-elect Barack Obama will convene a 'fiscal responsibility summit' in February . . . on solving the long term problems with the economy and with a special focus on entitlements, he said during an interview with Washington Post reporters and editors this afternoon."[6]

On February 10, 2009, shortly after his inauguration, Obama met with the so-called Blue Dog caucus, conservative Democratic members of Congress who, at the time, comprised over 50 members, nearly one out of every five House Democrats. (Thanks to election defeats and retirements, self-identified Blue Dogs now total only around nineteen members.)[7] Obama reportedly told the Blue Dogs that he favored a commission whose recommendations were subject to an up-or-down vote. That comment, together with the word that Pete Peterson would deliver a keynote, directly following the president and vice president at the fiscal responsibility summit, set off frantic, behind-the-scenes activity to convince the new president to change his mind.

The quiet pressure was enough to cause Obama to drop his push for a fast-track commission and scuttle the plan to invite Peterson to keynote his summit, though Peterson was still an attendee. Also invited was David Walker, who, as chapter 9 details, was then-president and CEO of the Peterson Foundation and star of the documentary *I.O.U.S.A.*, which had opened the August before. Both Peterson and Walker participated in the breakout group on Social Security. The White House report on the proceedings states: "Some participants emphasized the urgency of acting quickly on Social Security because of the looming fiscal challenges on the horizon. Pete Peterson presented the view that the Social Security system will begin running out of money in 2017, and that we cannot rely on the concept of a 'Trust Fund' because the money has been spent."[8]

The report also included David Walker's remarks at the closed, invitation-only meeting: "David Walker argued that an increase in the retirement age could be justified as part of a bipartisan reform to create certainty and security around the program. The reform could provide security to current retirees that their benefits are protected, and certainty to future generations that their defined benefit will be there. Thus, increasing the retirement age would encourage people to work longer but strengthen the safety net."[9]

At a different breakout session, this one on the budget process, the report stated:

> Senator [Kent] Conrad [Democratic chairman of the Senate Budget Committee] spoke strongly in favor of an extraordinary procedural mechanism such as the commission he and Senator [Judd] Gregg [Republican ranking minority member of the Senate Budget Committee] have proposed. . . . Senator Conrad did not feel that the regular rules of order (especially the amendment and cloture rules in the Senate) enable a solution to long-term problems such as Medicare and Medicaid, Social Security, and taxation. . . . [H]e noted that former Comptroller General David Walker [then president of the Peterson Foundation] has stated that "regular order is dysfunctional."[10]

Thanks to the president's apparent seal of approval, bypassing the normal legislative process to get at Social Security was now part of the mainstream discussion. Opponents of Social Security saw their opportunity in an arcane law limiting the amount of debt the U.S. Treasury could issue.

The debt limit has nothing to do with the amount of debt the United States carries. Rather, the level of debt is a function of the difference between how much the government spends and how much it taxes. Nevertheless, the limit has to be raised from time to time, or else the United States would be forced to default on its obligations, something it has never done. Raising the debt limit has to be done, but politicians hate taking that highly visible vote because, in our sound-bite world, those voting to do so can be made to look like they are in favor of incurring more debt. The Treasury was projecting that the upcoming fall was when, once again, politicians would need to take one of those visible votes increasing the debt limit.[11]

Seeing their chance, Conrad and Gregg organized conservative

Democrats to refuse to vote to raise the debt limit unless there was also a vote on their proposal to establish a fast-track commission.

The chairman of the Senate Finance Committee, which has jurisdiction over Social Security and Medicare, opposed the Conrad-Gregg commission, stating, "It is clear from their press release that senators Conrad and Gregg have painted a big red target on Social Security and Medicare. That's what this commission is all about."[12]

The Conrad-Gregg proposal failed to pass the Senate, but Obama stepped in and established the commission by executive order. Though he did not have the power to fast-track his recommendations, he reportedly convinced the leadership of Congress that, if at least fourteen of the eighteen members of the Commission agreed on recommendations, the package would receive a speedy up-down vote, without amendment in Congress.

As chapter 9 explains, Obama appointed Alan Simpson and Erskine Bowles, two well-known opponents of Social Security, to co-chair the new commission. The co-chairs were unsuccessful in securing the necessary votes for an up-or-down vote on their package, which contained proposals that would have radically transformed Social Security, inside a comprehensive package dealing with all of federal spending and taxation. If they had been successful, it might have been hard for members to vote against a bipartisan proposal, because it would have been framed as voting for or against the deficit. If enacted, Social Security as we know it would have disappeared.[13]

Frustrated by the failure of the Bowles-Simpson commission, which met for the last time on December 3, 2010, the anti–Social Security forces redoubled their quest for the elusive "Grand Bargain"—a comprehensive package that dealt with all of federal spending, including Social Security as well as federal taxation.[14] A Grand Bargain, everyone knew, could provide political cover, especially if it came out of closed-door meetings and was fast-tracked, not subject to hearings or amendments.

The anti–Social Security campaign again looked to the recurring need to raise the debt limit. This time the debt limit would be reached the following May, but the Treasury could, through the use of extraordinary measures, stretch that deadline to around August 2, 2011.[15]

On July 31, 2011, a bargain was struck, though it was not grand. The agreement called for a new group, this time labeled the Supercommittee, and composed only of senators and members of Congress. The Supercommittee's charge was similar to that of the Bowles-Simpson commission. "Everything" was deemed "on the table," and its recommendations were to be fast-tracked, with no chance for amendment.[16] The Supercommittee's reporting date was to be November 23, when the American people would be distracted by the Thanksgiving and Christmas holidays.

But what would keep the Supercommittee from going the way of the Bowles-Simpson commission? The Social Security foes did not want to go through that again. They needed a stick—automatic cuts; known in Washington circles as a sequester—that was so draconian that it would force Congress to reach an agreement. If the Supercommittee failed, then just under $1 trillion of cuts would be triggered over nine years, a little more than $100 billion a year, split evenly between defense and nondefense spending.[17] But, politicians being politicians, they delayed the imposition of the stick for two years, until 2013, and excluded cuts to Social Security, Medicare beneficiaries, Medicaid, civil and military employee pay, and veterans' benefits.[18]—apparently recognizing that these cuts would be deeply and widely unpopular, and so could trigger a tremendous backlash if implemented in an automatic, across-the-board fashion.

The Supercommittee failed to reach an agreement. Shockingly, the members, consisting of six Democrats and six Republicans, were reportedly prepared to cut Social Security.[19] According to the *New York Times*, "The only reason the committee failed was because Republicans refused to raise taxes on the rich, and, in fact, wanted to cut them even below their current bargain-basement level."[20] (This willingness to cut Social Security as part of a deficit deal is particularly shocking and outrageous, since Social Security does not add a penny to the nation's federal debt!)

This time, the anti–Social Security forces came close. They were foiled by Republicans who refused to violate their principle against any and all tax increases. But there is always another debt limit.

The next opportunity came at the end of 2012, when the stakes were the highest yet. In addition to having to once more raise the debt limit, the Bush tax cuts were expiring, which, if allowed to happen, would increase the taxes of virtually everyone in the country, but most especially on the very well-off. Extended unemployment insurance benefits were set to expire on January 1 and, absent a legislative patch to Medicare (a.k.a. "the doc fix"), physician reimbursements under Medicare would be cut by 27 percent. And the long-delayed stick of automatic cuts was finally about to happen. These cuts were aimed at programs like Head Start and Meals on Wheels, which assisted the most vulnerable among us, as well as spending on extremely important functions, like food safety and disease prevention. This perfect storm of pressure to finally cut Social Security was named the "fiscal cliff" by pundits. The image was stark. If not careful, the country would go over a cliff to its doom.

Incredibly, the fiscal cliff was resolved in a way that gave even more power to those determined to cut Social Security. Most of the Bush tax cuts were made permanent and the scheduled Medicare reimbursement cuts to doctors postponed for one year. But the across-the-board spending cuts were only postponed by a few months—to coincide more closely with the need to raise the debt limit (since the debt limit alone had already proven insufficient to force those Social Security cuts).

Sure enough, Obama released his 2014 budget, which eliminated the automatic spending cuts known as sequestration, replacing them with a combination of Social Security cuts and tax increases. Republicans in Congress immediately rejected the budget because of the tax increases, while progressive Democrats in Congress objected vociferously to the cuts to Social Security.

In the end, the multiyear quest for a Grand Bargain—an omnibus package, in which Social Security cuts are only one part, not subject to amendment—ended with a whimper. Harmful sequestration went into effect, though with some flexibility added, and the debt ceiling was raised once more. In the fall of 2013, Republicans shut down the federal government over so-called Obamacare. That proved to be extremely unpopular with the American public and their popularity suffered as a result. Struggles over federal spending and the debt limit continued, but pundits declared the death of the Grand Bargain.

THE UPCOMING SOCIAL SECURITY
DISABILITY FIGHT

As the effort to force action through a Grand Bargain failed, at least for now, Social Security's determined foes began focusing on another avenue to get their way. That is through the part of Social Security that insures workers and their families against the loss of wages as the result of serious and permanent disability.

Just as the Grand Bargain efforts were disappearing from the agenda, the media started reporting about problems with Social Security disability insurance. In March 2013, for example, National Public Radio ran several broadcasts on the program *All Things Considered*. Under the provocative headline, "Unfit for Work: The startling rise of disability in America," NPR's online story, which is a synthesis of the radio reports, begins, "In the past three decades, the number of Americans who are on disability has skyrocketed."

The next three paragraphs of their report paint a picture of something seriously amiss. It talks about the growth in the rolls despite "medical advances" and "new laws" against "workplace discrimination of the disabled." It mentions the alarmist but unremarkable fact that the government spends more on "disabled former workers" than on "food stamps and welfare," failing to point out that the latter are means-tested because they are welfare, while disability insurance is not, because it is insurance, and so has been earned and purchased with premiums.[21]

Similarly, a December 2012 *Bloomberg News* opinion piece on the same subject, confides, "There are now 8.8 million workers receiving disability payments from Social Security. I find this number haunting."[22] Perhaps NPR would have been less startled and *Bloomberg* less haunted if they had talked to the chief actuary of the Social Security Administration.

Just as the aging of the population has not been a surprise to Social Security's actuaries, they also had long projected that, as the baby boom generation aged, the numbers of workers receiving disability insurance benefits would increase. They knew that disabilities increase as people age. The oldest baby boomers, those born in 1946, would reach age 50 in 1996, and then the next oldest, every year until the youngest boomers, those born in 1964, would reach that milestone in 2014. They also knew that the baby boom generation had larger numbers of women join the paid workforce for full-length careers, making them eligible to receive disability benefits as workers.[23]

They also understood that a technicality accompanying the legislative increase to Social Security's statutorily defined retirement age would cause the Disability Insurance (DI) Trust Fund to have to pay more money. That is, disability benefits are paid from the Disability Insurance Trust Fund until the worker, on whose record the benefits are being paid, reaches his or her full retirement age. From that point on, the benefits are paid from the Old-Age and Survivors Insurance (OASI) Trust Fund. Consequently, when the full retirement age is increased, benefits are paid for a longer time from the DI Trust Fund and for a shorter time from the OASI Trust Fund. Moreover, as the statutorily defined retirement age is increased, it becomes more difficult for people with disabilities who had hoped to hang on in the workforce until that age to actually do so. Some become unable to continue working and end up applying for disability benefits.

Not only was this perfectly predictable, but Social Security's actuaries also understood that the rates of disability would slow down once these workers were old enough to receive retirement benefits. Those simple facts did not temper the scary headlines about the out-of-control growth in the disability rolls.

The NPR story does mention in passing, and implicitly dismisses, one of the unremarkable causes of the increase: "It's the story *not only of an aging workforce*, but also of a hidden, increasingly expensive safety net."[24] [Emphasis added]

Similarly, the *Bloomberg* piece dismisses the aging of the population as an explanation by referring to a paper produced by two economists—with no mention of the Social Security actuaries, whose job it is to understand these matters.[25] The larger number of women in the workforce is not mentioned in either story.

Not only has the chief actuary explained in detail what has caused these increased numbers, but he has written that "all of these trends have stabilized or are expected to do so in the future." Consequently, he projects that "the number of DI beneficiaries will continue to increase in the future, but only at about the rate of increase in workers."[26] None of this appeared in either story.

Even worse, many of the stories use anecdotes, without national data, to give the impression that the rolls have been growing as a result of fraud. What fails to get reported is that all large insurance programs experience some level of fraud, and the levels of fraud under Social Security disability insurance are extremely low.[27] Roughly 10 percent of the losses paid out by the property/casualty insurance industry are fraudulent, for example.[28] In contrast, in 2012, less than 1 percent of all Social Security disability insurance payments were more than should have been paid, and fraudulent payments were only a fraction of that.[29]

What also fails to get reported is that the Social Security Administration has zero tolerance for fraud. It vigilantly ferrets it out. Two-thirds of fraud investigations and successful prosecutions come from reports by the frontline workers of the Social Security Administration,[30] and the agency has a hotline for reporting suspected fraudulent claims.

What we are seeing in this reporting is the beginning of a new misconception about Social Security. Indeed, this misinformation has caused the Social Security Administration to undertake an initiative to set the record straight.

The facts of those promoting this storyline may be wrong, but those intent on undercutting support for and confidence in Social Security have one thing going for them. They have an action-forcing event. Congress will have to enact a technical change to Social Security in 2016 to maintain the uninterrupted flow of benefits to disabled workers and their families. When the Social Security Disability Insurance program was enacted in 1956, a new trust fund, the Disability Insurance Trust Fund, was established for the revenue dedicated specifically to it.[31] The annual Trustees Report projects both trust funds independently, but also projects them on a combined basis, since they are so intertwined. The same formula is used for calculating old age, disability, and survivors' benefits. The revenues for the two funds have always come from the same sources. Indeed, workers have a combined 6.2 percent of their salaries withheld, up to the maximum, without knowing how much goes to each trust.[32]

Over the years, the exact percentage allocated to one fund or the other has been changed by law many times, but from the worker's perspective, nothing noticeable changed. Indeed, sometimes the amounts going to one fund have decreased and the amounts going to the other have increased, and sometimes the reverse. In 1994, the percentage of the Social Security contribution going to the DI Trust Fund was increased, and that going to the OASI Trust Fund was reduced. At the time of the change, it was projected that another rebalancing would have to occur in 2016. Doing so would enable Social Security to pay all earned retirement, disability, and survivors' benefits through 2033.[33] The projection is that this will have to happen before the end of 2016.[34]

The need for simple legislation to rebalance the two funds provides new opportunity for those wanting to cut Social Security. The current drumbeat vilifying the disability insurance program seems to be setting the stage to demand changes affecting not just disability benefits, but, since all parts of the program are intertwined, retirement and survivors' benefits as well.

DEATH BY A THOUSAND CUTS

Even if Social Security is not cut legislatively, administrative cuts that make it hard for people to access their earned benefits can undermine program support. If people's experience in claiming benefits and getting information is a frustrating one, their general support for the program, and indeed for government, may be subtly compromised. Social Security is the face of the federal government for many Americans. Virtually all workers contribute directly to Social Security from every paycheck. Nearly one in five Americans receive a monthly Social Security check.

People contact the Social Security Administration at times of transition, ones often involving sadness, vulnerability, and stress. Americans claim benefits when a loved one of the person contacting Social Security has died, when the person contacting Social Security or a family member has become so seriously and permanently disabled that work is impossible, or when the person contacting Social Security or a family member has attained old age and generally is retiring from work.[35]

Determined that Americans who had earned Social Security receive the world-class service they deserve, the first commissioner of Social Security wrote:

> Employees who would come in direct contact with the public were impressed with the importance of making certain that people were given necessary assistance in understanding their rights and duties. This included assisting claimants in the preparation of their applications for benefits under the federal old age insurance system and ensuring that those who had valid claims received the benefits to which they were entitled.[36]

That emphasis on first-class customer service has been a hallmark of the Social Security Administration. Distressingly, at the same time that the anti–Social Security forces have been seeking to undermine the program legislatively, there have been starve-the-beast stealth attacks on the program's administration, including large cuts in its budget. Moreover, some people appointed during the administration of president George W. Bush were at odds with core Social Security principles.

Some of the effects of budget cuts and decisions made within the agency can be easily seen. Since 1996, when the number of Social Security field office peaked at 1,352 offices, 107 have been closed, 64 of them since 2010 alone. Public hours in the remaining offices have been reduced by the equivalent of one full day a week. Altogether, staff in field offices has been reduced by nearly 14 percent. More callers to the agency's 800 number experience busy signals—about 14 percent of all callers—and those who do get through have to wait an average of seventeen minutes to get assistance, up from five minutes in fiscal year 2012.[37]

All of those reductions have occurred as the numbers of older Americans are rapidly increasing and after they have entered the years when most long-term disabilities occurred. Not surprisingly, those applying for disability benefits often experience excessively long waits before hearing whether their claims are accepted. With large backlogs of disability claims and not enough funding for sufficient numbers of trained workers to process those claims, those applying for benefits must wait, on average, for three to four months before receiving a determination, and the average wait for those appealing a denial is over a year.[38]

The erosion of service can be seen in other ways as well. Until 2011, annual earnings statements, listing workers' wages and earned benefits, were automatically mailed, each and every year, from the Social Security Administration directly into the homes of each of those workers aged 25 and older. People valued the statements. Moreover, a Gallup Poll commissioned by the Social Security Administration found that Americans who received the statement had a better understanding of the program.[39]

Notwithstanding the value of these statements, their modest cost, and the legal requirement that they be mailed, the commissioner who President Bush appointed and who served until 2013, ordered the mailings stopped on budget grounds, with only a website notice. (That commissioner's successor resumed mailing the statements to workers every five years beginning at age 25, though not every year as the law requires.)

Another troubling development, the government has begun to aggressively go after overpayments, often decades in the past—even when the mistake is the government's.[40] And adding insult to injury, those who, through no fault of their own, have been over-paid, are labeled debtors. Sending letters from the government, out of the blue, claiming that a beneficiary owes tens of thousands of dollars, when the mistake was the government's, is wrong. In one case that came to the authors' attention, the anxiety caused by that government letter resulted in a temporary hospital stay.

The insensitive administration and death by a thousand cuts are harmful to all of us, but the degree of harm is not distributed evenly. Imagine the difficulty for those for whom English is not their primary language; who are developmentally disabled, physi-cally challenged, or mentally challenged in other ways, or who do not have a high school education.

The deterioration in service to the American people is especially outrageous because the Social Security trust funds, out of which Social Security's administrative costs are paid, have an accumulated surplus of more than $2.8 trillion. The problem is that Congress won't allow the agency to spend just a small amount more of this surplus on administration to restore the first-class service the American people have paid for.[41]

RECLAIMING OUR SOCIAL SECURITY SYSTEM

It is time to fight back. The anti–Social Security campaign can be defeated, but it will take vigilance. It is well-funded and its members are smart and determined. We must all resist cuts to Social Security, especially those attempted to be done behind closed doors.

But a strong defense against those who want to tear Social Security apart is only part of the solution. We must work to expand Social Security benefits and to restore the world-class service that Americans have paid for and deserve.

The good news is that the conversation has begun to shift. No longer is "saving" Social Security a disguised way of asking, how much do we cut? No longer is the only choice, how do we cut secretly, behind closed doors, and without accountability so the American people won't know whom to blame. Supporters of Social Security are raising awareness about the office closings and other cutbacks in service.

The question has started to become more even-handed: Do we cut Social Security or expand it? What is the fairest way to allocate the costs of an expanded program? When those are the questions, there is no need for secrecy, for fast tracks and undemocratic processes. No need, that is, unless those making the decision refuse to follow the will of the people.

There is the key. As the concluding chapter discusses, the American people will carry the day, as ultimately they always have, if—and this is crucial—they are informed, get involved, and insist on reminding politicians that those in Washington work for the American people, not the other way around.

12

PASSING SOCIAL SECURITY FORWARD: A LEGACY FOR ALL GENERATIONS

SOCIAL SECURITY DIDN'T JUST HAPPEN. PAST GENERATIONS have worked tirelessly to create and improve our Social Security system. They fought for it, defended it, safeguarded it, expanded it, and passed it forward, stronger than before, as a legacy to all of us, young and old alike. Now it is our turn.

Everyone who cares about the economic security of his or her family has a stake in this cause. Everyone who cares about what kind of nation we leave for our children and grandchildren has a stake.

How do we successfully build on the legacy that has been bequeathed to us, leaving it even better for the generations that follow? In short, how do we get our elected officials—who, after all, work for us—to vote to expand Social Security?

We already have some very dedicated and powerful senators and members of Congress championing the cause of expansion, but we need more of them. Getting the right people elected is tricky. All politicians these days claim to support Social Security. All say that their goal is to strengthen or save it. We cannot be satisfied with platitudes. We must demand more.

Electing more champions won't be done without knowledge, commitment, perseverance, and action. It won't be done without vision backed by the values that we all share. It won't be done without politics and policies that put the American people first.

And, it won't be done without a fight. Nor will the fight be an easy one. There is too much money on the side of those who want to dismantle our Social Security system. But we have growing numbers of emerging champions calling for expansion. They cannot win on their own, however. They need our help, just as past champions did.

We can expand Social Security, even in the face of distortions, misunderstanding, and outright lies promoted by moneyed interests. But we must all educate ourselves and those we know, we must get involved, and we must work together.

EXPANDING SOCIAL SECURITY IS ABOUT VALUES

We must understand that today's debate over the future of Social Security is most fundamentally a debate about confidence, security, and values. In the words of president Franklin Roosevelt, it's not about "the creation of new and strange values," but, as he explained more than eighty years ago: "It is rather the finding of the way once more to known, but to some degree forgotten, ideals and values. If the means and details are in some instances new, the objectives are as permanent as human nature. Among our objectives I place the security of the men, women and children of the Nation first."[1]

All the talk about Social Security going broke has robbed us of that security. As its name suggests, Social Security is intended to provide not only tangible cash benefits, but also the intangible benefit of peace of mind. For Social Security to accomplish its goal of providing peace of mind and security, people must feel confident that it will be there for them. Otherwise, the program ceases to function as intended; it provides income replacement only, not true security. Many no longer have that sense of security and peace of mind that they and their families are assured financial security in the event of disability, death, or old age. That sense of security has been lost as the result of the extremely effective thirty-year campaign against Social Security. It is now time to restore that intangible benefit of peace of mind. That is one value we all should be fighting for.

Americans appropriately have a sense of contributing toward their own retirement and feel good about receiving Social Security benefits. They understand the importance of providing disability protections for themselves and their families; the importance of protecting children and other family members if they die. The benefits are not based on need, but rather have been earned through labor and contributions from salaries and wages.

Yet some have lost the sense that Social Security benefits are earned compensation, thanks to the use of words and phrases like "entitlement," "makers versus takers," and "safety net." The language subtly implies that Social Security is a government handout, not insurance that we have earned and paid for. A safety net, after all, is something you fall into if you make a mistake on the high wire or trapeze. One is glad the safety net is there, but falling into it is to be avoided, if possible. Insurance, on the other hand, is what prudent people buy because they are aware of life's risks and are planning ahead. People who are prudent do not need or want safety nets. It is why they purchase insurance (and accumulate savings).

The phrase "social safety net" in connection with Social Security was introduced into the political lexicon and popularized by President Reagan.[2] Revealingly, Reagan rejected the idea that Social Security is insurance. He asserted, for example, in a stump speech he gave in 1964 in support of the election of Republican presidential nominee Barry Goldwater, that supporters of Social Security "only use the term 'insurance' to sell it to the people.[3]

The phrase "safety net" has become embedded in the language in the same way that the word "entitlement" has in relation to Social Security. The next step seems to be to redefine the image of a "safety net" into a "hammock" lulling able-bodied people to sleep.[4]

The false claim that Social Security is a government giveaway has become a standard talking point of those who would dismantle the program. On May 20, 2011, for example Fox Business launched a weeklong series, called *Entitlement Nation: Makers vs. Takers*, in which it pushed the idea that "the great divide in this country [is] between the folks who actually make things, and those who actually take what others make." Not surprisingly, those benefitting from Social Security, Medicare, and Medicaid were labeled as takers.[5]

The recognition that Social Security is part of our compensation for our hard work and contributions is another value this fight over Social Security is about. People who receive the Social Security benefits they have earned are not takers. They are not feckless souls who have fallen into a safety net. They are not spoiled, over-entitled adults taking advantage of working Americans. They are not dependent on government any more than are representative Paul Ryan, who routinely uses the "takers" language,[6] and other politicians, whose salaries are paid by the federal government. Social Security beneficiaries are our parents, our grandparents, our children, our friends, and our neighbors who have earned these benefits. They are all of us, who see mandatory contributions to Social Security deducted from every paycheck. None of us deserves to be assaulted by language that diminishes our accomplishments and risks undermining our dignity. We have earned our benefits and we should claim our benefits with pride.

Yet another value that underlies the fight over Social Security is compassion for our neighbors. After the tragic events of September 11, 2001, millions of Americans reached into their pockets to contribute to the Red Cross and other charitable organizations assisting the families of the 9/11 victims. What most Americans, to this day, do not know is that the most immediate, sustained, and generous support came from Social Security. Today, virtually all working Americans continue to contribute to those families every payday. The money withheld from every worker's paycheck for Social Security goes into the program's Old-Age and Survivors Insurance and Disability Insurance Trust Funds, out of which those victims' families receive benefits. Virtually every child who lost a parent or whose parent was severely disabled as a result of the terrorist attack will receive a Social Security check every month until his or her late teens.

Still another value the fight is about is recognition of Social Security's conservative, prudent management of our money. Of all federal programs, Social Security and Medicare are the most closely monitored. As discussed in chapter 2, Social Security is extremely conservatively financed and must balance its budget without any borrowing whatsoever. Yet this important value is disregarded by our politicians, who tend to lump it together with all other federal spending.

This is not a time for compromising the economic well-being of the middle class and poor, not when two-thirds of the income growth over the past twenty years has gone to the top 1 percent.[7] This is not a time to accept further cuts to our Social Security as "reasonable compromise," as little "tweaks" that will do no lasting harm. Rather, this is the time for reasonable people to talk about expanding Social Security, just as the majority of Americans want. This is the time to seriously discuss real increases in benefits, protections for young families, and protections for working people who must leave work due to illness.

At base, this is about what kind of nation we want to live in and leave for those who follow. Although couched largely in terms of economics, the debate over the future of Social Security is most fundamentally a debate about the role of government, about all of us working together, and about the societal values the nation seeks to achieve through Social Security.

EXPANDING SOCIAL SECURITY REQUIRES YOUR INVOLVEMENT

But facts and values alone are not enough. Those of us who want to expand Social Security must work for it.

We know we can expand Social Security, because by working together and bringing the voices of the American people into the policy debate, we have already done much. Together, the American people defeated president George W. Bush's effort to privatize Social Security. Together, the American people defeated president Barack Obama's effort to strike a "Grand Bargain" that would have traded cuts to our earned Social Security benefits in exchange for increased taxes.

These victories didn't happen by themselves. Working together, hundreds of national and state organizations and many millions of Americans won the day. (For a discussion of who those organizations are, please see appendix D.) These champions of Social Security were able to communicate the threats to Social Security to the American people, who in turn communicated to their elected officials in Washington and the media through petitions, phone calls, letters, blog posts, and opinion pieces. All of these efforts brought the voices of the American people to their representatives, in Washington and in their district offices, alerting those representatives that they were considering actions that violated the will of the American people.

In the last few years, our elected officials came closer than most people realize to cutting and, worse, beginning the dismantling of our Social Security system, as chapter 11 describes. When the president of the United States and the leadership of the opposition party all supported cutting Social Security, when hundreds of millions of dollars were directed at making the case for cutting Social Security, when so many in the mainstream media seemed so supportive of such cuts, it is truly inspiring that they were stymied by the coordinated efforts of public interest organizations and the American people.

But now is not the time to let up. The fight continues. Now is the time to redouble our efforts and fight harder. If you are not yet involved, we urge you to do so, in ways we explain below. The goal is clear: block destructive cuts and enact wise, responsible Social Security expansions.

EXPANDING SOCIAL SECURITY REQUIRES AN AMERICAN STRATEGY

In chapter 1, we spoke of an article titled "Achieving Social Security Reform: A 'Leninist' Strategy," published in 1983. Calling for "guerrilla warfare against the current social security system and the coalition that supports it," the authors explained: "We must be prepared for a long campaign. . . . [I]t could be many years before the conditions are such that a radical reform of Social Security is possible. But then, as Lenin well knew, to be a successful revolutionary, one must . . . be patient."[8]

We who want to protect and expand Social Security must develop our own strategy, an American strategy, and must be patient and be prepared for a long campaign. We must be prepared in the short term to lay the groundwork for ultimate success. Unlike the anti–Social Security ideologues, our strategy won't require deception or division. Quite the opposite. The American strategy involves truth-telling and joining forces, all of us together—young, old, and those in between; rich, poor, and those in the middle; Republicans, Democrats, and Independents alike.

Combating the Leninist strategy, which is with us still, and achieving greater economic security for all of America's working families will require all of us to become actively involved. A crucial first step in the American strategy is reversing the lack of confidence in the future of Social Security, believed most widely by young Americans, but infecting even those who are old. Because the misinformation is so deeply imbedded in the minds of the general public, but especially the elites, a multipronged approach is necessary.

This book is but one source of information. Other sources of accurate information are discussed in appendix D. Indeed, the Social Security Administration itself has an excellent website with much useful information, available at www.ssa.gov.

Social Security experts who are supportive of the program must educate students, teachers, professors, media, and elected officials alike. In addition to appearing on panels and at symposia, these experts should be increasingly drawn upon to hold Washington briefings for policymakers and influencers. All of their work should be backed by solid information.

But that is not enough. Citizen organizations, religious communities, and everyone whose lives are touched by Social Security (that's all of us) should get involved in the effort to restore confidence in this sound institution. Everyone should become informed and work to dispel the myths highlighted in chapter 10. But that is only a first step.

We know that Social Security works. Now we need to show how it can work even better—how expanding this institution is part of the solution to the economic insecurities facing many of today's old; to the retirement income crisis confronting today's workers; to the pressures—financial, time, and stress related—experienced by those caring for children or disabled and ill family members; to unacceptable inequality threatening the American Dream, ours, our children's, and grandchildren's.

If the American strategy to expand Social Security is to succeed, all of us together must convince those seeking election that championing the expansion of Social Security is the key to victory—and then demand that they carry through on their promise, in the sunshine, so that they can be held to account.

The American people are sometimes called a sleeping giant. The "Leninist" strategy is designed to lull that giant, to keep it asleep, by offering seniors comforting words that their benefits won't be cut, while convincing their grandchildren that they have nothing to lose, or worse, that Grandma is stealing from them.

But that is not how America's families think. Grandparents care about their grandchildren. They fight for Social Security because they love those grandchildren and want them to have the same economic security seniors know is so important in this insecure world. And grandchildren are too smart to buy the lie that they will be better off if their grandparents are worse off.

It is time for the sleeping giant to awaken. Poll after poll shows that the overwhelming majority of Americans supports Social Security, opposes benefit cuts, and wants responsible benefit improvements. And we are, after all, a democracy, where the majority is supposed to rule. But we must make sure our voices are heard. We must get involved.

We have noted that Social Security is often called the third rail of American politics. There's a reason for this. The American people may at times be slow to respond to threats to our Social Security, but when they do, their representatives take note. Senators and representatives know they ignore their constituents on this issue at the peril of their political careers. That's why, with rare exception, we never hear a politician speak directly about cutting benefits.

Rarely do those who support cutting our Social Security talk directly to the American people about cutting cost-of-living adjustments, reducing benefits for today's middle-aged and younger workers, or turning Social Security into what would virtually be, in time, a flat and much smaller benefit for most of the young. They talk instead in generalities, about "saving" or "fixing" Social Security. Don't be fooled. We must all demand straight talk from those who have been elected to serve us.

It is time for those of us who have a stake in the fight—and that is everyone—to take action. Educate your friends, co-workers, children, grandchildren, parents, and grandparents. Go to town hall meetings when your representative holds them. And ask hard questions. Don't let them off the hook with platitudes. And make clear that you and your allies will hold them accountable. Seek pledges, circulate petitions, write and call elected officials. Write letters to the editor and make calls to radio shows, especially when they spout the tired charges found in chapter 10. Support candidates not just with contributions, but with time. If you want to be involved with others, we have listed our organization and its website, together with the names of our coalition partners and other allies who would love to have your energy and talent. The bottom line: get involved however you can.

Social Security has transformed the United States. It has reshaped America, providing wage insurance for virtually all of today's working families. These benefits matter greatly to workers and families who are protected against the economic devastation that death, disability, and retirement might otherwise pose. But Social Security is more than dollars and cents. It is a cherished institution, embodying the noblest of American values and ideals.

As we have emphasized throughout this book, Social Security builds on, reinforces, and reflects what is best about our nation— working hard; taking responsibility to care for our parents, children, other family, neighbors, and selves; promoting the dignity of all persons throughout their lives; and sharing the burdens and bounty of our great nation.

Prior generations have created and improved our Social Security system, as a legacy for us. Now it is our turn to build on it and pass forward an even stronger, more robust institution for those who follow in our footsteps.

APPENDIX A

ADDITIONAL EXPLANATION ABOUT HOW
SOCIAL SECURITY WORKS

This appendix provides more detail about how Social Security works. Even more detailed explanations of the intricacies of Social Security can be found on the Social Security Administration website (www.ssa.gov).

Social Security provides cash benefits based on a worker's earnings record. Those benefits may be paid to workers, as well as to family members, including spouses, divorced spouses, dependent children (including adult children disabled before age 22), and occasionally to financially dependent grandchildren and parents. Monthly benefits vary according to such factors as type of benefit, prior contributions, age when benefits begin, and the number of people receiving benefits in a household. The maximum monthly benefit for people first retiring at full retirement age (66) is $2,642 in 2014.[1]

Workers covered by Social Security (virtually all workers other than about 25 percent of state and local government employees) contribute 6.2 percent of their earnings (with an equal employer match) up to a maximum taxable ceiling ($117,000 in 2014) into two trust funds: the Old-Age and Survivors Insurance Trust Fund and the Disability Insurance Trust Fund, or what is more conveniently called the combined OASDI Trust Fund.[2] Self-employed workers make contributions equal to those made by regular employees and their employers.

The maximum taxable ceiling is adjusted each year by the percentage that wages have increased, on average, nationwide. (The goal of indexing the maximum amount to average wages is for Social Security to receive a constant share, 90 percent, of national earnings.[3] Because wages at the top of the income scale have grown so much faster than the wages of everyone else over the last few decades, the percentage has dropped. In 1982, 90 percent of wages were covered by Social Security, as Congress intended. Through the inadvertent impact of the way wages have grown, that percentage was roughly 82.5 percent in 2014.[4] Another 1.45 percent contribution, paid by employees and matched by their employers, and assessed on all wages (with no maximum amount), goes to Medicare's Hospital Insurance (HI) Trust Fund.[5]

To qualify for benefits, workers must have contributed on large enough wages for a sufficient amount of time to become insured. There are several categories of insured status. To be what the Social Security Administration calls "fully" or "permanently" insured, workers must have contributed to Social Security for forty "quarters of coverage."[6] In 2014, one credit is given for contributions made on each $1,200 of earnings anytime in the calendar year, up to a maximum of four quarters or credits in any calendar year.[7] Because workers can become disabled or die at any time, workers under age 31 may become insured for those benefits with fewer than forty quarters, as few as six quarters out of the last three years for the youngest workers. Disability Insurance applicants must meet an additional requirement of recency of work, usually twenty out of the last forty quarters, except that in the case of workers under age 31, it may be as little as six quarters out of the last three years.

Expanding on the discussion in chapter 2, monthly benefits vary according to such factors as type of benefit, prior contributions, age when benefits begin, and the number of people receiving benefits in a household. Retirement, disability, survivor, spousal, widow(er), divorced, children's benefits—essentially all benefits—make use of the same benefit formula. The benefit formula produces what is called the primary insurance amount, which is best understood as the amount workers are eligible for if they claim benefits in the first month of their full retirement age, currently 66.[8] For purposes of calculating disability and survivor benefits, the disability or death is assumed to be at age 66 (or, more precisely, the statutorily defined full retirement age at the time of the death or disability).

Social Security's benefit formula is progressive, an acknowledgement that lower-wage workers have less discretionary income and less ability to save, and so need a larger percentage of their pre-retirement wages replaced to maintain the standard of living they enjoyed during their working years. The formula uses career earnings, so workers who have periods of unemployment usually receive larger proportionate benefits as well.

To calculate benefits, a worker's career earnings are indexed to adjust for real wage growth, averaged to determine a monthly amount (the average indexed monthly earnings, or AIME) inserted in Social Security's progressive formula, and then adjusted, based on the age at which the worker first retires and other factors. The formula for 2014 is:

The sum of:

> 90 percent of the first $816 of average indexed monthly earnings, plus
>
> 32 percent of average indexed monthly earnings over $816 and through $4,917, plus
>
> 15 percent of average indexed monthly earnings over $4,917.[9]

The percentage factors are fixed by law while the dollar amounts (known as bend points) are adjusted annually by the percentage increase of average wages nationwide.

Workers who have earned higher salaries over their careers receive benefits that are larger in absolute dollars, but are smaller in proportionate terms, than those received by lower-paid workers. For workers retiring at the full retirement age of 66 years old in January 2014, Social Security benefits replaced about 26 percent of earnings for those with earnings consistently at the maximum taxable earnings ceiling ($117,000 in 2014); about 41 percent for average earners, and about 55 percent for low-wage workers with earnings at 45 percent of median wage, just $26,965 in 2012.

In addition to Social Security's single benefit formula, other benefit formulas apply in specific circumstances, such as the special minimum benefit, which, as discussed in chapter 7, is payable to certain persons who have worked in covered employment or self-employment for many years at low earnings levels. (This formula is used only if it results in higher than the regularly computed benefit.[10])

Retired worker benefits. Retired worker benefit amounts are affected by a worker's prior contributions and earnings, and by his or her age and when benefits are first claimed. Although the Social Security Act defines the full retirement age as a single defined age (age 66 for individuals attaining age 62 after December 31, 2004, and before January 1, 2017),[11] Social Security provides what really amounts to a continuum of retirement ages, ranging from 62 to 70. Workers are eligible to claim benefits as early as age 62. For every month after age 62 up to age 70 that benefits are claimed, the initial benefit amount is increased in recognition that benefits will be received for a shorter time.[12] Benefits, once received, can also be affected by earnings. About 38 million persons, age 62 and over, received retired worker benefits in 2014.[13]

The full eligibility age for retired workers (a.k.a. the age of eligibility for full benefits, Social Security's statutory retirement age, the normal retirement age) has been increasing since 2000, from age 65 to 66 for those born from 1943 to 1954 and will be increased from 66 to 67 for those born in 1960 or later. This amounts to a roughly 6 to 7 percent across-the-board cut in benefits for persons becoming eligible for these benefits today, regardless of whether they accept retired worker benefits at age 62, 70, or any age in between; a 12 to 13 percent cut for those born after 1959 when age 67 is fully phased in as the full retirement age.[14]

Covered workers may accept retired worker benefits beginning with the first month that they turn 62, but if they do, their monthly benefits are permanently reduced, for example, by 25 percent for workers accepting retired worker benefits today; by 30 percent when age 67 is fully phased in as the full retirement age. Alternatively, those workers in a position to postpone receipt of benefits past the full retirement age get credits that permanently increase the value of their monthly benefits for each month benefit receipt is postponed past their full retirement age, up to age 70.[15]

As must be apparent by now, Social Security's terminology and rules sometimes defy "hard and fast" explanation. Here's another example. People who receive retired worker benefits can hold a paid job and, in many cases, receive some or all of their earned benefits. Retired worker benefits are not affected by any earnings received after reaching the full retirement age, but retired workers under full retirement age generally lose $1 in benefits for every $2 earned in excess of an earnings exempt amount—$15,480 in 2014. A more liberal exempt amount ($41,400 in 2014) and benefit reduction offset ($1 for every $3 of earnings above the exempt amount) are applied in the year a worker obtains the full retirement age.[16]

Disabled worker benefits. When covered workers become severely disabled, they may be eligible, after a five-month waiting period, to receive monthly Disability Insurance (DI) benefits. After an additional twenty-four months, disabled workers (as well as disabled widow(er)s age 50 through 64), and disabled adult children (of retired, disabled, or deceased workers) are eligible for all Medicare benefits.[17]

Roughly 9 million people receive DI benefits each month.[18] The disability criteria are strict. To be considered disabled, in 2014 a person must be unable to engage in substantial gainful activity (SGA), defined as earning $1,070 a month ($1,800 for the blind) in 2014, because of a physical or mental impairment that is expected to last at least a year or result in death. A worker does not actually have to earn this amount, just be able to earn it. A worker must be unable to do any kind of job that exists in significant numbers in the national economy. The local or regional availability of jobs is not taken into consideration, although age, education, and previous work experience are.

Surviving spouse benefits. Three types of benefits exist for widows and widowers of a covered spouse or, in some cases, of a divorced spouse whose marriage had lasted for at least ten years. Reduced benefits are available at age 60 (or age 50 if severely disabled) to the surviving spouses of deceased workers; full benefits at full retirement age or later.[19] Among the 4.3 million widow(er)s receiving benefits in 2013, the large majority, 3.9 million, are aged widow(er)s, 60 and over. About 150,000 widowed parents caring for a child under age 16 also receive monthly benefits.[20] As with many Social Security matters, there are some complexities. Aged widow(er)s with earnings histories receive a benefit equivalent to their spouse's, or what they have earned through their own work histories, whichever is higher. The benefit will also be affected by other factors, such as the age it is first accepted and decisions made to maximize household benefits when both spouses are eligible.[21]

Disabled widow(er)s benefits. Widow(er)s ages 50 to 60 who are not caring for young children may be eligible for monthly benefits if they meet disability eligibility standards that are somewhat more strict than those applied to workers with disabilities. About 257,000 people receive these benefits in 2014.[22]

Benefits for spouses of disabled and retired workers. About 2.3 million spouses of retired workers and 153,000 spouses of persons receiving DI benefits receive monthly benefits based on Social Security contributions made by their married, or in some cases, divorced spouses.[23] There are a number of complexities for spouses of retired worker beneficiaries. Those who have worked generally receive a benefit that is equivalent to what they have earned based on their earnings history or one-half of their spouse's benefit, whichever is larger.[24]

Young children's and grandchildren's benefits. Young children, and in some cases grandchildren, of deceased, retired, and disabled workers are eligible to receive benefits. Nearly all are under age 18, but some who are full-time elementary or secondary school students may receive benefits until age 19 and 2 months.[25] At one time, as discussed in chapter 7, these benefits were continued until age 22 if a child was a full-time college student or in an advanced vocational education program.[26]

Disabled adult children's benefits. A little-known Social Security benefit provides vital support for some people with very significant, lifelong disabilities. Social Security's disabled adult children (DAC) benefits essentially protect everyone who is, or hopes to be, a parent; every young child; those yet to be born; and 1 million adults whose severe disabilities began prior to age 22.[27] A DAC is usually the child of a parent who is deceased or receiving retirement or disability benefits. In some cases, a DAC may be a stepchild, grandchild, or stepgrandchild.[28]

Cost of living adjustment (COLA). The cost of living adjustment is one of Social Security's most important features. Its purpose is to assure that Social Security benefits, once received, maintain their purchasing power no matter how long someone lives. Although many, including ourselves, believe that it falls short of its goal, one thing is clear: virtually no other occupational pension or savings schemes provides inflation protection that compares favorably to Social Security's. Without the cost of living adjustment, inflation would halve the value of benefits after roughly twenty years with normal inflation rates (3 percent a year).[29]

APPENDIX B

ADDITIONAL INFORMATION ABOUT THE SOCIAL SECURITY WORKS ALL GENERATIONS PLAN AND OTHER PROPOSALS, INCLUDING COST AND REVENUE ESTIMATES

This appendix provides a more detailed discussion of the proposals highlighted in chapters 7 and 8, together with costs and revenues.

As explained in chapter 8, absolute dollar amounts over long periods of time are hard, if not impossible, to comprehend. Consequently, Social Security's actuaries express seventy-five-year projections of the financial status of Social Security, as well as the cost or savings from particular proposals in terms of percent of taxable payroll (i.e., as a percent of all covered earnings). In 2014, covered earnings include about 82.5 percent of all earnings in the economy. Expressing costs and savings as a percent of taxable payroll over Social Security's seventy-five-year estimating period is much more useful than dollar amounts because over seventy-five years the value of the dollar will change considerably and even so-called constant dollars involve extremely large numbers. Because the main source of Social Security's financing is from Social Security contributions assessed against covered earnings, expressing the projected deficit/surplus and the cost/savings of proposals in that form permits an easy comparison of costs. In addition, we also express these large numbers as a percent of gross domestic product.

Based on the actuaries' estimates, in 2014, Social Security's board of trustees reported that under the most widely accepted set of assumptions, the program had a shortfall of 1.02 percent of gross domestic product, which also equals 2.88 percent of taxable payroll. In other words, the entire shortfall could be eliminated totally if the FICA rates on employers and employees each were increased immediately from 6.2 percent to 7.64 percent.[1] That provides a sense of scale, but as the All Generations Plan details, we believe that there are better ways to eliminate the projected shortfall and finance the projected costs of the improvements advocated here. All estimates of costs or savings, unless otherwise noted, are for the traditional seventy-five-year valuation period and were derived by Social Security Administration's Office of the Chief Actuary. Most of the numbers can be found on that office's website at www.ssa.gov/oact.

INCREASING THE ECONOMIC SECURITY OF CURRENT AND FUTURE SENIORS

INCREASE BENEFITS FOR ALL CURRENT AND FUTURE BENEFICIARIES

As chapter 7 explains, across-the-board benefit increases can be designed in a variety of ways. Every benefit could simply be increased by the same flat percentage. A 5 percent across-the-board increase, for example, costs 0.78 percent of taxable payroll, or 0.28 percent of GDP.[2] Alternatively, all beneficiaries could be given the same dollar increase. That would provide lower-wage workers, as well as spouses and children, a larger percentage increase. Another approach is to modify the bend points. (The formula is set forth and the phrases "bend points" and "percentage factors" are described in appendix A.) That approach was followed, for example, in legislation sponsored by then-senator Tom Harkin[3] and now by Senator Sherrod Brown and Representative Linda Sanchez (D-CA).[4] That legislation gradually increases the Social Security formula's bend points by 15 percent, which translates, when fully phased in, into roughly a $70 increase for retired workers and a smaller increase for other family members.[5] If enacted, this proposal would cost 0.37 percent of taxable payroll, or 0.13 percent of GDP.[6]

The Social Security Works All Generations Plan would increase the benefits of all current and future beneficiaries by a full

10 percent, but just as there is a minimum benefit, the increase would be limited to a maximum amount of $150 a month, indexed annually by the average growth of wages. The proposal would cost 1.2 percent of taxable payroll, or 0.42 percent of GDP, as calculated by the authors.[7]

ENSURE THAT BENEFITS DO NOT ERODE OVER TIME BY ENACTING A MORE ACCURATE MEASURE OF THE COST OF LIVING EXPERIENCED BY SENIORS AND PEOPLE WITH DISABILITIES

As chapter 7 explains, virtually every expansion plan proposes the adoption of the more accurate cost of living adjustment for the elderly. (Technically, this change is not an increase, but it is an improvement, because it will do a better job of maintaining the purchasing power of benefits no matter how long someone lives.) This proposal would cost 0.37 percent of taxable payroll, or 0.13 percent of GDP.[8]

INCREASE THE SPECIAL MINIMUM BENEFIT

As chapter 7 explains, a number of expansion plans update the special minimum benefit, which is targeted toward low-income workers. There are many ways to structure this expansion. The Social Security Works All Generations Plan would update the special minimum benefit to equal 125 percent of the federal poverty level, when benefits are claimed at full retirement age, which is now age 66, but is gradually increasing to age 67, when workers have at least thirty years of credited work (i.e., 120 quarters of coverage.) For those with under thirty years of coverage, the benefit is proportionately lower. This improvement costs 0.19 percent of taxable payroll, or 0.07 percent of GDP.[9]

INCREASE BENEFITS FOR THE VERY OLD AND THOSE WHO HAVE BEEN RECEIVING BENEFITS FOR MANY YEARS

As mentioned in chapter 7, some proposals increase benefits at a certain age or after beneficiaries have been receiving benefits for a certain number of years. These proposals can be structured in a variety of ways. A 5 percent increase at age 85, for example, would cost 0.11 percent of taxable payroll, or 0.04 percent of GDP.[10] To target the increase disproportionately to those who are low income, some have proposed a flat dollar amount equal to 5 percent of the average retired worker's benefit. To also include those with disabilities that started at young ages, these proposals could be structured to increase benefits after twenty years of receipt or eligibility for benefits.

INCREASE THE BENEFITS OF WIDOWED SPOUSES, WHO HAVE DISPROPORTIONATELY HIGH RATES OF POVERTY

Private pensions may end or be greatly reduced when a worker dies. Social Security, which pays significantly higher benefits to widow(er)s than spouses, helps cushion the loss of other income, particularly when the one left behind has earned considerably less than the deceased spouse. However, Social Security is less adequate when the spouses earned around the same amounts. Consequently, some have proposed a higher amount in that situation. The cost is relatively small. In one variation, where the increased benefits are targeted to those of low income, the cost is just 0.06 percent of taxable payroll, or 0.02 percent of GDP.[11]

STRENGTHENING FAMILY PROTECTIONS AND REINFORCING CAREGIVING

PROVIDE PAID FAMILY LEAVE UPON THE BIRTH OR ADOPTION OF A CHILD, THE ILLNESS OF A FAMILY MEMBER, OR THE ILLNESS OF A WORKER

The Social Security Works All Generations Plan would provide those workers who are insured for Social Security disability benefits up to twelve weeks of paid leave in the event of the birth or adoption of a child, the illness of a family member, or the illness of the covered worker. The benefit would be two-thirds of gross salary, capped to a monthly ceiling that would be inflation indexed. For the first year after the enactment of the law, the maximum benefit would be $4,000.[12] This proposal would, according to The Center for American Progress, cost 0.40 percent of taxable payroll, or 0.14 percent of GDP.[13]

IN RECOGNITION OF THE VALUE OF CAREGIVING, CREDIT THAT WORK TOWARD FUTURE BENEFITS

Some have proposed giving credit for unpaid child care to improve the benefits of those who have taken the time out from the paid workforce to undertake this important work. The proposals can be structured in a variety of ways. The Social Security Works All Generations Plan would give credit to parents with a child under age 6 for earnings for up to five years. The earnings credited for a child-care year would equal one-half of the Social Security Administration average wage index (about $22,161 in 2012).[14] The credits would be available for all past years to newly eligible retired-worker and disabled-worker beneficiaries starting in 2014. The proposal would cost 0.25 percent of taxable payroll, or 0.09 percent of GDP.[15]

INCREASE BENEFITS FOR FAMILIES OF DISABLED, DECEASED, OR RETIRED WORKERS

Because the benefits of children and other qualified family members are derived from the same single benefit formula, expanding benefits across the board will increase the benefits of all current and future family members who themselves are beneficiaries.

FACILITATE THE ATTAINMENT OF HIGHER EDUCATION BY CHILDREN WHOSE PARENTS ARE INSURED UNDER SOCIAL SECURITY AND HAVE DIED OR BECOME SERIOUSLY AND PERMANENTLY DISABLED

Continuing Social Security benefits to age 22 for children whose parents have become disabled or died and who are in college, university, or vocational school would cost 0.07 percent of taxable payroll, or 0.02 percent of GDP.[16]

OTHER FAMILY BENEFIT IMPROVEMENTS

There is not room to discuss, even in this appendix, all the variations and all the minor expansions that have been recommended for Social Security. Here are two representative examples that are included in the All Generations Plan with relatively small costs. They would not affect many beneficiaries, but they nevertheless could make a huge difference to those they help.

Provide new child benefit of $1,000 at the birth or adoption of a child

The Social Security Works All Generations Plan would provide a $1,000 benefit at the birth or adoption of a child. The payment could be accompanied by information about the other Social Security protections earned on behalf of the child by the covered parent(s). This proposal would cost 0.07 percent of taxable payroll, or 0.02 percent of GDP.[17]

Encourage independence and work of disabled adult children and support families giving care to them

Social Security imposes a maximum family benefit, which limits the amount that can be paid based on a worker's earnings record. Children disabled prior to age 22 may receive disabled adult child (DAC) benefits if a parent (or, in a few cases, a grandparent or other relative providing the principal financial support and care) is retired, disabled, or deceased. These benefits are counted toward the family maximum, regardless of whether that disabled adult child lives at home. This can have the unfortunate side effect of reducing monthly benefits for the parent's household. While this adjustment may make sense when a DAC beneficiary lives in the family home and shares household expenses, it makes little sense for those DAC beneficiaries who do not live with their parents, and poses a significant barrier for DAC beneficiaries who wish to live more independently. Excluding the coverage of the family maximum for DAC beneficiaries who live independently would cost 0.01 percent of taxable payroll, or 0.004 percent of GDP.[18]

Provide equity for disabled widow(er)s by eliminating both the age 50 requirement and seven-year rule, and by providing unreduced benefits

Under current law, a disabled widow(er) may collect widow(er) benefits, reduced in amount if she or he is at least age 50, and the disability began within seven years of the worker's death or seven years after the last month he or she was eligible to receive a benefit as a surviving spouse with child in care. The Social Security Works All Generations Plan would extend protection to persons under age 50, eliminate the seven-year rule and increase the level of benefits to 100 percent of the deceased spouses' PIA, aligning the treatment of disabled widow(er)s more closely to that of other disability beneficiaries. This proposal would cost 0.04 percent of taxable payroll, or 0.01 percent of GDP.[19]

SECURING SOCIAL SECURITY'S FINANCING

GRADUALLY ELIMINATE THE MAXIMUM TAXABLE WAGE BASE, GIVING CREDIT FOR CONTRIBUTIONS

As chapter 8 explains, the maximum level of wages on which Social Security insurance premiums are assessed has been slipping as a percentage of all wages nationwide. The percentage has been slipping not because of any action by Congress, but simply because the level is indexed to average wages, and that average has been skewed because wages at the top have risen so much faster than everyone else's. As a consequence, even conservative proposals like the one put forward by Erskine Bowles and Alan Simpson, mentioned in chapter 11, proposed gradually restoring the maximum to where Congress intended.[20] Those paying the increased amount would have their benefits based on those higher earnings. This proposal, gradually phased in over about thirty years, would increase Social Security's revenue 0.62 percent of taxable payroll, or 0.22 percent of GDP.[21] Others have proposed restoring the maximum to 90 percent on employees but requiring employers to contribute on their entire payrolls, as they do to Medicare's Hospital Insurance Trust Fund. This proposal would increase Social Security's revenue 1.43 percent of taxable payroll, or 0.51 percent of GDP.[22]

The Social Security Works All Generations Plan would gradually eliminate the maximum taxable wage base, over about ten years, for both employers and employees. When fully phased in, this would result in the roughly 6 percent of workers with earnings above the maximum paying into Social Security all year, as other workers do. Consistent with how Social Security has always operated, all wages on which contributions are made would be counted in calculating benefits, but the formula would be modified so that those higher earners would receive Social Security benefits that would be a higher dollar amount but a lower percentage of their wages than lower-earning workers.

That is, consistent with Social Security's progressive benefit formula, which provides benefits that are a higher dollar amount but represent a lower rate of return for workers (and their families) who earn more and contribute more to Social Security, this proposal would provide benefits, in the event of retirement, disability, and death, that are higher dollar amounts though lower rates of return to those workers (and their families) who earn above the current-law maximum and contribute to Social Security on those wages, as a result of this proposal.

This proposal would add two additional brackets onto the formula to take into account the elimination of the current-law maximum benefits base. The new percentage factors will be 5 percent and 0.25 percent, and the bend points will be at about the level of the current-law maximum (divided by twelve to achieve a monthly amount), or $9,750 (indexed to the average wage index, or AWI), and twice that amount, or $18,500 (indexed to AWI). As a result, under this proposal, Social Security's benefit formula would be, in 2014 dollars:

The sum of:

(a) 90 percent of the first $816 of average indexed monthly earnings, plus

(b) 32 percent of average indexed monthly earnings over $816 and through $4,917, plus

(c) 15 percent of average indexed monthly earnings over $4,917 and through $9,750, plus

(d) 5 percent of average indexed monthly earnings over $9,750 and through $18,500, plus

(e) 0.25 percent of average indexed monthly earnings over $18,500 [23]

GRADUALLY INCREASE SOCIAL SECURITY CONTRIBUTION RATE FROM 6.2 PERCENT ON BOTH EMPLOYEES AND EMPLOYERS TO 7.2 PERCENT BY 2039

Social Security's contribution rate has not been increased since 1990. As chapter 8 explains, the rate could be increased a small or large amount, quickly or slowly. The Social Security Works All Generations Plan would increase the rate modestly and gradually. It would increase Social Security contribution rate by 1/20th of a percentage point per year from 2020 to 2039 until the rate reaches

7.2 percent on both employers and employees. Its impact each year would be to require a worker earning an average income to contribute about 50¢ more a week to our Social Security system. It would increase Social Security's revenue 1.41 percent of taxable payroll, or 0.50 percent of GDP.[24]

TREAT ALL SALARY REDUCTION PLANS THE SAME AS 401(K) PLANS WITH RESPECT TO THE DEFINITION OF WAGES UNDER SOCIAL SECURITY

By treating all salary reduction plans the same as 401(k)s, the Social Security Works All Generations Plan would generate modest revenues while also correcting an inconsistency in the law. This proposal would increase Social Security's revenue 0.25 percent of taxable payroll, or 0.09 percent of GDP.[25]

INCREASE SOCIAL SECURITY'S INVESTMENT INCOME

Social Security currently has an accumulated reserve of $2.8 trillion, which by law is invested solely in interest-bearing obligations of the United States.[26] Standard investment advice is to diversity one's portfolio, investing in both equities and bond instruments. This proposal would achieve that diversification. The more that is invested in equities, the higher the return generally. The Social Security Works All Generations Plan directs that 40 percent of trust fund assets be gradually, over fifteen years, invested in a broadly diversified, indexed equity fund or funds. A variety of safeguards would be introduced to assure no interference with the market or the entities in which the trust funds are invested. Assuming a 6.4 percent real rate of return, this proposal would increase Social Security's revenue 0.59 percent of taxable income, or 0.21 percent of GDP.[27]

DEDICATE REVENUES FROM NEW TAXES ON INCOME IN EXCESS OF $1 MILLION AND FROM OTHER PROGRESSIVE SOURCES

The Social Security Works All Generations Plan would create a new dedicated source of revenue from the taxation of incomes above $1 million. Those fortunate taxpayers pay no additional tax on their first $1 million of income. On their million and first dollar, and every dollar after that, they simply pay an additional 10¢ per dollar. This proposal would increase Social Security's revenue 1.5 percent of taxable payroll, or 0.53 percent of GDP, as calculated by the authors.[28]

As discussed in chapter 8, other proposals would dedicate other progressive taxes, such as the federal estate tax or a financial speculation tax. Dedicating to Social Security the federal estate tax, restored to its 2009 level, where it taxed estates in excess of $3.5 million ($7 million for married couples), would increase Social Security's revenue 0.51 percent of taxable payroll, or 0.18 percent of GDP.[29] Dedicating a new financial speculation tax would increase Social Security's revenue 2.8 percent of taxable payroll, or 0.99 percent of GDP, according to calculations made by the authors.[30]

SIMPLIFY AND STREAMLINE ACCOUNTING

Social Security's disability, survivors, and retirement benefits are all intertwined, generated from the same benefit formula. For this reason, the annual Trustees Report presents the two trust funds on both a separate and combined basis. The Social Security Works All Generations Plan simply makes that presentation of the combined funds—OASDI—a reality by combining the OASI Trust Fund with the DI Trust Fund. This change has no cost. It just simplifies and streamlines accounting.

The following table shows the costs of the benefit expansions and the increased revenue of the financing proposals contained in the All Generations Plan. As the table reveals, the plan leaves Social Security in long-range actuarial surplus for the next three-quarters of a century.

SOCIAL SECURITY WORKS
ALL GENERATIONS PLAN

	As percent of taxable payroll	As percent of GDP
Currently projected seventy-five-year shortfall (present value)	-2.88	-1.02
Addressing the Retirement Income Crisis	Cost/ Savings as percent of taxable payroll	Cost/ Savings as percent of GDP
Increase benefits for all current and future beneficiaries by 10%, up to a maximum of $150 a month	-1.20	-0.42
Ensure that benefits do not erode over time by enacting the more accurate CPI-E	-.37	-0.13
Provide a minimum benefit, at full benefit age, of 125% of poverty for covered workers who have 30 years of work	-.19	-0.07
Strengthening Family Protections for All Generations		
Provide up to 12 weeks of paid family leave upon the birth or adoption of a child, the illness of a covered worker or family member	-.40	-0.14
Give credits toward future Social Security benefits for up to five years of caring for a child under age 6	-.25	-0.09
Facilitate higher education by restoring student benefits for children up to age 22 whose covered parents have died or become disabled	-.07	-0.02
Provide $1,000 new child benefit at birth or adoption of a child	-.07	-0.02
Encourage work and independence by not applying the Family Maximum when Disabled Adult Children do not live at home	-.01	-0.004
Improve disabled widow(er) benefits by eliminating both the age 50 requirement and seven-year rule, and by providing unreduced benefits	-.04	-0.01

Securing Social Security's Financing for Generations to Come		
Starting in 2016, gradually eliminate the maximum taxable wage base, giving credit for these contributions	+1.95	+0.69
Enact a new dedicated 10% marginal income tax rate on yearly incomes in excess of $1 million (no additional tax on the first $1 million dollars of yearly income)	+1.50	+0.53
Treat all salary reduction plans the same as 401(k) plans with respect to the definition of wages under Social Security	+.25	+0.09
Increase Social Security contribution rate by 1/20th of a percentage point per year, on employers and employees each, from 2020–2039, until rate reaches 7.2% on both employers and employees	+1.41	+0.50
Invest 40% of Trust Funds in equities, phased in from 2014–2028	+.59	+0.21
Combine the OASI Trust Fund with DI Trust Fund	0	0
Long-Range Surplus	+0.22	+0.08

Note: These estimates are preliminary and do not include interaction effects. Long-range surplus totals differ from sum of cost estimates due to rounding. "Percent of taxable payroll" is the customary way of expressing the projected deficit/surplus of the Social Security Trust Fund—and the cost/savings generated by various proposals—over 75 years. Since the present value of 75-year GDP (2014-2088) is 2.83 times larger than that of taxable payroll, the amounts expressed as a share of taxable payroll are 2.83 times larger than when expressed as a share of GDP.

Source: Long-range actuarial shortfall: "2014 OASDI Trustees Report," Social Security Administration, 2014. Estimates of individual proposals: Office of the Chief Actuary, Social Security Administration, except where noted in the preceding text.

APPENDIX C

DESCRIPTIONS OF VARIOUS SOCIAL SECURITY EXPANSION
LEGISLATIVE BILLS AND ORGANIZATIONS' PLANS

TABLE A.1: LEGISLATORS' SOCIAL SECURITY EXPANSION BILLS

Bill Name	Bill Sponsor(s)	Number of Co-Sponsors	Increases/ Expands Benefits	Pays for Expanded Benefits	Extends Solvency
Strengthening Social Security Act of 2013 (S. 567 and H.R. 3118)	Sen. Tom Harkin (D–IA) and Rep. Linda Sanchez (D–CA-38)	4 Senate, 62 House; Endorsed by Congressional Progressive Caucus, which includes 74 members	✓	✓	✓
Protecting and Preserving Social Security Act (S. 308 and H.R. 649)	Sen. Mark Begich (D–AK) and Rep. Theodore Deutch (D–FL-21)	2 Senate, 27 House	✓	✓	✓
Social Security Enhancement and Protection Act of 2013 (H.R. 1374)	Rep. Gwen Moore (D–WI-4)	1 House	✓	✓	✓
The Retirement and Income Security (RAISE) Act of 2013 (S. 2455)	Sen. Mark Begich (D–AK) and Sen. Patty Murray (D–WA)	1 Senate	✓	✓	✓
Fair Raises for Seniors Act (S. 2382)	Sen. Jeff Merkley (D–OR)	0 Senate	✓	✓	✓

Major Points of Bill

Increases benefits for virtually all Social Security beneficiaries by approximately $70 per month, by an increase in the first so-called bend point of the Social Security benefit formula. Switches to the more accurate CPI-E. Pays for the improvements and extends solvency by gradually eliminating the Social Security maximum taxable wage base. For more information, go to www.gpo.gov/fdsys /pkg/BILLS-113s567is/pdf/BILLS-113s567is.pdf.

Switches to the more accurate CPI-E. Pays for the improvements and extends solvency by gradually eliminating the Social Security maximum taxable wage base. For more information, go to www.gpo.gov/fdsys/pkg/BILLS-113s308is /pdf/BILLS-113s308is.pdf.

Increases the special minimum benefit paid to workers who have spent long careers in low-wage jobs. Gives credits of up to five years toward the minimum benefit for a parent who leaves the workforce to raise a child younger than 6 years old. Provides a 5% increase for the very old and others who have been eligible to receive benefits for twenty years. Restores the student benefit for children of disabled or deceased workers. Pays for the improvements and extends solvency by gradually eliminating the Social Security maximum taxable wage base and gradually increasing the Social Security contributions rate by 0.3% on employees, matched by employers. For more information, go to www.gpo.gov /fdsys/pkg/BILLS-113hr1374ih/pdf/BILLS-113hr1374ih.pdf.

Extends benefits to divorced spouses married less than ten years; provides alternative, higher benefits to widow(er)s of 75% of combined benefit, if higher than current-law benefit. Restores student benefits to children of deceased, disabled, and retired workers. Pays for the improvements and extends solvency by requiring workers and their employers to contribute to Social Security 2% of earnings above $400K for which they would receive higher benefits. For more information, go to www.govtrack.us/congress/bills/113/s2455/text.

Switches to the more accurate CPI-E. Pays for the improvements and extends solvency by requiring workers to contribute to Social Security 2% of earnings above $250K. For more information, go to www.govtrack.us/congress /bills/113/s2382/text.

Bill Name	Bill Sponsor(s)	Number of Co-Sponsors	Increases/ Expands Benefits	Pays for Expanded Benefits	Extends Solvency
The Social Security 2100 Act (H.R. 5306)	Rep. John Larson (D-CT-1)	1 House	✓	✓	✓
Family and Medical Insurance Leave Act of 2013 (S. 181 and H.R. 3712)	Sen. Kirsten Gillibrand (D-NY) and Rep. Rosa De Lauro (D-CT-3)	6 Senate, 95 House	✓	✓	N/A
The Social Security and Marriage Equality (SAME) Act (S. 2305 and H.R. 4664)	Sen. Patty Murray (D-WA) and Rep. Ron Kind (D-WI-3)	7 Senate, 46 House	✓	N/A	N/A
The Social Security Caregiver Credit Act of 2014 (H.R. 5024)	Rep. Nita Lowey (D-NY-17)	33 House	✓	N/A	N/A

Major Points of Bill

Provides an across-the-board 2% increase for all beneficiaries so that all Social Security recipients would see an immediate benefit increase starting in 2015. Improves the cost of living adjustment (COLA) by moving to a CPI-E formula. Provides a tax break to Social Security recipients by raising the threshold for taxation on benefits to $50,000 for individuals ($100,000 for joint filers). Presently, Social Security beneficiaries making more than $25,000 ($32,000 for joint filers) per year pay taxes on their benefits. Protects the lowest income beneficiaries by ensuring that those who paid into the system receive a minimum benefit equal to 125% of the poverty line. This will prevent low-lifetime earners from falling into poverty in retirement. Over twenty years, increases the payroll tax on workers and employers from 6.2% to 7.2%. This is a 0.05% increase each year beginning in 2018, and would be the equivalent of 50 cents per week cumulatively. Lifts the cap by applying the payroll tax to earners making more than $400,000. Presently, payroll taxes are not collected on wages over $117,000. Gradually invests up to 25% of the assets in a broad-based, diversified index fund in order to bolster the Trust Fund as more baby boomers begin to retire. The investments would be overseen by an independent board with fiduciary responsibilities and would include sensible safeguards to ensure that all benefits are paid in full and on time. For more information, go to www.govtrack.us/congress/bills/113/hr5306.

Establishes the Office of Paid Family and Medical Leave within the Social Security Administration. Provides twelve weeks of paid leave each year to qualifying workers for the birth or adoption of a new child, the serious illness of an immediate family member, or a worker's own medical condition. Pays for the new benefit by having employees and employers each make contributions of 0.2% of wages. For more information, go to http://beta.congress.gov/113/bills/s1810/BILLS-113s1810is.pdf.

Confers survivors benefits to any individual legally married in United States. Eliminates the requirement that the surviving spouse reside in a state that recognizes same-sex marriage in order to be eligible for Social Security benefits. Ensures spouses legally married outside the United States are eligible for Social Security benefits. For more information, go to https://beta.congress.gov/bill/113th-congress/senate-bill/2305.

Modestly enhances caregivers' Social Security benefits. Anyone spending at least eighty hours a month providing care to a dependent relative under the age of 12 or a chronically dependent individual is eligible to claim credit for up to sixty months. The credit would be structured in a way to complement earnings and would be progressive, with those not receiving income earning a higher credit, eventually phasing out when an individual earns more than the average national wage. For more information, go to https://beta.congress.gov/bill/113th-congress/house-bill/5024.

Note: Table A.1. lists the key sponsors and a number of co-sponsors of plans put forward by senators and memebers of Congress at the time of this writing. N/A=not applicable.

TABLE A.2: ORGANIZATIONS' SOCIAL SECURITY EXPANSION PLANS

Name of Plan	Organization(s) Proposing Plan	Increases/ Expands Benefits	Pays for Expanded Benefits	Extends Solvency
Expanding Social Security Benefits for Vulnerable Populations	Center for Community Change and Older Women's Economic Security Task Force	✓	✓	✓
Plan for a New Future: The Impact of Social Security Reform on People of Color	The Commission to Modernize Social Security	✓	✓	✓
Keeping Social Security Strong	Economic Opportunity Institute	✓	✓	✓
Strengthening Social Security for Women	Institute for Women's Policy Research	✓	✓	✓
Breaking the Social Security Glass Ceiling	Institute for Women's Policy Research, National Organization for Women Foundation, National Committee to Preserve Social Security and Medicare	✓	✓	✓

Major Points of Plan

Creates a caregiving credit, restores and expands student benefits, increases the minimum benefit. Switches to the more accurate CPI-E. Ensures that LGBTQ couples receive Social Security benefits. Pays for the improvements and extends solvency by gradually eliminating the Social Security maximum taxable wage base. Also urges full employment and immigration reform, which will increase Social Security's revenue, and offers other options. For more information, go to www.iwpr.org/publications/pubs/expanding-social-security-benefits-for-financially-vulnerable-populations/at_download/file.

Increases benefits across the board by an amount equal to 5% of average benefits, restores student benefits, increases the minimum benefit. Improves survivors' benefits and increases benefits after age 85. Pays for the improvements and extends solvency by gradually eliminating the Social Security maximum taxable wage base, gradually increasing the Social Security contribution rate, treating all salary reduction plans as income for Social Security purposes. For more information, go to http://modernizesocialsecurity.files.wordpress.com/2013/04/new_future_social_security_10_24_11.pdf.

Increases benefits for low earners. Creates a caregiving credit, restores student benefits, and improves survivors' benefits. Pays for the improvements and extends solvency by eliminating the Social Security maximum taxable wage base. For more information, go to www.eoionline.org/wp/wp-content/uploads/social-security/KeepingSocialSecurityStrongFourSteps-May2012.pdf.

Increases benefits for low earners, creates a caregiver credit, increases eligibility for divorce benefits, and improves survivors' benefits. Pays for the improvements and extends solvency by eliminating the Social Security maximum taxable wage base and diversifying trust fund investments. For more information, go to www.iwpr.org/publications/pubs/strengthening-social-security-for-women-a-report-from-the-working-conference-on-women-and-social-security-1/at_download/file.

Increases benefits across the board by an amount equal to 5% of average benefits. Creates a caregiver credit, restores the student benefit, increases the minimum benefit, and improves survivor benefits. Switches to the more accurate CPI-E. Improves benefits for disabled adult children. Pays for the improvements and extends solvency by eliminating the Social Security maximum taxable wage base, gradually increasing the Social Security contribution rate, and treating all salary reduction plans as income for Social Security purposes. For more information, go to www.iwpr.org/publications/pubs/breaking-the-social-security-glass-ceiling-a-proposal-to-modernize-womens-benefits/at_download/file.

Name of Plan	Organization(s) Proposing Plan	Increases/ Expands Benefits	Pays for Expanded Benefits	Extends Solvency
Protecting Social Security: A Blueprint for Strengthening Social Security for All Americans	Latinos for a Secure Retirement	✓	✓	✓
Boost Social Security Now	National Committee to Preserve Social Security and Medicare	✓	✓	✓
Does the Social Security COLA Need to Be Changed?	National Senior Citizens Law Center	✓		
Expanded Social Security: A Plan to Increase Retirement Security for All Americans	New America Foundation	✓	✓	✓

Major Points of Plan

Restores the student benefit, increases the minimum benefit, and encourages legal immigration, which will increase Social Security's revenue. Pays for the improvements and extends solvency by gradually raising the Social Security maximum taxable wage base to cover 90% of all earnings, treating all salary reduction plans as income for Social Security purpose, and diversifying trust fund investments. For more information, go to http://latinosforasecureretirement .org/assets/LSR_Protecting_Social_Security_Plan.pdf.

Increases all benefits by $70 a month, creates a caregiver credit. Switches to the more accurate CPI-E. Pays for the improvements and extends solvency by gradually eliminating the Social Security maximum taxable wage base, gradually increasing the Social Security contribution rate, and treating all salary reduction plans as income for Social Security purposes. For more information, go to www.ncpssm.org/Portals/0/pdf/6WaystoBoostSS.pdf.

Switches to the more accurate CPI-E. For more information, go to: http:// www.nsclc.org/wp-content/uploads/2011/06/Issue-Brief-COLA-July-2012 .pdf.

Creates "Social Security B," a universal flat benefit of $11,669 per year for all retirees. To pay for all current benefits and this new benefit, the plan lists a variety of options, including general revenue for the new benefit. For more information, go to http://growth.newamerica.net/sites/newamerica.net/files/policy docs/LindHillHiltonsmithFreedman_ExpandedSocialSecurity_04_03_13.pdf.

Note: Table A.2 lists plans of which the authors were aware at the time of this writing and includes organizations involved in their development. The authors apologize for any inadvertent omissions.

APPENDIX D

LEADING ORGANIZATIONS WORKING TO EXPAND SOCIAL SECURITY

The victories described in chapter 11 were the work of many. They can be traced to the foresight and investments over several decades of Atlantic Philanthropies, Ford Foundation, Rockefeller Foundation, Retirement Research Foundation, and the donations of individuals whose generous support enabled organizations to create and disseminate research-based information. Such organizations include AARP, Center for American Progress, Center for Budget and Policy Priorities, Center for Economic Policy Research, Economic Policy Institute, Institute for America's Future, Institute for Women's Policy Research, National Academy of Social Insurance (discussed in more detail below), National Institute on Retirement Security, National Women's Law Center, Pension Rights Center, and Retirement Research Center at Boston College. These organizations provided the intellectual infrastructure so important to efforts to advance a sound Social Security system, to build the case against privatizing and cutting Social Security, and to expand its vital protections.

More proximately, the Ford Foundation made generous contributions that helped engage new citizen-based constituencies in the Social Security policy arena. Beginning in 2009, Atlantic Philanthropies funded Social Security Works, the organization the authors co-founded and that convened and staffs the Strengthen Social Security Coalition (SSSC), a broad-based diverse coalition of more than 350 national and state organizations, including many of the nation's leading union, women's, disability, aging, civil rights, and netroots/Internet advocacy organizations. (A list of all members of the coalition can be found at socialsecurityworks .org.)

Many, many organizations, including the labor-based Alliance for Retired Americans, Center for Community Change, AARP, Generations United, National Committee to Preserve Social Security and Medicare, National Organization for Women, NAACP, and National Senior Citizens Law Center made major investments to safeguard Social Security. Electronic advocates—including Campaign for America's Future, CREDO Action, Democracy for America, MoveOn.org, Progressive Change Campaign Committee, and Progressive Democrats of America—engaged their millions of members. Union organizations—including AFGE, AFL-CIO, AFSCME, AFT, IFPTE, NEA, National Nurses United, SEIU, Steelworkers, UAW, Teamsters, and others—used their networks to get information out about the risk to their members. These and other organizations worked tirelessly to educate their members, the public, media, and our representatives in Congress.

And they continue to work. If you want to learn more, there is much good information available. The late Robert M. Ball, the nation's longest serving Social Security commissioner (to whom the authors dedicate this book), established the National Academy of Social Insurance in 1987, consisting of more than a thousand of the nation's leading experts on Social Security and other social insurance programs. The academy issues excellent briefs and reports, which can be downloaded from its website. Similarly, Harvard University professor Theda Skocpol has created the Scholars Strategy Network, which states its mission as "bring[ing] together many of America's leading scholars to address pressing public challenges at the national, state, and local levels."[1] The network also issues informative briefs on a variety of social policy issues. Those briefs are, like the academy's, available for download on its website. Other excellent information can be found on the websites of the AARP, Center for Policy and Budget Priorities, Economic Policy Institute, Social Security Works, and many of the other groups mentioned above.

We urge those who want to get involved to check out the website of Social Security Works, a nonprofit organization founded by the co-authors, and sign up for alerts. (Social Security Works annually publishes fifty state reports (including eleven in Spanish and reports for the District of Columbia, Puerto Rico, American Samoa, Guam, the Northern Mariana Islands, and the U.S. Virgin Islands), highlighting the protections afforded to each state's citizens—children, seniors, veterans, persons with disabilities, persons of color, and women—and providing data about the numbers of people served and benefits provided across all congressional districts and in every county (see www.socialsecurityworks.org /resources/state-reports).

To keep informed about the latest developments in the battle for Social Security and to join the fight, please visit our website at socialsecurityworks.org.

NOTES

CHAPTER 1: THE CHANGING CONVERSATION

1. In our acknowledgments, we thank a number of people whose invaluable assistance helped in the preparation of this book. We also want to note that the book builds on and draws from previous individual and co-authored works of the authors, including: Altman, *The Battle for Social Security* (Hoboken, NJ: John Wiley & Sons, 2005); Kingson and E.D. Berkowitz, *Social Security and Medicare: A Policy Primer* (Westport, CT: Auburn House, 1993); Kingson, B.A. Hirshorn, and J.C. Cornman, *Ties That Bind: The Interdependence of Generations* (Cabin John, MD: Seven Locks, 1986); Kingson, Altman, and Stephen H. Gorin, "What Social Workers Need to Know about the Retirement Income Crisis," *Health and Social Work,* November 2014. Altman, and Kingson, "Social Security Reduces Inequality—Efficiently, Effectively and Fairly," in *Divided: The Perils of Our Growing Inequality,* ed. D.C. Johnston (New York: The New Press, 2014); Altman, "The Striking Superiority of Social Security in the Provision of Wage Insurance," *Harvard Journal on Legislation* 50 (2013); Kingson, D. Bell, and S. Shive, "American Social Security System," in *Encyclopedia of Social Work On Line* (New York: Oxford University Press, 2013); Altman, "The War Against Social Security" (review of *The People's Pension: The Struggle to Defend Social Security Since Reagan,* by Eric Laursen), in *Dissent* (Fall 2012); M. Checksfield and Kingson, "Social Security Remains the Key in Averting the Impending Retirement Income Crisis, Revisited," *Aging Today,* November/December 2012; Kingson and M. Morrissey, "Can Workers Offset Social Security Cuts by Working Longer?" (Washington, DC: Economic Policy Institute, May 30, 2012); Altman, "The Impact of Social Security on American Lives," and Kingson, "Framing Social Security for the 21st Century," both in *A Promise to All Generations: Stories and Essays About Social Security and Frances Perkins,* eds. K. Downey and C. Breiseth (Newcastle, ME: Frances Perkins Center, 2011); Kingson and Altman, "The Social Security Retirement Age(s) Debate: Perspectives and Consequences," in *Public Policy and Aging Report, "To Raise or Not to*

Raise: The Social Security Retirement Age" 21, no. 2 (2011): 1–7; Altman, "The Current Battle in the Long-Standing War Against Social Security," *Poverty and Public Policy* 3, no. 1 (2011); Kingson, "A Tale of Three Commissions: The Good, the Bad, and the Ugly," *Poverty and Public Policy* 2, no. 3 (2010); Altman, "A Silver Lining to the Economic Crisis: The Case for Improving Social Security and Medicare," *Generations* 33, no. 3 (Fall 2009); Kingson and A.L. Torre, "Supporting Care Across Generations: Perspectives for Assessing Social and Public Policy Issues," (unpublished paper, 2009); Altman, "Social Security and Intergenerational Justice," *George Washington Law Review* 77 (2009): 1383; J.R. Cornman, Kingson, and D.M. Butts, "Time for an All Generations Approach to Public Policy," *Generations* 33, no. 3 (Fall 2009): 86–88; Altman and Marmor, "Social Security from the Great Society to 1980: Further Expansion and Rekindled Controversy," in *Conservatism and American Political Development,* eds. Brian Glenn and Steven Teles (New York: Oxford University Press, 2009); Kingson and M.T. Brown, *Are Age-62/63 Retired Worker Beneficiaries at Risk?* (Chestnut Hill, MA: Center for Retirement Research at Boston College, 2009); Altman, "Protecting Social Security's Beneficiaries: Achieving Balance Without Benefit Cuts," *Briefing Paper,* no. 206 (November 20, 2007); Altman, "Social Security and the Low-Income Worker," *American University Law Review* 56 (June 2007): 1139; Kingson and J.H. Schulz, "Should Social Security Be Means-Tested?" in *Social Security in the 21st Century,* eds. Kingson and J.H. Schulz (New York: Oxford University Press, 1997); Altman, "Social Security and Social Insurance Benefits: What to Expect and How to Obtain Them," in *The Columbia Retirement Handbook,* ed. Abraham Monk (New York: Columbia University Press, 1994); Kingson and R.A. O'Grady-LeShane, "The Effects of Caregiving on Women's Social Security Benefits," *The Gerontologist* (April 1993); and Kingson, "Financing Social Security: Agenda-Setting and the Enactment of 1983 Amendments to the Social Security Act," *Policy Studies Journal* (September 1984).

2. Jasmine Tucker, Virginia Reno, and Thomas Bethell, "Strengthening Social Security: What Do Americans Want?" National Academy of Social Insurance, January 31, 2013, www.nasi.org/sites/default/files/research /What_Do_Americans_Want.pdf.

3. Social Security Works, "Social Security Polling," January 2014, www .socialsecurityworks.org/wp-content/uploads/2014/01/2013-Polling -Highlights.pdf; Pew Research Center, "Political Polarization in the American Public," June 2014, www.people-press.org/files/2014/06/6-12-2014 -Political-Polarization-Release.pdf.

4. Social Security Bill, H.R. 7260, 74th Cong., 1st Sess., *Congressional Record*, April 18, 1935, H5993, www.ssa.gov/history/pdf/h418.pdf.

5. Social Security Bill, H.R. 7260, 74th Cong., 1st Sess., *Congressional Record*, April 18, 1935, H6061, www.ssa.gov/history/pdf/h419.pdf.

6. Frances Perkins, *The Roosevelt I Knew* (New York: Viking Press, 1946), 299.

7. Franklin Roosevelt, "Statement of the President Upon Signing the Social Security Bill," August 14, 1935, www.fdrlibrary.marist.edu/_resources /images/sign/fdr_14.pdf#search=social%20security.

8. "Landon Hits Social Security as 'Cruel Hoax' in Milwaukee," *The Day*, September 28, 1936, http://news.google.com/newspapers?nid=1915& dat=19360928&id=XqktAAAAIBAJ&sjid=Z3EFAAAAIBAJ&pg =999,2342658; Alf Landon, "I Will Not Promise the Moon," *Oshkosh Daily Northwestern*, September 28, 1936, www.newspapers.com/newspage /43540453/; See generally Nancy J. Altman, *The Battle for Social Security: From FDR's Vision to Bush's Gamble* (Hoboken: John Wiley & Sons, 2005), 101–103.

9. Nicolaus Mills, "Alf Landon and Social Security Reform," *Dissent*, Spring 2005, www.dissentmagazine.org/article/alf-landon-and-social-securi ty-reform.

10. Franklin Delano Roosevelt, "Speech at Madison Square Garden," October 31, 1936, http://millercenter.org/president/speeches/detail/3307.

11. Blanche D. Coll, *Perspectives in Public Welfare* (Washington, DC: U.S. Department of Health, Education, and Welfare, 1973).

12. Patricia P. Martin and David A. Weaver, "Social Security: A Program and Policy History," *Social Security Bulletin* 66, no. 1 (September 2005), www.ssa.gov/policy/docs/ssb/v66n1/v66n1p1.html#mn6.

13. Harry S. Truman, "131. Veto of Resolution Excluding Certain Groups From Social Security Coverage," June 14, 1948, www.trumanlibrary.org /publicpapers/index.php?pid=1677&st=&st1=.

14. Bonnie K. Goodman, "Overviews and Chronologies: 1948," *Presidential Campaigns and Elections Reference* (blog), http://presidentialcampaigns electionsreference.wordpress.com/overviews/20th-century/1948-overview.

15. Arthur J. Altmeyer, *Formative Years of Social Security* (Madison: University of Wisconsin, 1966), 214.

16. Dwight Eisenhower, "Special Message to the Congress Transmitting Proposed Changes in the Social Security Program," August 1, 1953, www .ssa.gov/history/ikestmts.html#special.

17. U.S. Bureau of Labor Statistics, "The So-Called 'Core' Index: History and Uses of the Index for All Items Less Food and Energy," *Focus on Prices and Spending* 1, no. 15 (February 2011), www.bls.gov/opub/focus/volume1 _number15/cpi_1_15.pdf.

18. U.S. Bureau of Labor Statistics, "Consumer Price Index—All Urban Consumers," 2014, www.bls.gov/cpi.

19. U.S. Bureau of Labor Statistics, "Labor Force Statistics from the Current Population Survey," 2014, http://data.bls.gov/timeseries/LNU04000 000?years_option=all_years&periods_option=specific_periods&periods =Annual+Data.

20. John Haaga, "Just How Many Baby Boomers Are There?" Population Reference Bureau, December 2002, www.prb.org/Publications/Articles /2002/JustHowManyBabyBoomersAreThere.aspx.

21. Larry W. DeWitt, Daniel Béland, and Edward D. Berkowitz, *Social Security: A Documentary History* (Washington, DC: Congressional Quarterly Press, 2007), 318.

22. Ronald Reagan, "Second 1980 Presidential Debate," October 28, 1980, www.debates.org/index.php?page=october-28-1980-debate-transcript.

23. William Safire, "Third Rail," *New York Times,* February 18, 2007, www.nytimes.com/2007/02/18/magazine/18wwlnsafire.t.html?_r=0.

24. Ronald Reagan, "Remarks on Signing the Social Security Amendments of 1983," April 20, 1983, www.ssa.gov/history/reaganstmts.html.

25. Social Security Administration, *Annual Statistical Supplement, 2014*, (2014), table 5.A6, www.ssa.gov/policy/docs/statcomps/supplement/2014 /5a.html; About 4.4 million children received Social Security benefits directly in 2012, 3.2 million of whom were under age 18, 1 million were disabled adult children, and 146,000 were students age 18–19. Furthermore, about 4.8 million children under the age of 18 did not receive benefits directly, but lived in households that received Social Security benefits. The latter estimate is from December 2010, the most recent year data was available, so it likely understates the 2012 total; Thomas Gabe, *Social Security's Effect on Child Poverty* (Washington, DC: Congressional Research Service, December 22, 2011); There are 74 million children under age 18 living in the United States; U.S. Census Bureau, "ACS Demographic and Housing Estimates," *2010–2012 American Community Survey 3-Year Estimates*, 2013, http://fact finder2.census.gov.

26. Social Security Administration, "Survivors' Benefits," July 2013, www.ssa.gov/pubs/EN-05-10084.pdf.

27. Social Security Administration, "Monthly Statistical Snapshot, March 2014," April 2014, www.ssa.gov/policy/docs/quickfacts/stat_snapshot/index .html?qs.

28. Social Security Administration, "Income of the Population 55 or Older, 2012," April 2014, table 9.A1, www.ssa.gov/policy/docs/statcomps /income_pop55/2012/sect09.html#table9.a1.

29. Shawn Fremstad and Rebecca Vallas, "The Facts on Social Security Disability Insurance and Supplemental Security Income for Workers with Disabilities," Center for American Progress, May 2013, www .americanprogress.org/issues/poverty/report/2013/05/30/64681/the-facts -on-social-security-disability-insurance-and-supplemental-security -income-for-workers-with-disabilities.

30. Stuart Butler and Peter Germanis, "Achieving Social Security Reform: A 'Leninist' Strategy," *Cato Journal* 3, no. 2, The Cato Institute (Fall 1983), www.cato.org/cato-journal/fall-1983.

31. George W. Bush, "The 2001 President's Commission to Strengthen

Social Security: President's Remarks at the Announcement of the Commission," May 2, 2001, www.ssa.gov/history/reports/pcsss/potus.html.

32. George W. Bush, "Address Before a Joint Session of the Congress on the State of the Union," February 2, 2005, www.presidency.ucsb.edu/ws/index.php?pid=58746.

33. Editorial Board, "Social Security Proposals Are Wrongheaded," *Washington Post*, November 17, 2013, www.washingtonpost.com/opinions/social-security-proposals-are-wrongheaded/2013/11/17/38ebb486-4bde-11e3-ac54-aa84301ced81_story.html.

34. Jon Cowan and Jim Kessler, "Economic Populism Is a Dead End for Democrats," *Wall Street Journal*, December 2, 2013, http://online.wsj.com/news/articles/SB10001424052702304337404579213923151169790.

CHAPTER 2: SOCIAL SECURITY WORKS FOR ALL GENERATIONS

1. Social Security Trustees, *The 2014 Annual Report of the Board of Trustees of the Federal Old-Age and Survivors Insurance and Federal Disability Insurance Trust Funds*, July 28, 2014, table 4.B2, www.ssa.gov/oact/TR/2014/lr4b2.html

2. See table 2 in Social Security Administration, "Monthly Statistical Snapshot, December 2013," January 2014, www.ssa.gov/policy/docs/quickfacts/stat_snapshot/index.html?qs; Estimated annual benefits are calculated based on the total monthly benefits in December 2013.

3. Joannah Maleh, Robert Baldwin, and Jason Shultz, "A Death and Disability Life Table for Insured Workers Born in 1992," *Actuarial Note*, no. 2012.6, Social Security Administration, February 2013, www.socialsecurity.gov/OACT/NOTES/ran6/an2012-6.pdf; Social Security Administration, "Fact Sheet," April 2, 2014, www.ssa.gov/pressoffice/factsheets/basicfact-alt.pdf.

4. Michael Clingman, Kyle Burkhalter, and Chris Chapman to Alice H. Wade, memorandum, "The Insurance Value of Potential Survivor and Disability Benefits for an Illustrative Worker—Information," Social Security Administration, September 27, 2012. The worker must have achieved insured status. See appendix 1 for details.

5. Andrew Achenbaum, personal communication with author (Eric R. Kingson), March 31, 2014.

6. A portion of the proceeds are credited to the Hospital Insurance Trust Fund of Medicare.

7. Social Security Trustees, *The 2014 Annual Report of the Board of Trustees of the Federal Old-Age and Survivors Insurance and Federal Disability Insurance Trust Funds*, July 28, 2014, table 3.A6, www.ssa.gov/OACT/tr/2014/III_A_cyoper.html#147356.

8. Geoffrey Kollmann, "Social Security: Summary of Major Changes in the Cash Benefits Program," *CRS Legislative Histories* 2, May 18, 2000; Besides

Social Security's main benefit formula, other benefit formulas apply in specific circumstances, such as the special minimum benefit, payable to certain persons who have worked in covered employment or self-employment for many years at low earnings levels (it is used only if higher than the regularly computed benefit).

9. To the extent possible, we use the term "full retirement age" throughout this book.

10. There are some exceptions. For instance, if retired worker benefits are claimed after the full retirement age, then the aged widow(er) benefits of such workers will also be larger than a "full benefit."

11. Social Security Trustees, *The 2014 Annual Report of the Board of Trustees of the Federal Old-Age and Survivors Insurance and Federal Disability Insurance Trust Funds*, July 28, 2014, table 3.A6, www.ssa.gov/OACT/tr/2014/III_A_cyoper.html#147356.

12. Social Security Administration, "Fact Sheet on the Old-Age, Survivors, and Disability Insurance Program," July 2013, table 3.A6, www.ssa.gov/OACT/FACTS/fs2013_06.pdf.

13. Franklin D. Roosevelt, "Fireside Chat 5: On Addressing the Critics," June 28, 1934, http://millercenter.org/president/speeches/detail/3302.

14. Social Security Administration, "Frances Perkins," 1979, www.ssa.gov/history/fpbiossa.html.

15. J. Douglas Brown, *Essays on Social Security* (Princeton, NJ: Princeton University Press, 1977): 31–32.

16. Social Security Administration, *Annual Statistical Supplement, 2013*, February 2014, table 4.C2, www.ssa.gov/policy/docs/statcomps/supplement/2013/4c.html.

17. Social Security Administration, "Monthly Statistical Snapshot, December 2013," January 2014, www.ssa.gov/policy/docs/quickfacts/stat_snapshot/2013-12.html; Percentage of Americans receiving benefits calculated using total population from U.S. Census Bureau, "Annual Estimates of the Resident: April 1, 2010 to July 1, 2012," *2013 Population Estimates*, 2013, http://factfinder2.census.gov.

18. Social Security Administration, "Monthly Statistical Snapshot, March 2014," April 2014, www.ssa.gov/policy/docs/quickfacts/stat_snapshot/index.html?qs.

19. U.S. Census Bureau, "ACS Demographic and Housing Estimates," *2010–2012 American Community Survey 3-Year Estimates*, 2013, http://factfinder2.census.gov.

20. Social Security Administration, *Annual Statistical Supplement, 2014*, July 2014, table 5.A6, www.ssa.gov/policy/docs/statcomps/supplement/2014/5a.html.

21. Thomas Gabe, *Social Security's Effect on Child Poverty*, Congressional Research Service, December 22, 2011: 3–4, http://wlstorage.net/file/crs/RL33289.pdf; The estimated 4,777,000 children not receiving benefits di-

rectly, but living in households that do, include 1.816 million children under age 18 with a parent or guardian receiving benefits, and 2.961 million children under age 18 in families where a relative other than a parent is receiving benefits. Figure is from 2010, the most recent year data were available, so it likely understates the total for 2012.

22. Paul N. Van de Water et al., "Social Security Keeps 22 Million Americans Out of Poverty: A State-by-State Analysis," Center on Budget and Policy Priorities, October 25, 2013, www.cbpp.org/cms/?fa=view&id=4037.

23. AARP, "Grandfacts: State Fact Sheets for Grandparents and Other Relatives Raising Children," 2011, www.aarp.org/relationships/friends-family/grandfacts-sheets.

24. Maya Rockeymoore et al., *Plan for a New Future: The Impact of Social Security Reform on People of Color,* Commission to Modernize Social Security, 2011, http://modernizesocialsecurity.files.wordpress.com/2013/04/new_future_social_security_10_24_11.pdf.

25. Ibid

26. Social Security Administration, *Annual Statistical Supplement, 2014,* July 2014, table 5.A1, www.ssa.gov/policy/docs/statcomps/supplement/2014/5a.html.

27. OECD Better Life Index, "Health," Organisation for Economic Cooperation and Development, 2013, www.oecdbetterlifeindex.org/topics health.

28. Social Security Administration, Office of Retirement Policy, "Veteran Beneficiaries, 2013," January 2014, www.socialsecurity.gov/retirementpolicy/fact-sheets/veteran-beneficiaries.html; Note that the data presented in this chart shows that in 2013, Social Security paid benefits to more than 9.6 million people. It also indicates that the average benefit going to veterans in 2012 was $16,320.

29. Social Security Works, "Social Security: Serving Those Who Serve Our Nation," March 2011, www.socialsecurityworks.org/wp-content/uploads/2014/06/Veterans-Social-Security-Report-Final.pdf; Quoted figures have been updated to reflect 2012 data, the most recent as of this writing; Data obtained from Department of Defense, "2012 Demographics: Profile of the Military Community," accessed May 3, 2014, www.militaryonesource.mil/12038/MOS/Reports/2012_Demographics_Report.pdf.

30. Tragedy Assistance Program for Survivors, "TAPS Fact Sheet and Statistics on Families of the Fallen," May 2014, www.taps.org/uploadedFiles/TAPS/RESOURCES/Documents/FactSheet.pdf.

31. Anya Olsen and Samantha O'Leary, "Military Veterans and Social Security: 2010 Update," *Social Security Bulletin* 17, no. 2 (May 2011), www.ssa.gov/policy/docs/ssb/v71n2/v71n2p1.html.

32. Increasingly the acronym LGBTQ is used, the Q standing for queer or questioning. We respect that newer acronym, but we use in this book the still more widely used and commonly understood acronym LGBT.

CHAPTER 3: THE PRECARIOUS LIVES OF TODAY'S OLD

1. Fox News, "Transcript: Debt Commission Chairmen on 'Fox News Sunday'," April 26, 2010, www.foxnews.com/printer_friendly_story/0,3566 ,591463,00.html.

2. CNBC, "Simpson: Attack the Deficit," February 22, 2010, http:// video.cnbc.com/gallery/?video=1421510966.

3. Stephanie Condon, "Alan Simpson: Social Security Is Like a 'Milk Cow with 310 Million Tits!'," CBS News, August 25, 2010, www.cbsnews.com /news/alan-simpson-social-security-is-like-a-milk-cow-with-310-million-tits.

4. Dana Milbank, "America Has a Cow Over Alan Simpson's Candor on Deficits," *Washington Post*, September 5, 2010, www.washingtonpost.com /wp-dyn/content/article/2010/09/03/AR2010090302961.html.

5. Illustrative vignette created by the authors for the purpose of this publication.

6. James Sterngold, "Madoff Victims Recount the Long Road Back," *Wall Street Journal*, December 9, 2013, http://online.wsj.com/news/articles /SB10001424052702303560204579248221657387860; This vignette is the authors' paraphrase of the account given in Sterngold's article above.

7. U.S. Census Bureau, "Poverty Thresholds by Size of Family and Number of Children," 2012, www.census.gov/hhes/www/poverty/data /threshld/thresh12.xls.

8. Carol Morello, "Census Releases Alternative Formulas for Gauging Poverty," *Washington Post*, January 5, 2011, www.washingtonpost.com/wp -dyn/content/article/2011/01/04/AR2011010405677.html.

9. U.S. Census Bureau, "Poverty Thresholds by Size of Family and Number of Children," www.census.gov/hhes/povmeas/index.html.

10. U.S. Census Bureau, "Poverty—Experimental Measures," www .census.gov/hhes/povmeas/index.html.

11. Zachary Levinson et al., "A State-by-State Snapshot of Poverty Among Seniors: Findings from Analysis of the Supplemental Poverty Measure," Kaiser Family Foundation, May 20, 2013, http://kff.org/medicare /issue-brief/a-state-by-state-snapshot-of-poverty-among-seniors/; Defined as incomes less than twice the U.S. Census Bureau's Supplemental Poverty Measure (SPM) threshold, the SPM is a more refined and comprehensive measure of poverty than the Federal Poverty Level (FPL). Developed 50 years ago, the FPL equals three times the cost of a 1963 minimal food diet, adjusted for inflation, and simply counts before-tax cash income. In contrast, the Supplemental Poverty Measure equals the 33rd percentile of expenditures on food, clothing, shelter, and utilities, and in determining incomes takes into account government benefits and a range of expenses, such as taxes, out-of-pocket medical costs, and work expenses. Twice the poverty line is a measure of economic deprivation used routinely by researchers and government programs. It is the measure used in the Older Americans Act

Amendments of 2013 to determine the income level at which contributions for services are encouraged.

12. Elise Gould and David Cooper, "Financial Security of Elderly Americans at Risk," Economic Policy Institute, June 6, 2013, www.epi.org /publication/economic-security-elderly-americans-risk.

13. Julie Meyer, "Centenarians: 2010," U.S. Census Bureau, December 2012, https://www.census.gov/prod/cen2010/reports/c2010sr-03.pdf.

14. U.S. Census Bureau, "2012 National Population Projections: Summary Tables," December 2012, table 2, www.census.gov/population/projec tions/data/national/2012/summarytables.html.

15. U.S. Census Bureau, "Wealth and Asset Ownership—Net Worth and Asset Ownership of Households: 2011," March 21, 2013, www.census.gov /people/wealth.

16. U.S. Census Bureau, "Current Population Reports: Consumer Income," January 17, 1962, table 6, www2.census.gov/prod2/popscan/p60 -037.pdf; In 1960, income of families 65 or older was $2,897 in 1960 dollars; inflation adjusted to 2013 dollars using Bureau of Labor Statistics, "CPI Inflation Calculator," accessed February 18, 2014, http://data.bls.gov /cgi-bin/cpicalc.pl?cost1=2897&year1=1960&year2=2013.

17. Social Security Administration, "Income of the Population 55 or Older, 2012," April 2014, table 9.A1, www.ssa.gov/policy/docs/statcomps /income_pop55/2012/sect09.html#table9.a1.

18. Marilyn Watkins, "Keeping Social Security Strong: Four Steps We Can Take to Preserve America's Promise for Every Generation," Economic Opportunity Institute, May 2012, www.eoionline.org/wp/wp-content /uploads/social-security/KeepingSocialSecurityStrongFourSteps May2012 .pdf.

19. Ibid.

20. Social Security Administration, "Income of the Aged Chartbook, 2012," April 2014, www.ssa.gov/policy/docs/chartbooks/income_aged.

21. Alison Shelton, "Social Security: A Key Retirement Resource for Women," AARP Public Policy Institute, August 2013, www.aarp.org/con tent/dam/aarp/research/public_policy_institute/econ_sec/2013/ss-key -retirement-income-source-for-women-fs-AARP-ppi-econ-sec.pdf.

22. Social Security Administration, "Social Security Is Important to Women," March 2014, www.ssa.gov/pressoffice/factsheets/women.htm.

23. Paul N. Van de Water, Arloc Sherman, and Kathy Ruffing, "Social Security Keeps 22 Million Americans Out of Poverty: A State-By-State Analysis," Center on Budget and Policy Priorities, October 25, 2013, www .cbpp.org/cms/?fa=view&id=4037.

24. Illustrative vignette created by the authors for the purpose of this publication.

25. U.S. Census Bureau, Current Population Survey, 2013 Annual Social and Economic Supplement, "POV01: Age and Sex of All People, Family

Members, and Unrelated Individuals Iterated by Income-to-Poverty Ratio and Race: 2012," 2013, www.census.gov/hhes/www/cpstables/032013/pov/pov01_100_1.xls.

26. Illustrative vignette created by the authors for the purpose of this publication.

27. The Commission to Modernize Social Security notes that the circumstances of populations of color vary between groups. For example, with respect to life expectancies, "A 65-year-old Latino or Asian man is expected to live to 85 compared to 82 for all men; a Latina woman is expected to live to 89 and an Asian woman to 88 compared to 85 for all women . . . . On the other hand, African Americans and Native Americans have lower life expectancies than whites, Asians, and Latinos." And, within specific populations of color, there is also much diversity; see Maya Rockeymoore and Meizhu Lui, "Plan for a New Future: The Impact of Social Security Reform on People of Color," Commission to Modernize Social Security, October 2011, http://modernizesocialsecurity.files.wordpress.com/2013/04/new_future_social_security_10_24_11.pdf.

28. Maya Rockeymoore and Meizhu Lui, "Plan for a New Future: The Impact of Social Security Reform on People of Color."

29. Social Security Administration, "Income of the Population 55 or Older, 2012," April 2014, table 9.A3, www.ssa.gov/policy/docs/statcomps/income_pop55/2012/sect09.html#table9.a3.

30. Center on Budget and Policy Priorities, "Calculations of March 2012 Current Population" (unpublished survey data performed for Social Security Works).

31. Social Security Administration, "Annual Statistical Supplement, 2010," August 2010, table 6.B3, www.ssa.gov/policy/docs/statcomps/supplement/2010/6b.html#table6.b3.

32. Government Accountability Office, "Raising the Retirement Ages Would Have Implications for Older Workers and SSA Disability Rolls," November 2010, 17–18, www.gao.gov/new.items/d11125.pdf.

33. Hye Jin Rho, "Hard Work? Patterns in Physically Demanding Labor Among Older Workers," Center for Economic and Policy Research, July 2010, www.cepr.net/documents/publications/older-workers-public-2010-10.pdf.

34. Social Security Administration, "SSI Federal Payment Amounts for 2014," accessed April 3, 2014, www.ssa.gov/OACT/cola/SSI.html.

35. Social Security Administration, "Monthly Statistical Snapshot, March 2014," April 2014, www.ssa.gov/policy/docs/quickfacts/stat_snapshot.

36. Social Security Administration, "Income of the Population 55 or Older, 2014," April 2012, table 9.A1, www.ssa.gov/policy/docs/statcomps/income_pop55/2012/sect09.html#table9.a1.

37. Social Security Administration, "Income of the Population 55 or

Older, 2012," April 2014, tables 9.A2, 9.A3, and 9.B3, www.ssa.gov/policy /docs/statcomps/income_pop55/2012/index.html.

38. Social Security Works, "Shifting More Medicare Costs to Seniors Is an Indirect Social Security Cut," January 2014, www.socialsecurityworks. org/wp-content/uploads/2014/01/Shifting-More-Medicare-Costs-to -Seniors-Is-an-Indirect-Social-Security-Cut_Final.pdf.

39. Fidelity Investments, "Fidelity Estimates Couples Retiring in 2012 Will Need $240,000 to Pay Medical Expenses Throughout Retirement," May 9, 2012, www.fidelity.com/inside-fidelity/individual-investing/retiree -health-care-costs-2012; The Fidelity estimate applies to couples with traditional Medicare coverage—that is, it assumes no employer-provided retiree health care coverage. "The calculation takes into account cost sharing provisions (such as deductibles and coinsurance) associated with Medicare Part A and Part B (inpatient and outpatient medical insurance). It also considers Medicare Part D (prescription drug coverage) premiums and out-of-pocket costs, as well as certain services excluded by Medicare. The estimate does not include other health-related expenses, such as over-the-counter medications, most dental services and long-term care."

40. Blake Ellis, "Nursing Home Costs Top $80,000 a Year," CNN Money, April 9, 2013, http://money.cnn.com/2013/04/09/retirement /nursing-home-costs.

CHAPTER 4: THE COMING RETIREMENT INCOME CRISIS

1. Rodney Brooks, "5 Questions with Sen. Harkin on Retirement Crisis," USA Today, February 1, 2014, www.usatoday.com/story/money /personalfinance/2014/02/01/retirement-crisis-pension-tom-harkin /5084689.

2. Elizabeth Warren, "The Retirement Crisis," November 18, 2013, www.warren.senate.gov/files/documents/Speech%20on%20the%20 Retirement%20Crisis%20-%20Senator%20Warren.pdf.

3. Barack Obama, "State of the Union Address," January 28, 2014, www.whitehouse.gov/the-press-office/2014/01/28/president-barack -obamas-state-union-address.

4. Senate Committee on Aging, "Testimony by Joanne Jacobsen," September 25, 2013, www.aging.senate.gov/imo/media/doc/04_Jacobsen_9_25 _13.pdf.

5. Retirement USA, "Faces of the Retirement Income Deficit," 2014, www.retirement-usa.org/stories/story-145.

6. Ibid.

7. Ibid.

8. L.W. Squier, "Old Age Dependency in the United States," as quoted in Facing Old Age, Abraham Epstein (New York: Alfred K. Knopf, 1922), 21.

9. Allianz Life Insurance Company of North America, Reclaiming the

Future, May 2010, https://www.allianzlife.com/content/public/Literature/Documents/ENT-991.pdf.

10. Ruth Helman, Nevin Adams, Craig Copeland, and Jack VanDerhei, "2013 Retirement Confidence Survey: Perceived Savings Needs Outpace Reality for Many," *EBRI Issue Brief*, no. 384 (March 2013), www.ebri.org/pdf/briefspdf/EBRI_IB_03-13.No384.RCS2.pdf.

11. Larry DeWitt, "Research Note #1: Origins of the Three-Legged Stool Metaphor for Social Security," Social Security Administration, May 1996, www.ssa.gov/history/stool.html.

12. Emily Brandon, "The Retirement Pogo Stick," *U.S. News & World Report*, February 5, 2009, http://money.usnews.com/money/blogs/planning-to-retire/2009/02/05/the-retirement-pogo-stick.

13. Virginia Reno, "What's Next for Social Security? Essential Facts for Action," National Academy of Social Insurance, October 2013, www.nasi.org/sites/default/files/research/Whats_Next_for_Social_Security_Oct2013.pdf.

14. The "statutorily defined retirement age" is the age at which a worker is eligible to receive full Social Security retired worker benefits, more commonly termed by the Social Security Administration as the "Normal Retirement Age (NRA)" or the "Full Retirement Age (FRA)." For further explanation, see discussion in chapter 2.

15. Janice M. Gregory et al., "Strengthening Social Security for the Long Run," National Academy of Social Insurance, *Social Security Brief*, no. 35 (November 2010), www.nasi.org/sites/default/files/research/SS_Brief_035.pdf.

16. Virginia Reno, "What's Next for Social Security? Essential Facts for Action."

17. Social Security Administration, "Benefits Planner: Income Taxes and Your Social Security Benefits," 2014, accessed April 11, 2014, www.ssa.gov/planners/taxes.htm.

18. Virginia Reno, "What's Next for Social Security? Essential Facts for Action."

19. This assumes federal income tax rates remain what they are today.

20. Employee Benefit Research Institute, "FAQs About Benefits—Retirement Issues," 2014, www.ebri.org/publications/benfaq/index.cfm?fa=retfaq14.

21. Ilana Boivie, "Who Killed the Private Sector DB Plan?" *Issue Brief*, National Institute on Retirement Security, March 2011, www.nirsonline.org/storage/nirs/documents/Who%20Killed%20DBs/final-_who_killed_the_private_sector_db_plan.pdf.

22. Gordon Lafer, "The Legislative Attack on American Wages and Labor Standards, 2011–2012," *Briefing Paper*, no. 364, Economic Policy Institute, October 31, 2013, http://s4.epi.org/files/2013/EPI-Legislative-Attack-on-American-Wages-Labor-Standards-10-31-2013.pdf.

23. Ibid.

24. Monique Morrissey and Natalie Sabadish, "Retirement Inequality: How the 401(k) Revolution Created a Few Big Winners and Many Losers," Economic Policy Institute, September 3, 2013, http://s1.epi.org/files/2013/epi-retirement-inequality-chartbook.pdf.

25. Mark Maremont, "Romney's Unorthodox IRA," *Wall Street Journal*, January 19, 2012, http://online.wsj.com/news/articles/SB10001424052970204468004577168972507188592.

26. Monique Morrissey and Natalie Sabadish, "Retirement Inequality: How the 401(k) Revolution Created a Few Big Winners and Many Losers."

27. Diane Oakley, "How Washington Rates on Retirement Security and Defined Benefit Plan Issues," National Institute on Retirement Security, April 8, 2014, http://sdc.wastateleg.org/wp-content/uploads/2014/04/WADefinedBenefitRetirementSecurityPP.pdf.

28. Nari Rhee, "The Retirement Savings Crisis: Is It Worse than We Think?" National Institute on Retirement Security, June 2013, www.nirsonline.org/storage/nirs/documents/Retirement%20Savings%20Crisis/retirementsavingscrisis_final.pdf.

29. Ibid.

30. Lori Trawinski, "Nightmare on Main Street," AARP Public Policy Institute, July 2012, www.aarp.org/money/credit-loans-debt/info-07-2012/nightmare-on-main-street-AARP-ppi-cons-prot.html.

31. Tyler Atkinson, David Luttrell, and Harvey Rosenblum, "How Bad Was It? The Costs and Consequences of the 2007–09 Financial Crisis," *Staff Papers*, no. 20, Federal Reserve Bank of Dallas, July 2013, http://dallasfed.org/assets/documents/research/staff/staff1301.pdf.

32. Federal Reserve Bank of St. Louis, *Annual Report 2012*, May 2013, https://www.stlouisfed.org/publications/ar/2012/pdfs/ar12_complete.pdf.

33. Ibid.

34. Fidelity Investments, "Fidelity Estimates Couples Retiring in 2013 Will Need $220,000 to Pay Medical Expenses Throughout Retirement," May 15, 2013, www.fidelity.com/inside-fidelity/individual-investing/fidelity-estimates-couples-retiring-in-2013-will-need-220000-to-pay-medical-expenses-throughout-retirement.

35. Paul Fronstin, Dallas Salisbury, and Jack VanDerhei, "Savings Needed for Health Expenses for People Eligible for Medicare: Some Rare Good News," *Notes* 33, no. 10, Employee Benefit Research Institute, October 2012, www.ebri.org/pdf/notespdf/EBRI_Notes_10_Oct-12.HlthSvg-only.pdf.

36. Genworth Financial Life Insurance, "Cost of Care Survey 2013," 2013, https://www.genworth.com/dam/Americas/US/PDFs/Consumer/corporate/130568_032213_Cost%20of%20Care_Final_nonsecure.pdf.

37. Virginia Reno and Joni Lavery, "Social Security and Retirement Income Adequacy," *Social Security Brief*, no. 25 (May 2007), www.nasi.org/sites/default/files/research/SS_Brief_025.pdf.

38. Alicia Munnell, Anthony Webb, and Francesca Golub-Sass, "The National Retirement Risk Index: An Update," no. 12-20, Center for Retirement Research at Boston College, October 2012, http://crr.bc.edu /wp-content/uploads/2012/11/IB_12-20-508.pdf.

39. Alicia Munnell et al., "Health Care Costs Drive Up the National Retirement Risk Index," no. 8-3, Center for Retirement Research at Boston College, February 2008, http://crr.bc.edu/wp-content/uploads/2008/02 /ib_8-3.pdf.

40. Alicia Munnell et al., "The National Retirement Risk Index: An Update."

41. Ibid.

42. In its 2010 at-risk estimates, the Center for Retirement Research did not include an estimate of the additional share of households that would be at risk if health and long-term care costs were taken into account. If in 2010 this additional share were equivalent to the 20 percent it amounted to in 2006, then more than 7 in 10 households would be at risk after taking into account health and long-term care costs.

43. Jack VanDerhei and Craig Copeland, "The EBRI Retirement Readiness Rating: Retirement Income Preparation and Future Prospects," *Issue Brief*, no. 344, Employee Benefit Research Institute, July 2010, www.ebri .org/pdf/briefspdf/EBRI_IB_07-2010_No344_RRR-RSPM.pdf.

44. Nari Rhee, "The Retirement Savings Crisis: Is It Worse than We Think?" National Institute on Retirement Security, June 2013, www .nirsonline.org/storage/nirs/documents/Retirement%20Savings%20Crisis /retirementsavingscrisis_final.pdf.

45. Alicia Munnell et al., "National Retirement Risk Index: How Much Longer Do We Need to Work?" no. 12-12, Center for Retirement Research at Boston College, June 2012, http://crr.bc.edu/wp-content/uploads/2012 /06/IB_12-12-508.pdf.

46. Joanne Jacobsen, testimony before the Senate Committee on Aging, September 25, 2013, www.aging.senate.gov/imo/media/doc/04_Jacobsen _9_25_13.pdf.

47. Social Security Administration, *Annual Statistical Supplement, 2013*, February 2014, table 6.B3, www.ssa.gov/policy/docs/statcomps/supplement /2013/6b.html.

48. Ibid., table 6.B5.

49. Government Accountability Office, "Social Security Reform: Raising the Retirement Ages Would Have Implications for Older Workers and SSA Disability Rolls," November 2010, www.gao.gov/new.items/d11125 .pdf.

50. Social Security Administration, "Fact Sheet: Social Security," July 26, 2013, www.ssa.gov/pressoffice/factsheets/basicfact-alt.pdf.

51. Eric Kingson and Monique Morrissey, "Can Workers Offset Social Security Cuts by Working Longer?" *Briefing Paper*, no. 343, Economic Policy

Institute, May 30, 2013, http://s3.epi.org/files/2012/bp343-social-security
-retirement-age.pdf.

52. "Long-Term Unemployment: A National Crisis for Older Workers," *Huffington Post*, September 9, 2012, www.huffingtonpost.com/2012/09/05 /long-term-unemployment-a-_n_1857516.html.

53. Ben Casselman, "For Middle-Aged Job Seekers, a Long Road Back," *Wall Street Journal*, June 22, 2012, http://online.wsj.com/news/articles /SB10001424052702303506404577448751320412974.

CHAPTER 5: THE DEBT OWED TO THOSE WHO CARE

1. Centers for Disease Control and Prevention, "Facts About Birth Defects," February 6, 2014, www.cdc.gov/ncbddd/birthdefects/facts.html.

2. U.S. Department of Health and Human Services, Health Resources and Services Administration, *The National Survey of Children with Special Health Care Needs Chartbook 2009–2010*, June 2013, http://mchb.hrsa.gov /cshcn0910/more/pdf/nscshcn0910.pdf.

3. Susannah Fox, Maeve Duggan, and Kristen Purcell, "Family Caregivers Are Wired for Health," Pew Research Center, June 20, 2013, www .pewinternet.org/files/old-media//Files/Reports/2013/PewResearch _FamilyCaregivers.pdf.

4. U.S. Census Bureau, "Annual Estimates of the Resident Population for Selected Age Groups by Sex for the United States, States, Counties, and Puerto Rico Commonwealth and Municipios: April 1, 2010 to July 1, 2012," June 2013, http://factfinder2.census.gov/faces/tableservices/jsf/pages/pro ductview.xhtml?pid=PEP_2012_PEPAGESEX&prodType=table.

5. Susannah Fox et al., "Family Caregivers Are Wired for Health." Taking into account that some adults care for both groups, 39 percent of adults care for other adults or children with significant limitations.

6. National Alliance for Caregiving, "Caregiving in the U.S., 2009," November 2009, www.caregiving.org/data/Caregiving_in_the_US_2009 _full_report.pdf.

7. Lynn Feinberg et al., "Valuing the Invaluable: 2011 Update, the Growing Contributions and Costs of Family Caregiving," *Insight on the Issues*, no. 51, AARP Public Policy Institute, June 2011, http://assets.aarp.org/rg center/ppi/ltc/i51-caregiving.pdf.

8. Richard Harris, "Heading Toward the Caregiving Cliff," *Washington Post*, March 4, 2013, www.washingtonpost.com/national/health-science /heading-toward-the-caregiving-cliff/2014/03/04/eb1661ec-9846-11e3 -afce-3e7c922ef31e_story.html.

9. Tara Bahrampour and Nikki Kahn, "As Americans Age, Families Are Critical to Nation's Health-Care System," *Washington Post*, March 4, 2014, www.washingtonpost.com/local/as-americans-age-families-are-critical -to-nations-health-care-system/2014/03/04/d40ab934-9446-11e3-84e1 -27626c5ef5fb_story.html.

10. Richard Harris, "Heading Toward the Caregiving Cliff."

11. Alzheimer's Association, "2011 Alzheimer's Disease Facts and Figures," *Alzheimer's and Dementia* 7, no. 2 (2011), www.alz.org/downloads /facts_figures_2011.pdf.

12. U.S. Department of Health and Human Services, Health Resources and Services Administration, *The National Survey of Children with Special Health Care Needs Chartbook 2009–2010.*

13. Autism Society, "Keisha's Story," August 18, 2013, https://www.face book.com/pages/Autism/125110860933803.

14. Gail Hunt et al., "Young Caregivers in the U.S.," National Alliance for Caregiving, September 2005, www.caregiving.org/data/youngcaregiv ers.pdf.

15. AARP, "GrandFacts," 2014, www.aarp.org/relationships/friends-fam ily/grandfacts-sheets.

16. Raising Your Grandchildren, "Raising 4 Grandchildren at 60," 2014, http://raisingyourgrandchildren.com/More_Stories.htm.

17. The Council of State Governments Justice Center, "Council of State Governments Justice Center Releases Estimates on the Prevalence of Adults with Serious Mental Illnesses in Jails," June 1, 2009, http://orca.dc.gov/sites /default/files/dc/sites/orca/publication/attachments/prevalence_brief.pdf.

18. Mark Lino, *Expenditures on Children by Families, 2012*, U.S. Department of Agriculture, Center for Nutrition Policy and Promotion, August 2013, www.cnpp.usda.gov/Publications/CRC/crc2012.pdf.

19. G.J. Duncan and J.N. Morgan, eds., "The Redistribution of Income by Families and Institutions and American Help Patterns," *Five Thousand American Families: Patterns of Progress* 10 (Ann Arbor: Institute for Social Research, University of Michigan, 1983), 11.

20. Judy Feder, "Testimony Before the Senate Committee on Aging, on the Future of Long-Term Care Policy: Continuing the Conversation," December 18, 2013, www.aging.senate.gov/imo/media/doc/Feder_12_18_13 .pdf.

21. Lynn Feinberg et al., "Valuing the Invaluable: 2011 Update, the Growing Contributions and Costs of Family Caregiving."

22. Congressional Budget Office, "Rising Demand for Long Term Services and Supports for Elderly People," June 2013, www.cbo.gov/sites /default/files/cbofiles/attachments/44363-LTC.pdf.

23. Alzheimer's Association, "2011 Alzheimer's Disease Facts and Figures," *Alzheimer's and Dementia* 7, no. 2 (2011), www.alz.org/downloads /facts_figures_2011.pdf.

24. Generations United, "Grandfamilies Statistics," 2013, http://www2 .gu.org/OURWORK/Grandfamilies/GrandfamiliesStatistics.aspx.

25. E.R. Kingson et al., *Ties That Bind: The Interdependence of Generations* (Cabin John, MD: Seven Locks Press, 1986); Eric R. Kingson et al., *Support-*

ing Care Across Generations: Perspectives for Assessing Social and Public Policy Issues (unpublished paper, 2006).

26. Kim Parker and Wendy Wang, "Modern Parenthood: Roles of Moms and Dads Converge as They Balance Work and Family," Pew Research Center, March 14, 2013, www.pewsocialtrends.org/files/2013/03/FINAL _modern_parenthood_03-2013.pdf.

27. National Alliance for Caregiving, "Caregiving in the U.S., 2009," November 2009, www.caregiving.org/data/Caregiving_in_the_US_2009 _full_report.pdf.

28. Ibid.

29. Ibid.

30. Sarah Jane Glynn and Jane Farrell, "Caregiving in America," Center for American Progress, February 5, 2014, www.americanprogress.org /issues/labor/report/2014/02/05/83427/family-matters.

31. U.S. Department of Health and Human Services, Health Resources and Services Administration, *The National Survey of Children with Special Health Care Needs Chartbook 2009–2010*, June 2013, http://mchb.hrsa.gov /cshcn0910/more/pdf/nscshcn0910.pdf.

32. Nancy Folbre, *Valuing Children: Rethinking the Economics of the Family* (Cambridge, MA: Harvard University Press, 2008), 5.

33. Lynn Feinberg et al., "Valuing the Invaluable: 2011 Update, the Growing Contributions and Costs of Family Caregiving."

34. MetLife Mature Market Institute, "Caregiving Costs to Working Caregivers Double Jeopardy for Baby Boomers Caring for Their Parents," June 2011, www.caregiving.org/wp-content/uploads/2011/06/mmi-care giving-costs-working-caregivers.pdf.

35. U.S. Department of Labor, "The Family and Medical Leave Act of 1993," 2014, www.dol.gov/whd/regs/statutes/fmla.htm.

36. Bryce Covert, "Workers in a Third State Can Now Take Paid Family Leave," *Think Progress*, January 2, 2014, http://thinkprogress.org /economy/2014/01/02/3110281/rhode-island-paid-family-leave-effect/#.

37. Organisation for Economic Co-operation and Development, "PF2.1: Key Characteristics of Parental Leave Systems," October 10, 2012, www .oecd.org/els/family/PF2.1_Parental_leave_systems%20-%20updated%20 %2018_July_2012.pdf.

38. Eric R. Kingson et al., "Supporting Care Across Generations: Perspectives for Assessing Social and Public Policy Issues" (unpublished paper, 2006); Lynn Feinberg et al., "Valuing the Invaluable: 2011 Update, the Growing Contributions and Costs of Family Caregiving."

39. Ibid.

40. National Alliance for Caregiving, "Caregiving in the U.S., 2009."

41. Metropolitan Life Insurance Company, "The MetLife Study of Working Caregivers and Employer Health Care Costs," February 2010, https://

www.metlife.com/assets/cao/mmi/publications/studies/2011/mmi-care
giving-costs-working-caregivers.pdf.

42. Metropolitan Life Insurance Company, "The MetLife Caregiving
Cost Study: Productivity Losses to U.S. Business," July 2006, www.caregiv
ing.org/data/Caregiver%20Cost%20Study.pdf.

43. U.S. Census Bureau, *2012 National Population Projections*, December 2012, table 2, www.census.gov/population/projections/files/summary
/NP2012-T2.xls.

44. Ibid.

45. Donald Redfoot, Lynn Feinberg, and Ari Houser, "The Aging of the
Baby Boom and the Growing Care Gap: A Look at Future Declines in the
Availability of Family Caregivers," *Insight on the Issues*, no. 85, AARP Public Policy Institute, August 2013, www.aarp.org/content/dam/aarp/research
/public_policy_institute/ltc/2013/baby-boom-and-the-growing-care-gap
-insight-AARP-ppi-ltc.pdf.

46. C. Wright Mills, *Sociological Imagination* (London: Oxford University
Press, 1959).

47. Ai-jen Poo with Ariane Conrad, *The Age of Dignity: Caring for a Changing America* (New York: The New Press, forthcoming 2015).

CHAPTER 6: THE NEW GILDED AGE

1. Thomas Piketty, *Capital in the Twenty-First Century* (Cambridge: The
Belknap Press of Harvard University Press, 2014), table 8.5, 291.

2. "Remarks by the President on Economic Mobility," December 4, 2013,
www.whitehouse.gov/the-press-office/2013/12/04/remarks-president
-economic-mobility.

3. Estelle Sommeiller et al., "The Increasingly Unequal States of America," Economic Policy Institute, February 19, 2014, www.epi.org/publication
/unequal-states.

4. Emmanuel Saez, "Striking It Richer: The Evolution of Top Incomes
in the United States (Updated with 2012 Preliminary Estimates)," September 3, 2013, http://eml.berkeley.edu/~saez/saez-UStopincomes-2012.pdf;
Also see Thomas Piketty and Emmanuel Saez, "Income Inequality in the
United States, 1913–1998," *Quarterly Journal of Economics*, February 2003;
Updated to 2012 by Emmanuel Saez and available at http://elsa.berkeley
.edu/users/saez, which points out that from 1948 to 1979, the average income of all Americans grew by $22,004. From 1979 to 2012, average income
grew by $9,442. These averages mask distributional inequality. From 1979
to 2012, the aggregate income of the bottom 90 percent actually declined.
Since it is impossible to depict negative growth in a pie chart, the pie chart
for 1979–2012 excludes the bottom 90 percent. When one takes negative
growth into account as well, however, that is, quantifies the shares of various income segments not just in positive growth (which occurred only in
the top 10 percent), but in all income shifts (whether positive or negative)

across the population, then from 1979 to 2012 growth was redistributive: the bottom 90 percent experienced negative 30.8% of total growth, while the top 1 percent got 84.5%, the top 1–5 percent got 31.6%, and the top 5–10 percent got 14.8% of total net growth. (These shares of total net growth add up, unrounded, to 100%.)

5. Lawrence Mishel and Natalie Sabadish, "CEO Pay in 2012 Was Extraordinarily High Relative to Typical Workers and Other High Earners," Economic Policy Institute, June 26, 2013, www.epi.org/publication /ceo-pay-2012-extraordinarily-high.

6. Tom Kertscher, "Michael Moore Says 400 Americans Have More Wealth Than Half of All Americans Combined," PolitiFact Wisconsin, March 10, 2011, www.politifact.com/wisconsin/statements/2011/mar/10 /michael-moore/michael-moore-says-400-americans-have-more-wealth-.

7. G. William Domhoff, "Wealth, Income, and Power," accessed June 8, 2014, http://whorulesamerica.net/power/wealth.html.

8. Ida Tarbell, *The History of the Standard Oil Company* (New York: McClure, Phillips, 1904).

9. Herbert Hoover, *The Memoirs of Herbert Hoover* 3 (New York: The MacMillan Company, 1952), www.ecommcode.com/hoover/ebooks/pdf /FULL/B1V3_Full.pdf.

10. Nancy J. Altman, *The Battle for Social Security: From FDR's Vision to Bush's Gamble*, (Hoboken, NJ: John Wiley & Sons, 2005), 14–20.

11. National Labor Relations Board, "The 1935 Passage of the Wagner Act," 2014, www.nlrb.gov/who-we-are/our-history/1935-passage-wagner-act.

12. Franklin Delano Roosevelt, *Public Papers and Addresses* 6 (May 24, 1937) (New York: The Macmillan Company, 1941), 209–14.

13. Jonathan Grossman, "Fair Labor Standards Act of 1938: Maximum Struggle for a Minimum Wage," *Monthly Labor Review*, U.S. Department of Labor, June 1978, www.dol.gov/dol/aboutdol/history/flsa1938.htm#21.

14. Senate Finance Committee, *Economic Security Act: Hearings Before the Committee on Finance, Seventy-Fourth Congress First Session, on S. 1130 A Bill to Alleviate the Hazards of Old Age, Unemployment, Illness, and Dependency, to Establish a Social Insurance Board in the Department of Labor, to Raise Revenue, and for Other Purposes* (January 25, 1935), 129, www.ssa.gov/history/pdf /s35perkins.pdf.

15. Ibid.

16. Internal Revenue Service, "SOI Tax Stats—Historical Table 23," December 2013, www.irs.gov/uac/SOI-Tax-Stats-Historical-Table-23.

17. Dwight D. Eisenhower to Edgar Newton Eisenhower, "Document #1147," *The Papers of Dwight David Eisenhower* 15, *The Presidency: The Middle Way*, ed. Louis Galambos (Baltimore: Johns Hopkins University Press, 1996).

18. Ronald Reagan, "Inaugural Address," January 20, 1981, www.presidency.ucsb.edu/ws/?pid=43130.

19. Bruce Bartlett, "'Starve the Beast,' Origins and Development of a Budgetary Metaphor," *Independent Review* 12, no. 1 (Summer 2007), www.independent.org/pdf/tir/tir_12_01_01_bartlett.pdf.

20. Americans for Tax Reform, "About Americans for Tax Reform," March 23, 2009, www.atr.org/americans-tax-reform-a2878.

21. All Politics (CNN/Time), "Mondale's Acceptance Speech, 1984," July 19, 1984. www.cnn.com/ALLPOLITICS/1996/conventions/chicago/facts/famous.speeches/mondale.84.shtml

22. George H.W. Bush, "Address Accepting the Presidential Nomination at the Republican National Convention in New Orleans," August 18, 1988, www.presidency.ucsb.edu/ws/?pid=25955.

23. White House Office of the President, "Why President Clinton's 'Save Social Security First' Position Is Right for America," *President Clinton's Remarks on Social Security—1993–1998*, October 30, 1998, www.ssa.gov/history/clntstmts.html#12.

24. Congressional Budget Office, *The Budget and Economic Outlook: Fiscal Years 2002–2011*, January 1, 2001, summary table 1, http://cbo.gov/sites/default/files/cbofiles/ftpdocs/27xx/doc2727/entire-report.pdf.

25. Andrew Fieldhouse and Ethan Pollack, "Tenth Anniversary of the Bush-era Tax Cuts," Economic Policy Institute, June 1, 2011, www.epi.org/publication/tenth_anniversary_of_the_bush-era_tax_cuts.

26. Sarah Anderson et al., "Executive Excess 2011: The Massive CEO Rewards for Tax Dodging," Institute for Policy Studies, August 31, 2011, www.ips-dc.org/reports/executive_excess_2011_the_massive_ceo_rewards_for_tax_dodging.

27. David Cay Johnston, "Beyond the 1 Percent," Reuters, October 25, 2011, http://blogs.reuters.com/david-cay-johnston/2011/10/25/beyond-the-1-percent.

28. See Social Security Financing Amendments of 1977, U.S. House of Representatives, Report of the Committee on Ways and Means to Accompany H.R. 9346, House Report No. 702, Part 1 (Washington, DC: U.S. Government Printing, October 12, 1977) 18; Because the wages covered by the maximum taxable wage base represented only 85 percent of total wages in 1977, Congress also enacted several ad hoc increases to the wage base, over and above the automatic adjustments, so that the base would be restored to covering 90 percent of all wages. The 90 percent level was reached in 1982.

29. Social Security Administration, "Fast Facts and Figures about Social Security, 2013," August 2013, www.ssa.gov/policy/docs/chartbooks/fast_facts/2013/fast_facts13.pdf.

30. Social Security Trustees, *The 2014 Annual Report of the Board of Trustees of the Federal Old-Age and Survivors Insurance and Federal Disability Insurance Trust Funds*, July 28, 2014, table 4.A1, www.ssa.gov/oact/TR/2014/IV_A_SRest.html#506116. In 2014, Social Security's ratio of taxable payroll (earnings under the cap of $117,000) to total covered earnings is pro-

NOTES 259

jected to be 82.5 percent, generating $644 billion in payroll contributions. If 90 percent of covered earnings were under the cap, this could be expected to generate around $702 billion in payroll contributions, or an additional $58 billion of revenue.

31. Josh Levin, "The Welfare Queen," *Slate*, December 19, 2013, www.slate.com/articles/news_and_politics/history/2013/12/linda_taylor_welfare_queen_ronald_reagan_made_her_a_notorious_american_villain.html.

32. Ellen Dannin, "Federal Privatization and the Expensive Philosophy of the Circular A-76 Process," *Truthout*, March 14, 2014, www.truth-out.org/news/item/22440-federal-privatization-and-the-expensive-philosophy-of-the-circular-a-76-process.

33. The acclaimed 2006 documentary film *Iraq for Sale: The War Profiteers* exposes how these contractors endangered the lives of Americans and Iraqis, while costing the government more and doing the work less well than would likely have been done by the government itself.

34. See, for example, Monique Morrissey, "Third Way's Surprising Retirement Proposal," www.epi.org/blog/ways-retirement-proposal.

35. For a discussion of how the one-step approach and two-step approach are essentially the same, see Altman, "The Striking Superiority of Social Security in the Provision of Wage Insurance," 133–142, *Harvard Journal on Legislation* 50 (2013), http://ssrn.com/abstract=2231267.

36. Kaiser Family Foundation (prepared by Health Policy Alternatives), "Prescription Drug Coverage for Medicare Beneficiaries: A Summary of the Medicare Prescription Drug Improvement and Modernization Act of 2003," December 10, 2003, http://kaiserfamilyfoundation.files.wordpress.com/2013/01/prescription-drug-coverage-for-medicare-beneficiaries-a-summary-of-the-medicare-prescription-drug-improvement-and-modernization-act-of-2003.pdf.

37. Kaiser Family Foundation, "Medicare Advantage Fact Sheet," May 1, 2014, http://kff.org/medicare/fact-sheet/medicare-advantage-fact-sheet; The Affordable Care Act of 2010 reduced federal payments to Medicare Advantage plans over time, bringing them more in line with the costs of care under the traditional Medicare program.

38. Brad Plumer, "Study: Privatizing Government Doesn't Actually Save Money," *Washington Post*, September 15, 2011, www.washingtonpost.com/blogs/wonkblog/post/study-privatizing-government-doesnt-actually-save-money/2011/09/15/gIQA2rpZUK_blog.html; See also "Privatization Myths Debunked," In the Public Interest, 2014, www.inthepublicinterest.org/node/457.

39. American Federation of State County and Municipal Employees, *How to Prevent Privatization*, 2014, www.afscme.org/news/publications/privatization/pdf/How-To-Prevent-Privatization.pdf.

40. Dick Meister, "Ronald Reagan's War on Labor," 2014, www.dick

meister.com/id89.html; See also Harold Meyerson, "Class Warrior," *Washington Post*, June 9, 2004, www.washingtonpost.com/wp-dyn/articles/A2 6543-2004Jun8.html.

41. U.S. Bureau of Labor Statistics, "Labor Force Statistics from the Current Population Survey," 2014, table 4, www.bls.gov/cps/cpslutabs.htm.

42. Craig K. Elwell, "Inflation and the Real Minimum Wage: A Fact Sheet," January 8, 2014, www.fas.org/sgp/crs/misc/R42973.pdf.

43. U.S. Department of Labor, "History of Federal Minimum Wage Rates Under the Fair Labor Standards Act, 1938–2009," accessed June 2, 2014, www.dol.gov/whd/minwage/chart.htm.

44. Social Security Works, "Restoring Minimum Wage Would Strengthen Social Security Protections for Low-Wage Workers and Improve System Finances," February 21, 2014, www.socialsecurityworks.org /restoring-minimum-wage-strengthen-social-security-protections-low -wage-workers-improve-system-finances.

45. Dick Meister, "Ronald Reagan's War on Labor."

46. Paul Krugman, "Reagan Did It," *New York Times,* May 31, 2009, www.nytimes.com/2009/06/01/opinion/01krugman.html?_r=0.

47. Karin Kamp, "By the Numbers: The Incredibly Shrinking American Middle Class," Moyers & Company, September 20, 2013, http:// billmoyers.com/2013/09/20/by-the-numbers-the-incredibly-shrinking -american-middle-class.

48. Marin Clarkberg, "The Time-Squeeze in American Families: From Causes to Solutions," *Futurework*, U.S. Department of Labor, September 6, 1999, www.dol.gov/oasam/programs/history/herman/reports/futurework /conference/families/couples.htm.

49. Doug Lederman, "A Historical Look at Student Debt," *Inside Higher Ed*, July 6, 2006, www.insidehighered.com/news/2006/07/06/debt.

50. Josh Sanburn, "The Loss of Upward Mobility in the U.S." *Time,* January 5, 2012, http://business.time.com/2012/01/05/the-loss-of-upward -mobility-in-the-u-s.

51. Andrew G. Berg and Jonathan D. Ostry (International Monetary Fund), "Equality and Efficiency," *Finance and Development* 48, no. 3 (September 2011), www.imf.org/external/pubs/ft/fandd/2011/09/berg .htm#author.

52. Dean Baker, "The Impact of the Upward Redistribution of Wage Income on Social Security Solvency," *CEPR Blog*, February 3, 2013, www .cepr.net/index.php/blogs/cepr-blog/the-impact-of-the-upward-redistri bution-of-wage-income-on-social-security-solvency; Monique Morrissey, "Wages and Social Security," *Working Economics*, Economic Policy Institute Blog, July 16, 2012, www.epi.org/blog/wages-social-security.

53. Andrew Fieldhouse, "Rising Income Inequality and the Role of Shifting Market-Income Distribution, Tax Burdens, and Tax Rates, Economic

Policy Institute," June 14, 2013, www.epi.org/publication/rising-income -inequality-role-shifting-market.

CHAPTER 7: EXPAND SOCIAL SECURITY FOR ALL GENERATIONS

1. The plan was first released as a free-standing description in late October 2013 at a conference convened by our organization, Social Security Works. See Nancy J. Altman and Eric R. Kingson, *Social Security Works All Generations Plan*, October 2013, www.socialsecurityworks.org/wp-content/uploads /2014/03/Social-Security-Works-All-Generations-Plan.pdf.

2. Social Security Administration, "Monthly Statistical Snapshot, March 2014," April 2014, www.ssa.gov/policy/docs/quickfacts/stat_snapshot; The average monthly benefit for retired workers in March 2014 was $1,297.55, or $15,570.60 on an annualized basis.

3. Organisation for Economic Co-operation and Development, "OECD Pensions at a Glance, 2013," 2013, www.oecd.org/pensions/pensionsata glance.htm.

4. Gary Koenig and Mikki Waid, "Proposed Changes to Social Security's Cost-of-Living Adjustment: What Would They Mean for Beneficiaries?" *Insight on the Issues* 71, AARP Public Policy Institute, October 2012, www.aarp.org/content/dam/aarp/research/public_policy_institute/econ _sec/2012/proposed-changes-cola-insight-AARP-ppi-econ-sec.pdf.

5. Benjamin W. Veghte et al., "Should Social Security's Cost-of-Living Adjustment Be Changed?" *Social Security Fact Sheet*, no. 2, National Academy of Social Insurance, April 2011, www.nasi.org/sites/default/files/research /SS%20Fact%20Sheet%20No.02_Should%20Social%20Secur ity's%20Cost-of-%20Living%20Adjustment%20Be%20Changed.pdf; Chain-weighting, as has recently been advocated as a strategy to cut Social Security, would lower official "inflation," and hence Social Security cost of living adjustments, based on the degree to which the population as a whole buys more of the goods and services whose prices rise less, and less of those whose prices rise more. The assumption is that people are no worse off if they call rather than visit their grandchildren when the price of fuel goes up, or if they use an herbal rather than a pharmaceutical remedy when the price of their prescription goes up. Chain-weighting an index that already under-measures the inflation experienced by seniors and people with disabilities would simply sink beneficiaries faster.

6. Social Security Works, calculations based on Social Security OCACT, Memorandum to Rep. Becerra, June 21, 2011; Social Security Administration, *Annual Statistical Supplement, 2012*, 2012, table 2.A26.

7. The Center for Community Change and Older Women's Economic Security Task Force, "Expanding Social Security Benefits for Financially Vulnerable Populations," October 2013, www.iwpr.org/publications/pubs /expanding-social-security-benefits-for-financially-vulnerable-populations.

8. American Academy of Actuaries, "Women and Social Security," *Issue Brief*, June 2007, www.actuary.org/pdf/socialsecurity/women_07.pdf.

9. Stephen C. Goss, memorandum to senator Robert Bennett, February 12, 2009, 3–4, www.ssa.gov/oact/solvency/RBennett_20090212.pdf; Stephen C. Goss, memorandum to Fiscal Commission co-chairs, December 1, 2010, table B1, www.ssa.gov/OACT/solvency/FiscalCommission_20101201.pdf.

10. Paul N. Van de Water et al., "Social Security Keeps 22 Million Americans Out of Poverty: A State-by-State Analysis," Center on Budget and Policy Priorities, October 25, 2013, www.cbpp.org/cms/?fa=view&id=4037.

11. Welfare and social insurance are not the only means of reinforcing income security. Another policy tool is "demogrants"—flat, universal benefits provided either to all citizens or to those who have reached a certain age (e.g., in New Zealand), regardless of need or work status. Demogrants may also be used as a foundational tier of a country's retirement income system, supplementing its social insurance program. For example, the New America Foundation's Expanded Social Security plan proposes improving Social Security's existing income protections by providing a universal, flat benefit (called Social Security B) in addition to the program's traditional, earnings-based benefits. For more information about the New America Foundation's plan, see appendix C.

12. Center on Budget and Policy Priorities, "Policy Basics: Introduction to Supplemental Security Income," February 27, 2014, www.cbpp.org/cms/index.cfm?fa=view&id=3370; Many states supplement federal SSI benefits, although budget pressures have scaled such assistance back in recent years.

13. Social Security Administration, "OASDI and SSI Program Rates and Limits, 2014," October, 2013, www.ssa.gov/policy/docs/quickfacts/prog_highlights/index.html.

14. Social Security Administration, "A Guide to Supplemental Security Income (SSI) for Groups and Organizations," January 2014, www.ssa.gov/pubs/EN-05-11015.pdf.

15. Social Security Administration, "Monthly Statistical Snapshot, March 2014," April 2014, www.ssa.gov/policy/docs/quickfacts/stat_snapshot/index.html?qs.

16. As we write this, the Supplemental Security Income Restoration Act has been introduced in the U.S. Senate by senators Sherrod Brown (D-OH) and Elizabeth Warren (D-MA), with a companion bill in the House of Representatives by congressman Raúl Grijalva (D-AZ). The bills provide a modest roadmap of what should be done to jump-start long-overdue basic reforms to SSI. It would increase the amount of earned and unearned income individuals could receive without losing some, and possibly all, of their SSI benefit. It would allow persons eligible for SSI benefits to earn $357 a month without loss of benefits, instead of just $65 as is now the case. Similarly, it would also increase the dollar amount of so-called unearned income that

could be disregarded, and not counted against someone's SSI benefits, from $20 to $110 a month. It would also increase assets limits to $10,000 for individuals and $15,000 for couples and eliminate the financial penalty that SSI recipients incur when friends or family provide them with food, housing, and other modest help.

17. SSI has a federal and a state component. Federal SSI payments assure a uniform income floor, and states may provide additional payments to supplement this floor. When the SSI program was introduced in 1972, the Social Security Administration was chosen to administer the program because the basic system for paying monthly benefits to a large number of individuals was already in place; Social Security Administration, "SSI Annual Statistical Report, 2012," July 2013, www.ssa.gov/policy/docs/statcomps/ssi_asr/2012/background.pdf.

18. Center on Budget and Policy Priorities, "Introduction to the Supplemental Security Income (SSI) Program," February 27, 2014, www.cbpp.org/cms/?fa=view&id=3367; Note, too, that if Social Security is increased without changes to SSI, the result could ironically be that those policymakers are seeking to help could be no better off or may even be worse off. That is because Social Security benefits are deducted dollar for dollar after an initial disregard of just $20. Consequently, an increase in Social Security benefits could simply supplant a person's SSI benefits. Worse, if the increased benefits make the person ineligible for any SSI benefit, he or she might lose Medicaid coverage, and thus be much worse off! Hence, the importance of holding SSI beneficiaries harmless from any negative consequences that might result from Social Security benefit expansions.

19. Social Security Administration, "Monthly Statistical Snapshot, March 2014," April 2014, www.ssa.gov/policy/docs/quickfacts/stat_snapshot/index.html?qs.

20. U.S. Department of Labor, "The Family and Medical Leave Act," 2014, www.dol.gov/whd/regs/compliance/1421.htm.

21. H.R. 3712, 113th Cong., 1st Sess., December 12, 2013, www.gpo.gov/fdsys/pkg/BILLS-113hr3712ih/pdf/BILLS-113hr3712ih.pdf.

22. S 1810, 113th Cong., 1st Sess., December 11, 2013, www.gpo.gov/fdsys/pkg/BILLS-113s1810is/pdf/BILLS-113s1810is.pdf.

23. The germinal work, which inspired these various proposals, was done by Heather Boushey of the Center for American Progress. See Heather Boushey, Ann O'Leary, and Alexandra Mitukiewicz, "The Economic Benefits of Family and Medical Leave Insurance," Center for American Progress, December 12, 2013, www.americanprogress.org/issues/economy/report/2013/12/12/81036/the-economic-benefits-of-family-and-medical-leave-insurance.

24. Organisation for Economic Co-operation and Development, "OECD Family Database," December 2013, www.oecd.org/els/soc/oecdfamilydatabase.htm.

25. Benefits also provided to the minor children of retired workers.

26. Social Security Administration, "Research Note #11: The History of Social Security 'Student' Benefits," January 2001, www.socialsecurity.gov /history/studentbenefit.html.

27. Center on Budget and Policy Priorities, "Policy Basics: Top Ten Facts About Social Security," November 6, 2012, www.cbpp.org/cms /?fa=view&id=3261#_edn25.

28. Unpublished calculations from the Social Security Administration (SSA) based on Survey of Income and Program Participation (SIPP) calendar year 2009, matched to SSA Master Beneficiary Record file, April 2014.

29. Disabled Adult Child (DAC) benefits are sometimes called Childhood Disability (CDB) benefits.

30. In addition to receiving benefits on the death of an insured parent, the child can also receive benefits if the parent—or under some circumstances, the grandparent—is retired or disabled. For a more detailed discussion, see appendix A.

31. Social Security Administration, "1972 Social Security Amendments," 2014, www.ssa.gov/history/1972amend.html.

CHAPTER 8: PAYING THE BILL

1. Central Intelligence Agency, *The World Factbook*, "United States," January 2014, https://www.cia.gov/library/publications/the-world-factbook /geos/us.html.

2. In calendar year 2013, our GDP was $16.8 trillion, another number none of us will ever experience personally; U.S. Bureau of Economic Analysis, "Current Dollar and 'Real' GDP," January 2014, www.bea.gov /national/xls/gdplev.xls.

3. Television History–The First 75 Years, "What Things Cost in 1935," last viewed February, 21, 2014, www.tvhistory.tv/1935%20QF.htm.

4. Grant McArther, "The World 70 Years from Now," News.com.au, August 19, 2013, www.news.com.au/finance/real-estate/the-world-70-years -from-now/story-fncq3gat-1226699742008.

5. Bureau of Labor Statistics, "CPI Inflation Calculator," January 2014, www.bls.gov/data/inflation_calculator.htm.

6. "CPI Calculator to Calculate Future or Historical Inflation," Accessed June 2, 2014, www.free-online-calculator-use.com/cpi-calculator .html#calculator.

7. Bureau of Labor Statistics, "CPI Inflation Calculator," January 2014, www.bls.gov/data/inflation_calculator.htm.

8. Social Security Trustees, *The 2014 Annual Report of the Board of Trustees of the Federal Old-Age and Survivors Insurance and Federal Disability Insurance Trust Funds*, July 28, 2014, table 6.G4, www.ssa.gov/OACT/tr/2014 /VI_G2_OASDHI_GDP.html#200732.

9. 2009 is the most recent year of comparative data at the time of this

writing. In 2009, Social Security cost 4.9 percent of GDP. Social Security Trustees, *The 2013 Annual Report of the Board of Trustees of the Federal Old-Age and Survivors Insurance and Federal Disability Insurance Trust Funds*, table 2.D4, May 31, 2013, www.ssa.gov/oact/TR/2013/tr2013.pdf; Plot points to table 2.D4 available at www.socialsecurity.gov/OACT/TR/2013/LD_figIID4.html; Calculations of these countries' public spending on those components of their old-age, survivors, and disability benefits that are comparable to the U.S. Social Security system are conservatively and roughly estimated based on data from the Social Expenditure Database of the Organisation for Economic Co-operation and Development (OECD), *Social Expenditure Database, 2012*, www.oecd.org/social/expenditure.htm#socx_data.

10. Social Security Trustees, *The 2014 Annual Report of the Board of Trustees of the Federal Old-Age and Survivors Insurance and Federal Disability Insurance Trust Funds*, July 28, 2014, table 6.G4, www.ssa.gov/OACT/tr/2014/VI_G2_OASDHI_GDP.html#200732.

11. U.S. Bureau of Economic Analysis, "Current Dollar and 'Real' GDP," January 2014, www.bea.gov/national/xls/gdplev.xls; Contains historical GDP data; projections of future GDP taken from Congressional Budget Office, "Supplemental Data: 2. Economic Variables Underlying the Long-Term Budget Projections and Projections of GDP and Population," *The 2013 Long-Term Budget Outlook,* September 2013, www.cbo.gov/publication/45308.

12. Social Security spending as a share of the economy has increased from 4.03 percent of GDP in 2000 to 4.84 percent in 2012 and a projected 4.92 percent in 2014. Social Security Trustees, *The 2014 Annual Report of the Board of Trustees of the Federal Old-Age and Survivors Insurance and Federal Disability Insurance Trust Funds*, July 28, 2014, www.ssa.gov/oact/TR/2014/tr2014.pdf.

13. Dean Baker, "The Economic Impact of the Iraq War and Higher Military Spending," Center for Economic and Policy Research, May 2007, www.cepr.net/documents/publications/military_spending_2007_05.pdf.

14. Viriginia P. Reno and Joni Lavery, "Can We Afford Social Security When Baby Boomers Retire?" *Social Security Brief,* no. 22, National Academy of Social Insurance, May 2006, www.nasi.org/sites/default/files/research/SS_Brief_022.pdf.

15. Committee on Economic Security, *Economic Security Act*, January 1935, table 13, www.ssa.gov/history/reports/ces16.html.

16. U.S. Census Bureau, *Profile of General Demographic Characteristics: 2000*, 2000, http://factfinder2.census.gov.

17. U.S. Census Bureau, "Age and Sex," *2010–2012 American Community Survey 3-Year Estimates*, 2012, http://factfinder2.census.gov.

18. U.S. Administration on Aging, "Older Population as a Percentage of the Total Population: 1900 to 2050," 2009, www.aoa.gov/AoARoot/(S(2ch3qw55k1qylo45dbihar2u))/Aging_Statistics/future_growth/docs/By_Age_Total_Population.xls.

19. Congressional Budget Office, *The Budget and Economic Outlook: 2014 to*

2024, February 2014, www.cbo.gov/sites/default/files/cbofiles/attachments /45010-Outlook2014_Feb.pdf.

20. Tax Policy Center, "Tax Benefit of Certain Retirement Savings Incentives; Baseline: Current Law; Distribution of Federal Tax Change by Expanded Cash Income Level, 2015," December 18, 2013, www.taxpolicy center.org/numbers/displayatab.cfm?DocID=4029.

21. Because of the uncertainties inherent in such long-range forecasts, Social Security's actuaries make three forecasts based on different sets of assumptions—optimistic, intermediate, and pessimistic. In making these forecasts, they make assumptions about dozens of factors, including, for example, price changes, wage changes, unemployment, economic growth, labor force participation, birth rates, life expectancies, and immigration rates. Long-range projections are subject to error and, indeed, to greater error the further out in time they go. Nevertheless, the projections are intended to be useful to policymakers who want to chart a stable course for Social Security's financing and provide a reasonable basis for mid-course corrections that are necessary from time to time.

22. Pension Protection Act of 2006, Pub. L. No. 109-280, 120 Stat. 280 (2006), www.gpo.gov/fdsys/pkg/PLAW-109publ280/pdf/PLAW-109 publ280.pdf; For an example of the colloquial use of the color-coded zones, see Harvey M. Katz, "Do You Know the Financial Status of Your Union Pension Fund?" Fox, Rothschild, LLP, www.foxrothschild.com/newspubs /newspubsArticle.aspx?id=16156.

23. Social Security Administration, "Social Security and Medicare Tax Rates," March 8, 2012, www.socialsecurity.gov/OACT/ProgData/taxRates .html.

24. Automatic IRA Act of 2013, H.R. 2035, 113th Cong., 1st Sess., May 16, 2013, http://beta.congress.gov/bill/113th/house-bill/2035/text.

25. Virginia P. Reno and Joni Lavery, "Fixing Social Security," National Academy of Social Insurance, 2009, www.nasi.org/sites/default/files /research/Fixing_Social_Security.pdf; Perhaps the first to propose this were Bruce Webb and Dale Coberly in their Northwest Plan. To be clear, as appendix B discusses in more detail, this is an average annual increase of about 50 cents every week in the first year, and slightly more each of the 19 subsequent years.

26. Jasmine V. Tucker, Virginia P. Reno, and Thomas N. Bethell, "Strengthening Social Security: What Do Americans Want?" National Academy of Social Insurance, January 2013, www.nasi.org/sites/default/files /research/What_Do_Americans_Want.pdf.

27. Internal Revenue Service, "Publication 15—Main Content: 5. Wages and Other Compensation," 2014, www.irs.gov/publications/p15/ar02.html #en_US_2014_publink1000202313; Wages lost to nontaxed health insurance could diminish somewhat if the number of people with employer-provided insurance falls as the result of the Patient Protection and Affordable

Care Act, but it is much too early to know whether that will happen; Patient Protection and Affordable Care Act, H.R. 3590, 111th Cong., 2nd Sess., January 5, 2010, www.gpo.gov/fdsys/pkg/BILLS-111hr3590enr/pdf/BILLS -111hr3590enr.pdf.

28. Internal Revenue Service, "Topic 424—401(k) Plans," December 12, 2013, www.irs.gov/taxtopics/tc424.html.

29. Social Security Administration, "Social Security Announces 1.5 Percent Benefit Increase for 2014," October 30, 2013, www.socialsecurity.gov /pressoffice/pr/2014cola-pr.html.

30. Dean Baker, "The Impact of the Upward Redistribution of Wage Income on Social Security Solvency," Center for Economic and Policy Research, February 3, 2013, www.cepr.net/index.php/blogs/cepr-blog/the -impact-of-the-upward-redistribution-of-wage-income-on-social-secu rity-solvency.

31. Kevin Whitman and Dave Shoffner, Social Security Administration, "The Evolution of Social Security's Taxable Maximum," September 2011, *Policy Brief No. 2011-02*, Office of Retirement and Disability Policy, www .ssa.gov/policy/docs/policybriefs/pb2011-02.html.

32. National Bipartisan Commission on the Future of Medicare, "Medicare Financing Sources," November 20, 1998, http://medicare.commission .gov/medicare/anne.html.

33. Social Security Administration, Office of the Actuary, "Long Range Solvency Provisions—Summary Measures and Graphs," September 11, 2013, www.ssa.gov/oact/solvency/provisions/charts/chart_run116.html.

34. Social Security Administration, "Frequently Asked Questions About the Social Security Trust Funds," 2014, www.ssa.gov/oact/progdata/fund FAQ.html#a0=1.

35. Social Security Administration, "Social Security Income, Outgo, and Assets," 2014, www.ssa.gov/oact/progdata/assets.html.

36. Social Security Trustees, *The 2014 Annual Report of the Board of Trustees of the Federal Old-Age and Survivors Insurance and Federal Disability Insurance Trust Funds*, July 28, 2014, www.ssa.gov/oact/TR/2014/tr2014.pdf.

37. Social Security Administration, "Frequently Asked Questions About the Social Security Trust Funds."

38. Virginia P. Reno, "What's Next for Social Security? Essential Facts for Action," National Academy of Social Insurance, October 2013, www .nasi.org/sites/default/files/research/Whats_Next_for_Social_Security _Oct2013.pdf; In the Social Security Amendments of 1983, up to 50 percent of Social Security benefits were made subject to income taxation for couples with more than $32,000 (singles: $25,000) in countable income. These revenues go to the Social Security trust fund. In 1993, up to 85 percent of Social Security benefits were made taxable for couples with more than $44,000 (singles: $34,000) in countable income. These additional revenues go to Medicare's hospital insurance fund.

39. Social Security Trustees, *The 2014 Annual Report of the Board of Trustees of the Federal Old-Age and Survivors Insurance and Federal Disability Insurance Trust Funds*, July 28, 2014, www.ssa.gov/oact/TR/2014/tr2013.pdf

40. Ibid.; A tiny percentage of Social Security's revenue—about $1,000 in 2012—consisted of gifts received under the provisions authorizing the deposit of money gifts or bequests in the trust funds.

41. Catherine Mulbrandon, "Top Marginal Tax Rates 1916–2011," *Visualizing Economics* (blog), January 23, 2012, http://visualizingeconomics.com/blog /2012/01/24/comparing-tax-rates.

42. Tax Policy Center, "U.S. Individual Income Tax: Personal Exemptions and Lowest and Highest Tax Bracket: Tax Rates and Tax Base for Regular Tax, Tax Years 1913–2014," May 12, 2014, www.taxpolicycenter .org/taxfacts/Content/PDF/historical_parameters.pdf.

43. Additionally there is sound policy logic in dedicating these revenues to Social Security. First is to pay down the so-called legacy debt, costs incurred at the start-up of the program or when new benefits were added, primarily by providing benefits to those close to retirement age. Today's premiums pay not only current costs but also these legacy costs. There is good reason for these costs to be paid from a progressive tax.

44. One example is the California "Millionaire's Tax" ballot initiative of 2012. Ballotpedia, "California 'Millionaire's Tax Initiative' (2012)," April 5, 2014, http://ballotpedia.org/California_%22Millionaire's_Tax_Initiative %22.

45. Tax Policy Center, "Estate and Gift Taxes," 2014, www.taxpolicycen ter.org/taxtopics/estatetax.cfm.

46. Social Security Administration, "Thomas Paine," 2014, https://www .socialsecurity.gov/history/tpaine3.html.

47. Spouses inherit without the imposition of any tax; GDP information available from Office of Management and Budget, "Historical Tables," 2014, www.whitehouse.gov/omb/budget/historicals.

48. Thornton Matheson, "Taxing Financial Transactions: Issues and Evidence," working paper, International Monetary Fund, March 2011, https:// www.imf.org/external/pubs/ft/wp/2011/wp1154.pdf.

49. The so-called Section 31 Transactions Fee was enacted in 1934, the year before Social Security was enacted. It was, as its name suggests, included as section 31 of the Securities and Exchange Act of 1934 to fund the proposed Securities and Exchange Commission. It is imposed on the national stock exchanges and other self-regulating securities organizations on the volume of transactions.

50. U.S. Securities and Exchange Commission, "'SEC Fee'—Section 31 Transaction Fees," 2014, https://www.sec.gov/answers/sec31.htm.

CHAPTER 9: THE BILLIONAIRES' WAR AGAINST SOCIAL SECURITY

1. "The Second Presidential Debate," *New York Times*, October 7, 2008, http://elections.nytimes.com/2008/president/debates/transcripts/second -presidential-debate.html.

2. Lori Montgomery, "The Debt Fallout: How Social Security Went 'Cash Negative' Earlier Than Expected," *Washington Post*, October 29, 2013, www.washingtonpost.com/business/economy/the-debt-fallout-how-social -security-went-cash-negative-earlier-than-expected/2011/10/27/gIQACm 1QTM_story.html.

3. U.S. House of Representatives, "Final Vote Results for Roll Call 151," March 29, 2012, http://clerk.house.gov/evs/2012/roll151.xml.

4. House Budget Committee, *The Path to Prosperity: A Blueprint for American Renewal*, March 20, 2012, http://paulryan.house.gov/uploadedfiles /pathtoprosperity2013.pdf.

5. Commission on Presidential Debates, "October 11, 2012, Debate Transcript," October 11, 2012, www.debates.org/index.php?page=october-11 -2012-the-biden-romney-vice-presidential-debate.

6. "How Flawed Is the Health Care Law and the Politics of Parenting," *Meet the Press*, October 27, 2013, www.nbcnews.com/video/meet -the-press/53387818#53387818.

7. Trudy Lieberman, "How the Media Has Shaped the Social Security Debate," *Columbia Journalism Review*, April 18, 2012, www.cjr.org/campaign _desk/how_the_media_has_shaped_the_s.php?page=all.

8. See Eric R. Kingson, "A Tale of Three Commissions: The Good, the Bad, and the Ugly," *Poverty & Public Policy* 2, no. 3 (August 2010): doi: 10.2202/1944-2858.1120; Eric R. Kingson, "The Deficit and the Debt," *Congressional Digest* 89, no. 2 (February 2010): 47–58; "Two Commissions: Lessons for the Proposed Debt Commission," published background paper written for congressional briefing, "Demystifying the Deficit, Social Security Finances, and Commissions," organized by the National Academy of Social Insurance; Information about the briefing is available at https://www .nasi.org/civicrm/event/info?reset=1&id=117%20).

9. Robert M. Ball, *The Greenspan Commission: What Really Happened* (New York: Century Foundation Press, 2010).

10. Social Security Administration, "Social Security Amendments of 1977: Legislative History and Summary of Provisions," March 1978, www .ssa.gov/policy/docs/ssb/v41n3/v41n3p3.pdf.

11. Social Security Trustees, *1978 Annual Report of the Federal Old-Age and Survivors Insurance and Disability Insurance Trust Funds*, May 15, 1978, 2, www. ssa.gov/history/reports/trust/1978/1978.pdf; Also see E.R. Kingson, "Financing Social Security: Agenda–Setting and the Enactment of 1983 Amendments to the Social Security Act," *Policy Studies Journal* (September 1984). The latter piece notes that the 1977 amendments to the Social Security Act

addressed a flaw in introduced by the 1972 amendments, the main reason that the projected long-term shortfall was reduced from 8.2 percent of taxable payroll to 1.5 percent. The 1977 amendments also made adjustments to address a projected short-term shortfall. If the economy had operated as anticipated between 1977 and 1983, Social Security's financing would not have gained much traction as an issue. The remaining 1.5 percent of taxable payroll shortfall might have given those with an axe to grind something to complain about. But given that the projected shortfall was thirty-five years in the future there would have been little incentive for Congress to act. For more information on this, see www.ssa.gov/history/reports/trust/1978/1978.pdf.

12. Social Security Trustees, *1979 Annual Report of the Federal Old-Age and Survivors Insurance and Disability Insurance Trust Funds*, April 13, 1979, 48, www.ssa.gov/history/reports/trust/1979/1979b.pdf.

13. Social Security Trustees, *1981 Annual Report of the Federal Old-Age and Survivors Insurance and Disability Insurance Trust Funds*, July 2, 1981, 2, www.ssa.gov/history/reports/trust/1981/1981.pdf.

14. David Stockman, *The Triumph of Politics* (New York: Harper and Row, 1986), 228.

15. William Greider, "The Education of David Stockman," *The Atlantic*, December 1, 1981, www.theatlantic.com/magazine/archive/1981/12/the-education-of-david-stockman/305760.

16. Steven Greene Livingston, *U.S. Social Security: A Reference Handbook* (Santa Barbara, CA: ABC-CLIO, 2008), 24.

17. Nancy J. Altman, *The Battle for Social Security: From FDR's Vision to Bush's Gamble* (Hoboken, NJ: John Wiley & Sons, 2005), 231.

18. William Safire, "Language: Tracking the Source of the 'Third Rail' Warning," *New York Times*, February 18, 2007, www.nytimes.com/2007/02/18/opinion/18iht-edsafmon.4632394.html.

19. Nancy J. Altman, *The Battle for Social Security: From FDR's Vision to Bush's Gamble* (Hoboken, NJ: John Wiley & Sons, 2005), 234.

20. Matthew Skomarovsky, "Obama Packs Debt Commission with Social Security Looters," *Alternet*, March 28, 2010, www.alternet.org/story/146183/obama_packs_debt_commission_with_social_security_looters?page=entire.

21. Social Security Administration, "Executive Order 12335," December 16, 1981, www.ssa.gov/history/reports/gspan8.html.

22. White House, "Executive Order 13531—National Commission on Fiscal Responsibility and Reform," February 18, 2010, www.whitehouse.gov/the-press-office/executive-order-national-commission-fiscal-responsibility-and-reform.

23. Social Security Administration, "Oral History Collection: Robert M. Ball—Interview #5," May 22, 2001, www.ssa.gov/history/orals/ball5.html.

24. Social Security Administration, "Appendix C of the 1983 Greens-

pan Commission on Social Security Reform," January 1983, www.ssa.gov /history/reports/gspan5.html.

25. Social Security Administration, "Greenspan Commission: Report of the National Commission on Social Security Reform," January 1983, www .ssa.gov/history/reports/gspan.html.

26. See Eric R. Kingson, "A Tale of Three Commissions: The Good, the Bad, and the Ugly," *Poverty & Public Policy* 2, no. 3 (August 2010): doi: 10.2202/1944-2858.1120; Eric R. Kingson, "The Deficit and the Debt," *Congressional Digest* 89, no. 2 (February 2010): 47–58. Published background paper, "Two Commissions: Lessons for the Proposed Debt Commission," written for congressional briefing, "Demystifying the Deficit, Social Security Finances, and Commissions" organized by the National Academy of Social Insurance. Information about the briefing is available at https://www .nasi.org/civicrm/event/info?reset=1&id=117.

27. Ibid.

28. Although Clinton's executive order established his commission as the "Bipartisan Commission on Entitlement Reform," the entitlements commission later came to be known as the "Bipartisan Commission on Entitlement *and Tax* Reform" (emphasis added)—the name used in the commission's final report.

29. Social Security Administration, "Report of the Bipartisan Commission on Entitlement and Tax Reform," December 1994, www.ssa.gov /history/reports/KerreyDanforth/KerreyDanforth.htm.

30. Remarks by Celinda Lake of Lake Research Partners based on focus groups conducted March 2010 in Richmond ,Virginia, and Chicago, Illinois, and on behalf of NCPSSM, May 17, 2010.

31. Edward Schumacher-Matos, "Is 'Entitlements' A Dirty Word?" National Public Radio, August 11, 2011, www.npr.org/blogs/ombudsman /2011/08/11/139557647/is-entitlements-a-dirty-word.

32. Bipartisan Commission on Entitlement and Tax Reform, *Interim Report to the President* (Washington, DC: Superintendent of Documents, April 1995). Summary available at Rita L. DiSimone, *Social Security Bulletin* 58, no. 2 (Summer 1995), www.ssa.gov/policy/docs/ssb/v58n2/index.html

33. Robert A. Rosenblatt, "Entitlements Seen Taking Up Nearly All Taxes by 2012," *Los Angeles Times*, August 9, 1994, http://articles .latimes.com/1994-08-09/news/mn-25181_1_entitlement-programs.

34. Eric Laursen, *The People's Pension: The Struggle to Defend Social Security Since Reagan* (Oakland, CA: AK Press, 2012), 206.

35. All three commissions included elected officials and representatives of business, labor, and the public.

36. Social Security Administration, "Report of the Bipartisan Commission on Entitlement and Tax Reform," December 1994, www.ssa.gov /history/reports/KerreyDanforth/KerreyDanforth.htm.

37. Government Printing Office, "Appointment of Deputy Chief of Staff

for White House Operations," September 23, 1994, www.gpo.gov/fdsys /pkg/WCPD-1994-09-26/html/WCPD-1994-09-26-Pg1830-2.htm.

38. Kim Geiger, "Alan Simpson Pens Scathing Letter to 'Greedy Geezers' Retiree Group," *Los Angeles Times*, May 23, 2012, http://articles .latimes.com/2012/may/23/news/la-pn-alan-simpson-pens-scathing-letter -to-greedy-geezers-retiree-group-20120523.

39. Stephanie Condon, "Alan Simpson: Social Security Is Like a 'Milk Cow with 310 Million Tits!'" CBS News, August 25, 2010, www.cbsnews.com/news /alan-simpson-social-security-is-like-a-milk-cow-with-310-million-tits.

40. "The 400 Richest Americans: #147 Peter Peterson," *Forbes*, September 17, 2008, www.forbes.com/lists/2008/54/400list08_Peter-Peterson_U WZU.html.

41. John Harwood, "Spending $1 Billion to Restore Fiscal Sanity," *New York Times*, July 14, 2008, www.nytimes.com/2008/07/14/us /politics/14caucus.html?ref=petergpeterson; In the 2013 *Forbes* ranking, his net worth was listed as $1.5 billion: *Forbes*, "Peter Peterson," September 2013, www.forbes.com/profile/peter-peterson.

42. Peter G. Peterson Foundation, "PGPF Mission," 2014, http://pgpf .org/about.

43. Peter G. Peterson, "Social Security: The Coming Crash," *New York Review of Books*, December 2, 1982, www.nybooks.com/articles/archives /1982/dec/02/social-security-the-coming-crash.

44. Peter G. Peterson, "The Salvation of Social Security," *New York Review of Books*, December 16, 1982, www.nybooks.com/articles/archives/1982 /dec/16/the-salvation-of-social-security.

45. The Concord Coalition, *The Zero Deficit Plan* (Washington, DC: 1993); Neil Howe and Phillip Longman, "The Next New Deal," *Atlantic Monthly*, April 1992, https://www.theatlantic.com/past/politics/budget /newdeal.htm; Peter G. Peterson, "Entitlement Reform: The Way to Eliminate the Deficit," *New York Review of Books*, April 7, 1994, www .nybooks.com/articles/archives/1994/apr/07/entitlement-reform-the-way -to-eliminate-the-defici/; In the 1990s, he and others warned that without means-testing, "Social Security will be unable to meet its commitments to baby boomers and those who follow them into old age." Eric R. Kingson and J.H. Schulz, "Should Social Security be Means-Tested?," in *Social Security in the 21st Century*, eds. E.R. Kingson and J.H. Schulz (New York: Oxford University Press, 1997), 49.

46. Peter G. Peterson, *The Education of an American Dreamer: How a Son of Greek Immigrants Learned His Way from a Nebraska Diner to Washington, Wall Street, and Beyond* (New York: Hachette Book Group, Twelve, 2009).

47. Peter G. Peterson et al., "The Future of Social Security: An Exchange," *New York Review of Books*, March 17, 1983, www.nybooks.com/articles /archives/1983/mar/17/the-future-of-social-security-an-exchange.

48. Social Security Trustees, *1983 Annual Report of the Federal Old-Age and*

Survivors Insurance and Disability Insurance Trust Funds, June 27, 1983, 2, www.ssa.gov/history/reports/trust/1983/1983.pdf.

49. The Concord Coalition, "Peter G. Peterson," 2014, www.concord coalition.org/peter-g-peterson.

50. The Concord Coalition, "About the Concord Coalition," 2014, www.concordcoalition.org/about-concord-coalition.

51. Columbia Teachers College, "Teaching Kids About the National Debt," February 4, 2010, www.tc.columbia.edu/i/a/document/12947_PRE SS_RELEASE_UFR04Feb2010.pdf.

52. Addison Wiggin, "I.O.U.S.A.," 2014, www.addisonwiggin.com/iousa.

53. Thomas White, "I.O.U.S.A. Makes TV Debut on CNN," International Documentary Association, January 9, 2009, www.documentary.org /content/iousa-makes-tv-debut-cnn.

54. YouTube, "IOUSA.flv," April 10, 2011, www.youtube.com/watch ?v=EPdHq9CdqtI.

55. Eric Laursen, *The People's Pension: The Struggle to Defend Social Security Since Reagan* (Oakland, CA: AK Press, 2012), 606.

56. Peter G. Peterson Foundation, "Comeback America Initiative," December 16, 2010, http://pgpf.org/grants/comeback-america-initiative.

57. Bill Gaston, "The Demise of the Comeback America Initiative," *Stamford Advocate,* October 9, 2013, www.stamfordadvocate.com/opinion/article /The-demise-of-the-Comeback-America-Initiative-4882316.php.

58. Tom Curry, "Bill Clinton, Paul Ryan Headline Fiscal Summit Talks," MSNBC, May 15, 2012, http://nbcpolitics.nbcnews.com/_news /2012/05/15/11713917-bill-clinton-paul-ryan-headline-fiscal-summit -talks?lite; See also www.fiscalsummit.com.

59. Louis Proyect, "Bipartisan Threats Against Social Security," *The Unrepentant Marxist* (blog),September 7, 2008, http://louisproyect.org/2008/09 /07/bipartisan-threats-against-social-security.

60. Peter G. Peterson Foundation, "Michael A. Peterson," January 26, 2011, http://pgpf.org/board/michael-peterson.

61. Fix the Debt, "Who We Are," 2014, www.fixthedebt.org/who-we-are.

62. Nicholas Confessore, "Public Goals, Private Interests in Debt Campaign," *New York Times,* January 9, 2013, www.nytimes.com/2013/01/10 /us/politics/behind-debt-campaign-ties-to-corporate-interests.html.

63. Sarah Anderson and Scott Klinger, "A Pension Deficit Disorder: The Massive CEO Retirement Funds and Underfunded Worker Pensions at Firms Pushing Social Security Cuts," Institute for Policy Studies, November 27, 2012, www.ips-dc.org/reports/pension-deficit-disorder.

64. Sarah Anderson and Scott Klinger, "Platinum Plated Pensions," The Institute for Policy Studies and the Center for Effective Government, November 19, 2013, www.foreffectivegov.org/files/budget/platinum-plated _pensions.pdf.

65. Anderson and Klinger, "A Pension Deficit Disorder: The Massive

CEO Retirement Funds and Underfunded Worker Pensions at Firms Pushing Social Security Cuts."

66. Mary Bottari, "Astroturf 'Fix the Debt' Caught Ghostwriting for College Students," *PR Watch*, Center for Media and Democracy, November 15, 2013, www.prwatch.org/news/2013/11/12307/astroturf-%E2%80%9Ccampaign-fix-debt%E2%80%9D-caught-ghost-writing-college-kids.

67. Allen McDuffee, "Koch Brothers vs. Cato: Charles Koch Releases Full Statement," *Washington Post*, March 8, 2012, www.washingtonpost.com/blogs/think-tanked/post/koch-brothers-vs-cato-charles-koch-releases-full-statement/2012/03/08/gIQAcWz0zR_blog.html.

68. Peter J. Ferrara, *Social Security: The Inherent Contradiction* (Washington, DC: Cato Institute, 1980).

69. The Heartland Institute, "Peter Ferrara," 2014, https://heartland.org/peter-ferrara.

70. American Civil Rights Union, "Peter Ferrara, Legal Director," April 1, 2007, http://web.archive.org/web/20071012051737/www.theacru.org/blog/2007/04/peter_ferrara.

71. Edwin Feulner, "Coors, R.I.P.," *National Review*, March 18, 2003, www.nationalreview.com/articles/206203/coors-r-i-p/edwin-j-feulner.

72. James A. Dorn, "Social Security: Continuing Crisis or Real Reform?" *Cato Journal* 3, no. 2 (Fall 1983), The Cato Institute, http://object.cato.org/sites/cato.org/files/serials/files/cato-journal/1983/11/cj3n2-1.pdf.

73. Stuart Butler and Peter Germanis, "Achieving Social Security Reform: A 'Leninist' Strategy," *Cato Journal* 3, no. 2 (Fall 1983) 547, The Cato Institute, www.cato.org/cato-journal/fall-1983.

74. Ibid., 556.

75. Laurence Kotlikoff, "Social Security: Time for Reform," June 1978, www.econ.ucla.edu/workingpapers/wp121.pdf.

76. Institute for Contemporary Studies, "About ICS and BAICLA," February 6, 2013, www.icspress.com/BAICLA.htm.

77. Scott Burns and Laurence J. Kotlikoff, *The Coming Generational Storm: What You Need to Know about America's Economic Future* (Cambridge, MA: MIT Press, 2004).

78. Scott Burns and Laurence J. Kotlikoff, *The Clash of Generations: Saving Ourselves, Our Kids, and Our Economy* (Cambridge, MA: MIT Press, 2012).

79. Trudy Lieberman, "How the Media Has Shaped the Social Security Debate," *Columbia Journalism Review*, April 18, 2012, www.cjr.org/campaign_desk/how_the_media_has_shaped_the_s.php?page=all.

CHAPTER 10: THE CONVENTIONAL "WISDOM" IS JUST PLAIN WRONG

1. Michael Hiltzik, "Abby Huntsman Wants to Lead Her Own Generation into Poverty," *Los Angeles Times,* March 14, 2014, www.latimes.com/business/hiltzik/la-fi-mh-abby-huntsman-20140314-story.html.

2. Lori Montgomery, "The Debt Fallout: How Social Security Went 'Cash Negative' Earlier Than Expected," *Washington Post,* October 29, 2011, www.washingtonpost.com/business/economy/the-debt-fallout-how -social-security-went-cash-negative-earlier-than expected/2011/10/27/gIQ ACm1QTM_story.html.

3. David C. John, "Misleading the Public: How the Social Security Trust Fund Really Works," Heritage Foundation, September 2, 2004, www.heritage.org/research/reports/2004/09/misleading-the-public-how -the-social-security-trust-fund-really-works.

4. Robert J. Samuelson, "Let's Get Rid of (the Term) Entitlements," *Washington Post,* October 20, 2013, www.washingtonpost.com/opinions /robert-j-samuelson-lets-get-rid-of-the-term-entitlements/2013/10/20 /e3bd464c-3809-11e3-8a0e-4e2cf80831fc_story.html.

5. Aspen Gorry and Sita Slavov, "To Protect Future Generations, Fix Social Security," *The Daily Caller,* February 13, 2013, http://dailycaller .com/2013/02/13/to-protect-future-generations-fix-social-security.

6. Ben Casselman, "What Baby Boomers' Retirement Means for the U.S. Economy," *FiveThirtyEight,* May 7, 2014, http://fivethirtyeight.com /features/what-baby-boomers-retirement-means-for-the-u-s-economy.

7. David C. John, "Time to Raise Social Security's Retirement Age," Heritage Foundation, November 22, 2010, www.heritage.org/research/reports /2010/11/time-to-raise-social-securitys-retirement-age.

8. Laurence Kotlikoff, "America's Ponzi Scheme: Why Social Security Needs to Retire," PBS, April 7, 2014, www.pbs.org/newshour/making-sense /americas-ponzi-scheme-why-social-security-needs-to-retire/.

9. Paul Krugman, "Little Black Lies," *New York Times,* January 28, 2005, www.nytimes.com/2005/01/28/opinion/28krugman.html.

10. Michael Tanner, "Still a Better Deal: Private Investment vs. Social Security," *Policy Analysis,* no. 692, Cato Institute, February 13, 2012, http:// object.cato.org/sites/cato.org/files/pubs/pdf/PA692.pdf.

11. Yuval Levin, "Old and Rich? Less Help for You," *New York Times,* February 19, 2013, www.nytimes.com/2013/02/20/opinion/old-and-rich -less-help-for-you.html.

12. Gary Galles, "Social Security: The Most Successful Ponzi Scheme in History," Ludwig von Mises Institute, November 22, 2013, https:// mises.org/daily/6594/Social-Security-The-Most-Successful-Ponzi -Scheme-in-History.

13. The Senior Citizens League, "Ask the Advisor: Do Members of Congress Pay into Social Security?" October 4, 2011, http://seniorsleague.org/2011 /ask-the-advisor-do-members-of-congress-pay-into-social-security.

14. Robert Rector, "Amnesty Will Cost U.S. Taxpayers at Least $2.6 Trillion," Heritage Foundation, June 6, 2007, www.heritage.org/research /reports/2007/06/amnesty-will-cost-us-taxpayers-at-least-26-trillion.

15. Even the most careful actuaries have trouble projecting seventy-five

years into the future. Sometimes their projections may be too optimistic, showing more income and/or less outgo than actually occurs. Sometimes, their projections may be too pessimistic, showing less income and/or more outgo than occurs.

16. Social Security Trustees, *The 2014 Annual Report of the Board of Trustees of the Federal Old-Age and Survivors Insurance and Federal Disability Insurance Trust Funds*, July 28, 2014, www.ssa.gov/oact/TR/2014/tr2014.pdf.

17. Social Security Act, Title II, section 201(d); 42 U.S.C. § 401(d), August 14, 1935, http://ssa.gov/OP_Home/ssact/title02/0201.htm.

18. "Landon Hits Social Security as 'Cruel Hoax' in Milwaukee," *The Day*, September 28, 1936, http://news.google.com/newspapers?nid=1915&dat=19360928&id=XqktAAAAIBAJ&sjid=Z3EFAAAAIBAJ&pg=999,2342658; Alf Landon, "I Will Not Promise the Moon," *Oshkosh Daily Northwestern*, September 28, 1936, www.newspapers.com/newspage/43540453/; See generally Nancy J. Altman, *The Battle for Social Security: From FDR's Vision to Bush's Gamble* (Hoboken, NJ: John Wiley & Sons, 2005), 101–103.

19. Advisory Council on Social Security, 1937–1938 (April 29, 1938), appendix in report to Congress available at www.ssa.gov/history/reports/38advise.html.

20. Social Security Trustees, *The 2014 Annual Report of the Board of Trustees of the Federal Old-Age and Survivors Insurance and Federal Disability Insurance Trust Funds*, July 28, 2014, www.ssa.gov/oact/TR/2014/tr2014.pdf.

21. Indeed, to keep Social Security's books completely separate from the books of the general fund of the United States, Congress, in 1990, enacted Pub. L. 101-508, title XIII, Sec. 13301(a), Nov. 5, 1990, 104 Stat. 1388-623, which unambiguously states that Social Security "shall not be counted . . . for purposes of - (1) the budget of the United States Government as submitted by the President, [or] (2) the congressional budget. . . ."; Social Security Administration, "P.L. 101-508, Approved November 5, 1990 (104 Stat. 143)," 2014, www.ssa.gov/OP_Home/comp2/F101-508.html.

22. Center on Budget and Policy Priorities, "Economic Downturn and Legacy of Bush Policies Continue to Drive Large Deficits," February 28, 2013, www.cbpp.org/files/10-10-12bud.pdf; All components include the associated debt-service costs.

23. Centers for Medicare and Medicaid Services, "Closing the Coverage Gap—Medicare Prescription Drugs Are Becoming More Affordable," May 2013, www.medicare.gov/pubs/pdf/11493.pdf; During the past few years, health care costs have been rising more slowly than in the past and out-of-pocket expenses for prescription drugs are expected to decline as the Medicare donut hole will be fully closed by 2020.

24. All projections seventy-five years into the future are difficult, but those difficulties compound when what is being projected can change dramatically and quickly. Think about the cost of immunizing against polio, in

contrast to having no option other than treating those who fall prey to it with iron lungs and long stays in hospitals and rehabilitation facilities.

25. Lisa Potetz, Juliette Cubanski, and Tricia Neuman, "Medicare Spending and Financing: A Primer," Kaiser Family Foundation, February 2011, 5, http://kaiserfamilyfoundation.files.wordpress.com/2013/01/7731-03.pdf.

26. Paul Krugman, "Administrative Costs," *New York Times*, July 6, 2009, http://krugman.blogs.nytimes.com/2009/07/06/administrative-costs/?_php=true&_type=blogs&_r=0.

27. Centers for Medicare and Medicaid Services, Office of the Actuary, National Health Statistics Group, "National Health Expenditure Accounts," accessed March 21, 2014, historical table 19, www.cms.gov/Research-Statistics-Data-and-Systems/Statistics-Trends-and-Reports/NationalHealth ExpendData/Downloads/tables.pdf.

28. David Rosnick, "Health Care Budget Deficit Calculator," Center for Economic and Policy Research, accessed July 30, 2014, www.cepr.net /calculators/hc/hc-calculator.html.

29. The Committee for a Responsible Federal Budget, "The Social Security and Medicare Trustee Reports in Charts," June 26, 2013, http://crfb .org/blogs/social-security-and-medicare-trustee-reports-charts.

30. The report of the commission co-chaired by Bowles and Simpson included the following statement: "When Franklin Roosevelt signed Social Security into law, average life expectancy was 64 and the earliest retirement age in Social Security was 65. Today, Americans on average live 14 years longer, retire three years earlier, and spend 20 years in retirement. In 1950, there were 16 workers per beneficiary; in 1960, there were 5 workers per beneficiary. Today, the ratio is 3:1—and by 2025, there will be just 2.3 workers "paying in" per beneficiary." The National Commission on Fiscal Responsibility and Reform, *The Moment of Truth*, December 2010, www .fiscalcommission.gov/sites/fiscalcommission.gov/files/documents/The MomentofTruth12_1_2010.pdf.

31. Social Security Trustees, *The 2014 Annual Report of the Board of Trustees of the Federal Old-Age and Survivors Insurance and Federal Disability Insurance Trust Funds*, July 28, 2014, www.ssa.gov/oact/TR/2014/tr2014.pdf; See also Nancy J. Altman, *The Battle for Social Security: From FDR's Vision to Bush's Gamble* (Hoboken, NJ: John Wiley & Sons, 2005), 274–275.

32. Center for Economic and Policy Research, "Catherine Rampell Is Right: Medicare Is a Steal, but for Whom?" April 10, 2014, www .cepr.net/index.php/blogs/beat-the-press/catherine-rampell-is-right -medicare-is-a-steal-but-for-whom.

33. Pew Research Center, "Baby Boomers Retire," December 10, 2010, www.pewresearch.org/daily-number/baby-boomers-retire.

34. Social Security Trustees, *The 2014 Annual Report of the Board of Trustees of the Federal Old-Age and Survivors Insurance and Federal Disability Insurance Trust Funds*, July 28, 2014, table 5.A2, www.socialsecurity.gov/OACT

/TR/2014/lr5a2.html; The slightly higher ratios that President Bush was fond of using, quoted in response to the previous charge, is a result of comparing Social Security beneficiaries, which include children, disabled workers and others, not just seniors, to the working-age population.

35. Dependency ratios are also expressed as ratios—for instance, we could say that the age dependency ratio in 2012 is about 1 to 4 and will grow to roughly 1 to 2.4 in 2065.

36. Jennifer M. Ortman, "U.S. Population Projections: 2012 to 2060," U.S. Census Bureau, February 7, 2013, www.gwu.edu/~forcpgm/Ortman.pdf.

37. Ryan Grim, "Alan Simpson Attacks AARP, Says Social Security Is 'Not a Retirement Program'," Huffington Post, July 6, 2011, www.huffingtonpost.com/2011/05/06/alan-simpson-aarp-social-security-retirement-program_n_858738.html.

38. Robert D. Grove and Alice Hetzel, "Vital Statistics Rates in the United States, 1940–1960," U.S. Department of Health, Education and Welfare, Public Health Service, 1968, table 38, www.cdc.gov/nchs/data/vsus/vsrates1940_60.pdf.

39. Marian F. MacDorman et al., "Recent Declines in Infant Mortality in the United States, 2005–2011," NCHS Data Brief, no. 120, April 2013, U.S. Department of Health and Human Services, Centers for Disease Control and Prevention, www.cdc.gov/nchs/data/databriefs/db120.pdf.

40. Robert D. Grove et al., "Vital Statistics Rates in the United States, 1940–1960."

41. Social Security Administration, "Life Expectancy for Social Security," 2014, www.ssa.gov/history/lifeexpect.html.

42. See table 5.A3, "Period Life Expectancy" in Social Security Trustees, The 2014 Annual Report of the Board of Trustees of the Federal Old-Age and Survivors Insurance and Federal Disability Insurance Trust Funds, July 28, 2014, table 5.A3, www.socialsecurity.gov/OACT/TR/2014/lr5a3.html.

43. Lawrence Mishel, Monique Morrissey, and Harry C. Ballantyne, "Social Security and the Federal Deficit: Not Cause and Effect," Briefing Paper, no. 273, Economic Policy Institute, August 6, 2010, http://epi.3cdn.net/99133adf653fd78719_qym6b95et.pdf; The data cited compare female life expectancy at age 65 for the bottom half of the income spectrum in 1982 vs. 2006.

44. Social Security Administration, Annual Statistical Supplement, 2014, 2014, table 5.A6, www.ssa.gov/policy/docs/statcomps/supplement/2014/5a.html#table5.a1.1. About 4.4 million children receive Social Security benefits directly as of this writing; Thomas Gabe, Social Security's Effect on Child Poverty (Washington, DC: Congressional Research Service, December 22, 2011); About 4.8 million nonbeneficiary children live in households that receive Social Security benefits. That figure is from 2010, the most recent year it was available, so it likely understates the current total; U.S. Census

Bureau, "ACS Demographic and Housing Estimates," *2010–2012 American Community Survey 3-Year Estimates*, 2013, http://factfinder2.census.gov/; There are 74 million children under age 18 living in the United States as of this writing.

45. Paul N. Van de Water et al., "Social Security Keeps 22 Million Americans Out of Poverty: A State-By-State Analysis," Center on Budget and Policy Priorities, October 25, 2013, www.cbpp.org/cms/?fa=view&id=4037.

46. Dean Baker, "The Kids versus Seniors Line Doesn't Fit the Facts," Center for Economic and Policy Research, September 19, 2013, www.cepr.net/index.php/blogs/cepr-blog/the-kids-versus-seniors-line-doesnt-fit-the-facts.

47. James H. Schulz and Robert Binstock, *Aging Nation: The Economics and Policies of Growing Older in America* (Baltimore: Johns Hopkins University Press, 2006); Eric R. Kingson, Barbara Hirshorn, and John Comman, *Ties That Bind: The Interdependence of Generations* (Cabin John, MD: Seven Locks Press, 1986).

48. Stanford School of Medicine, "Life Expectancy: The Crossover Phenomenon," 2014, http://geriatrics.stanford.edu/ethnomed/african_american/health_risk_patterns.

49. Social Security Administration, "Social Security Is Important to African Americans," April 2014, www.ssa.gov/news/press/factsheets/ss-customer/aa-ret.pdf.

50. Center on Budget and Policy Priorities, "Policy Basics: Top Ten Facts About Social Security," November 6, 2012, www.cbpp.org/cms/?fa=view&id=3261#_edn25.

51. Social Security Administration, "Social Security Is Important to African Americans."

52. Social Security Administration, *Income of the Population 55 or Older, 2012*, April 2014, table 9.A3, www.ssa.gov/policy/docs/statcomps/income_pop55/2012/sect09.html.

53. Center on Budget and Policy Priorities, unpublished calculations of March 2012 *Current Population Survey* data performed for Social Security Works.

54. Dean Baker and Hye Jin Rho, "The Potential Savings to Social Security from Means Testing," Center for Economic and Policy Research, March 2011, www.cepr.net/documents/publications/ss-2011-03.pdf.

55. Social Security Administration, "Frequently Asked Questions: Q5: Is it True That Members of Congress Do Not Have to Pay into Social Security?," accessed July 30, 2014, www.ssa.gov/history/hfaq.html.

56. Stephen Goss et al. "Effects of Unauthorized Immigration on the Actuarial Status of the Social Security Trust Funds," Social Security Administration, April 2013, www.socialsecurity.gov/OACT/NOTES/pdf_notes/note151.pdf.

57. Franklin Delano Roosevelt, "Speech at Madison Square Garden,"

The Miller Center, October 31, 1936, http://millercenter.org/president
/speeches/detail/3307.

CHAPTER 11: THERE THEY GO AGAIN: WHY SOCIAL SECURITY SUPPORTERS MUST REMAIN VIGILANT

1. Dwight D. Eisenhower to Edgar Newton Eisenhower, "Document #1147," *The Papers of Dwight David Eisenhower* 15, *The Presidency: The Middle Way*, ed. Louis Galambos (Baltimore: Johns Hopkins University Press, 1996).

2. Yasha Levine, "The Birth of the Koch Clan: It All Started in a Little Texas Town Called Quanah," *The Exiled*, November 7, 2011, http://exile donline.com/the-birth-of-the-koch-clan-it-all-started-in-a-little-texas -town-called-quanah.

3. Kitty Kelley, *The Family: The Real Story of the Bush Dynasty* (New York: Doubleday, 2004), 57.

4. Tom Curry, "Tweak in Inflation Formula or Significant Cut in Social Security Benefits?" NBC News, December 18, 2012, http://nbcpolitics .nbcnews.com/_news/2012/12/18/15997750-tweak-in-inflation-formula -or-significant-cut-in-social-security-benefits?lite.

5. James T. Kloppenberg, *Reading Obama: Dreams, Hope, and the American Political Tradition* (Princeton, NJ: Princeton University Press, 2010).

6. Chris Cillizza, "Obama to Hold Fiscal Responsibility Summit," *Washington Post*, January 15, 2009, http://voices.washingtonpost.com/thefix /white-house/obama-to-hold-fiscal-responsib.html.

7. Blue Dog Coalition, "Members," 2014, http://bluedog.schrader.house .gov/about/members.htm.

8. The White House, *Fiscal Responsibility Summit*, March 20, 2009, 19–20, www.whitehouse.gov/assets/blog/Fiscal_Responsibility_Summit_Report .pdf.

9. Ibid., 21.

10. Ibid., 29.

11. D. Andrew Austin and Mindy R. Levit, "The Debt Limit: History and Recent Increases," Congressional Research Service, October 15, 2013, www.fas.org/sgp/crs/misc/RL31967.pdf.

12. Carl Hulse, "Baucus: Don't Outsource My Committee," *New York Times*, December 10, 2009, http://thecaucus.blogs.nytimes.com/2009/12 /10/baucus-dont-outsource-my-committee.

13. For a detailed explanation of why and how the proposal would lead over time to the radical transformation of Social Security, see Nancy J. Altman, "The Striking Superiority of Social Security in the Provision of Wage Insurance," *Harvard Journal on Legislation* 50 (2013): 109–168.

14. E.J. Dionne Jr., "Audacity Without Ideology," *Washington Post*, January 15, 2009, www.washingtonpost.com/wp-dyn/content/article/2009

/01/14/AR2009011403128.html?referrer=emailarticle; Obama used the phrase "grand bargain" even before he was inaugurated in 2009.

15. D. Andrew Austin et al., "The Debt Limit: History and Recent Increases."

16. Jennifer Epstein, "Gene Sperling: Obama 'Didn't Give One Inch'," *Politico*, August 1, 2011, www.politico.com/news/stories/0811/60362.html.

17. Richard Kogan, "How Across-the-Board Cuts in the Budget Control Act Will Work," Center on Budget and Policy Priorities, April 27, 2012, www.cbpp.org/cms/?fa=view&id=3635; If the Supercommittee failed to reach agreement, the Budget Control Act of 2011 required cuts of $1.2 trillion, less assumed interest savings on the debt ($216 billion), over nine years, or $109.3 billion per year, split evenly between defense and nondefense programs.

18. Richard Kogan, "How Across-the-Board Cuts in the Budget Control Act Will Work;" Cuts to Medicare providers and insurance plans were not excluded; those cuts were limited to 2 percent of such payments. In other words, Medicare providers could continue to bill Medicare in the normal way but were reimbursed at a rate of 98 cents on the dollar.

19. Alex M. Parker, "On the 'Super Committee's' Menu: Social Security Cuts and Tax Hikes," *U.S. News & World Report*, November 7, 2011, www.usnews.com/news/articles/2011/11/07/on-the-super-committees-menu-social-security-cuts-and-tax-hikes.

20. The Editorial Board, "The Supercommittee Collapses," *New York Times*, November 21, 2011, www.nytimes.com/2011/11/22/opinion/the-deficit-supercommittee-collapses.html.

21. Chana Joffe-Walt, "Unfit for Work: The Startling Rise of Disability in America," National Public Radio, March 2013, http://apps.npr.org/unfit-for-work.

22. Edward Glaeser, "2013 Is the Year to Go to Work, Not Go on Disability," *Bloomberg*, December 26, 2012, www.bloomberg.com/news/2012-12-27/2013-is-the-year-to-go-to-work-not-go-on-disability.html.

23. David Pattison and Hilary Waldron, "Growth in New Disabled-Worker Entitlements, 1970–2008," *Social Security Bulletin* 73, no. 4 (November 2013), www.ssa.gov/policy/docs/ssb/v73n4/v73n4p25.html.

24. Chana Joffe-Walt, "Unfit for Work: The Startling Rise of Disability in America," National Public Radio, March 2013, http://apps.npr.org/unfit-for-work.

25. Edward Glaeser, "2013 Is the Year to Go to Work, Not Go on Disability."

26. Stephen C. Goss, "Statement Before the House Committee on Ways and Means, Subcommittee on Social Security," March 14, 2013, www.ssa.gov/legislation/testimony_031413a.html.

27. KPMG Forensic, Fraud Survey, 2003, Coalition Against Insurance Fraud, www.insurancefraud.org/index.htm#.U3YTM3Zruf4.

28. Insurance Information Institute, "Insurance Fraud," March 2014, www.fiii.org/issues_updates/insurance-fraud.html#_ftn1.

29. Carolyn W. Colvin, Acting Commissioner of the Social Security Administration, "Statement before the House Ways and Means Committee Subcommittee on Social Security," February 26, 2014, www.ssa.gov /legislation/testimony_022614.html.

30. Xavier Becerra, "Becerra Opening Statement at Social Security Subcommittee Hearing on Preventing Disability Scams, Ways and Means Committee Democrats," February 26, 2014, http://democrats.waysandmeans .house.gov/press-release/becerra-opening-statement-social-security -subcommittee-hearing-preventing-disability.

31. Social Security Administration, "Disability Insurance Trust Fund," November 2009, www.ssa.gov/oact/progdata/describedi.html.

32. Social Security Administration, "OASDI and SSI Program Rates and Limits, 2014," October 2013, www.ssa.gov/policy/docs/quickfacts/prog _highlights/index.html.

33. Social Security Administration, "Projected Future Course for SSA Disability Programs," *Trends in the Social Security and Supplemental Security Income Disability Programs*, August 2006, www.ssa.gov/policy/docs/chart books/disability_trends/index.html.

34. Social Security Trustees, *The 2014 Annual Report of the Board of Trustees of the Federal Old-Age and Survivors Insurance and Federal Disability Insurance Trust Funds*, July 28, 2014, www.ssa.gov/oact/TR/2014/tr2014.pdf.

35. Material drawn from authors' contribution to Strengthen Social Security Coalition, Transition Report for the New Commissioner of Social Security: How to Ensure the World-Class Service the American People Deserve (March 2013).

36. Arthur J. Altmeyer, *The Formative Years of Social Security* (Madison: University of Wisconsin Press, 1966), 55.

37. United States Senate Special Committee on Aging, "Reductions in Face-to-Face Services at the Social Security Administration, Summary of Committee Staff Investigation," March 2014, www.aging.senate.gov/imo /media/doc/SSA%20Hearing%20Staff%20Memo1.pdf.

38. Social Security Administration, Annual Performance Plan for Fiscal Year 2015 and Revised Final Performance Plan for Fiscal Year 2014 and Annual Performance Report for Fiscal Year 2013, 13.

39. Social Security Administration, "Social Security Begins Issuing Annual Statements to 125 Million Workers," September 30, 1999, www.ssa .gov/pressoffice/statement.html.

40. Marc Fisher, "Social Security Treasury Targets Taxpayers for Their Parents' Decades-Old Debts," *Washington Post,* April 10, 2014, www .washingtonpost.com/politics/social-security-treasury-target-hundreds-of -thousands-of-taxpayers-for-parents-old-debts/2014/04/10/74ac8eae -bf4d-11e3-bcec-b71ee10e9bc3_story.html?wpmk=MK0000200.

41. Despite funding administration from its own dedicated resources, and despite an accumulated reserve of $2.8 trillion, the Social Security program's administrative funds are subject to the annual appropriations process, essentially treated like expenditures that lack dedicated revenue. In addition to administering the Social Security program, SSA also administers the Supplemental Security Income (SSI) program. SSI is funded from general revenue, and accordingly SSA receives annual appropriations from general revenue for the administration of SSI. For more see Scott Szymendera, "Social Security Administration (SSA): Budget Issues," March 19, 2013, www.fas.org/sgp /crs/misc/R41716.pdf.

CHAPTER 12: PASSING SOCIAL SECURITY FORWARD: A LEGACY FOR ALL GENERATIONS

1. Franklin D. Roosevelt, "Message to Congress Reviewing the Broad Objectives and Accomplishments of the Administration," June 8, 1934, www.ssa.gov/history/fdrcon34.html.

2. David E. Rosenbaum, "Reagan's 'Safety Net' Proposal: Who Will Land, Who Will Fall; News Analysis," *New York Times,* March 17, 1981, www.nytimes.com/1981/03/17/us/reagan-s-safety-net-proposal-who-will -land-who-will-fall-news-analysis.html.

3. Ronald Reagan, "A Time for Choosing," October 27, 1964, www .reagan.utexas.edu/archives/reference/timechoosing.html.

4. National Public Radio, "Transcript: GOP Response from Rep. Paul Ryan," January 25, 2011, www.npr.org/2011/01/26/133227396/transcript -gop-response-from-rep-paul-ryan.

5. Fox Business, "Entitlement Nation: Makers vs. Takers," May 20, 2011, www.foxbusiness.com/industries/2011/05/20/entitlement-nation-ma kers-vs-takers; Later in 2011, Paul Ryan, the future Republican vice-presidential candidate, warns, ". . . we're going to a majority of takers versus makers"; Brett Brownell and Nick Baumann, "Video: Paul Ryan's Version of '47 Percent'—the 'Takers' vs. the 'Makers'," *Mother Jones,* October 5, 2012; Not far behind, Fox News host Eric Boling observes, "People who are takers are almost more than 50 percent of America;" Terry Krepel, "Makers vs. Takers: Romney's '47 Percent' Rhetoric Echoes Fox News," Media Matters, September 18, 2012, http://mediamatters.org/research/2012/09/18/makers -vs-takers-romneys-47-percent-rhetoric-ec/189987; Echoing this theme, during the 2012 presidential election, presidential nominee Mitt Romney is caught unexpectedly on camera saying, "There are 47 percent of the people . . . who are dependent upon government, who believe that they are victims, who believe that government has a responsibility to care for them"; *Mother Jones,* "Full Transcript of the Mitt Romney Secret Video," September 19, 2012, www.motherjones.com/politics/2012/09/full -transcript-mitt-romney-secretvideo#.

6. Zach Carter, "Paul Ryan: 60 Percent of Americans Are 'Takers,' Not

'Makers'," *The Huffington Post,* October 5, 2012, www.huffingtonpost
.com/2012/10/05/paul-ryan-60-percent-of-a_n_1943073.html.

7. Emmanuel Saez, "Striking It Richer: The Evolution of Top Incomes in the United States (Updated with 2012 Preliminary Estimates)," September 3, 2013, http://eml.berkeley.edu/~saez/saez-UStopincomes-2012.pdf.

8. Stuart Butler and Peter Germanis, "Achieving Social Security Reform: A 'Leninist' Strategy," *Cato Journal* 3, no. 2 (Fall 1983), 556, The Cato Institute, www.cato.org/cato-journal/fall-1983.

APPENDIX A: ADDITIONAL EXPLANATION ABOUT HOW SOCIAL SECURITY WORKS

1. Social Security Administration, "OASDI and SSI Program Rates and Limits, 2014," October 2013, www.ssa.gov/policy/docs/quickfacts/prog _highlights/index.html.

2. Ibid.

3. See Social Security Financing Amendments of 1977, U.S. House of Representatives, Report of the Committee on Ways and Means to Accompany H.R. 9346, House Report No. 702, Part 1 (Washington, DC: U.S. Government Printing Office, October 12, 1977), 18. Because the wages covered by the maximum taxable wage base represented only 85 percent of total wages in 1977, Congress also enacted several ad hoc increases to the wage base, over and above the automatic adjustments, so that the base would be restored to covering 90 percent of all wages. The 90 percent level was reached in 1982.

4. Social Security Trustees, *The 2014 Annual Report of the Board of Trustees of the Federal Old-Age and Survivors Insurance and Federal Disability Insurance Trust Funds,* July 28, 2014, 138, www.ssa.gov/oact/TR/2014/tr2014.pdf.

5. Social Security Administration, "OASDI and SSI Program Rates and Limits, 2014," October 2013, www.ssa.gov/policy/docs/quickfacts/prog _highlights/index.html.

6. Ibid.

7. Ibid.

8. Ibid.

9. Social Security Administration, "Primary Insurance Information," 2014, www.ssa.gov/OACT/cola/piaformula.html.

10. Geoffrey Kollmann, "Social Security: Summary of Major Changes in the Cash Benefits Program," CRS Legislative Histories 2, May 18, 2000.

11. Social Security Act, Title II, section 216(l); 42 U.S.C § 416. www.ssa. gov/OP_Home/ssact/title02/0216.htm

12. Social Security Administration, "Retirement Benefits," April 2013. www.ssa.gov/pubs/EN-05-10035.pdf.

13. Social Security Administration, "Monthly Statistical Snapshot, March 2014," April 2014. www.ssa.gov/policy/docs/quickfacts/stat_snapshot/in dex.html?qs.

14. Social Security Administration, "Effect of Early or Delayed Retirement on Retirement Benefits," August 2010, www.ssa.gov/oact/ProgData/ar_drc.html.

15. Ibid.

16. Social Security Administration, "OASDI and SSI Program Rates and Limits, 2014."

17. Social Security Administration, *Annual Statistical Report on the Social Security Disability Insurance Program, 2012*, November 2013, www.ssa.gov/policy/docs/statcomps/di_asr/2012/background.html.

18. Social Security Administration, "Monthly Statistical Snapshot, March 2014," April 2014, www.ssa.gov/policy/docs/quickfacts/stat_snapshot/index.html?qs.

19. Social Security Administration, *Annual Statistical Supplement, 2012*, February 2013, www.ssa.gov/policy/docs/statcomps/supplement/2012/oasdi.html.

20. Social Security Administration, "Monthly Statistical Snapshot, March 2014."

21. Social Security Administration, *Annual Statistical Supplement, 2012*.

22. Social Security Administration, "Monthly Statistical Snapshot, March 2014."

23. Ibid.

24. Social Security Administration, "Retirement Benefits," April 2013, www.ssa.gov/pubs/EN-05-10035.pdf.

25. Social Security Administration, "Survivors Benefits," July 2013, www.ssa.gov/pubs/EN-05-10084.pdf.

26. Social Security Administration, "Research Note #11: The History of Social Security 'Student' Benefits," January 2001, www.socialsecurity.gov/history/studentbenefit.html.

27. Social Security Administration, *Annual Statistical Supplement, 2014*, July 2014, table 5A.6, www.ssa.gov/policy/docs/statcomps/supplement/2014/5a.html.

28. Social Security Administration, "Benefits for Children," August 2012, www.socialsecurity.gov/pubs/EN-05-10085.pdf.

29. Kathryn Anne Edwards, Anna Turner, and Alexander Hertel-Fernandez, *A Young Person's Guide to Social Security*, Economic Policy Institute and National Academy of Social Insurance, July 2012, www.nasi.org/sites/default/files/research/Young_Person's_Guide_to_Social_Security.pdf.

APPENDIX B: ADDITIONAL INFORMATION ABOUT SOCIAL SECURITY WORKS ALL GENERATIONS PLAN AND OTHER PROPOSALS, INCLUDING COST AND REVENUE ESTIMATES

1. Social Security Trustees, *The 2014 Annual Report of the Board of Trustees of the Federal Old-Age and Survivors Insurance and Federal Disability Insurance Trust Funds*, July 28, 2014, www.ssa.gov/oact/TR/2014/tr2014.pdf.

2. Social Security Administration, "Summary of Provisions That Would Change the Social Security Program," October 2013, http://ssa.gov/oact/solvency/provisions/summary.pdf.

3. A Bill to Improve the Retirement Security of American Families by Strengthening Social Security, S. 567, 113th Cong., 1st Sess., March 14, 2013, www.gpo.gov/fdsys/pkg/BILLS-113s567is/pdf/BILLS-113s567is.pdf.

4. A Bill to Improve the Retirement Security of American Families by Strengthening Social Security, H.R. 3118, 113th Cong., 1st Sess., September 17, 2013, www.gpo.gov/fdsys/pkg/BILLS-113hr3118ih/pdf/BILLS-113hr3118ih.pdf.

5. Office of Senator Tom Harkin, "Harkin Legislation Will Strengthen Social Security Benefits; Ensure Program for Future Generations," March 14, 2013, www.harkin.senate.gov/press/release.cfm?i=341035.

6. Social Security Administration, "Letter to Senator Harkin," March 18, 2013, www.ssa.gov/OACT/solvency/THarkin_20130318.pdf.

7. Nancy J. Altman and Eric R. Kingson, *Social Security Works All Generations Plan*, Social Security Works, October 2013, www.socialsecurityworks.org/wp-content/uploads/2014/03/Social-Security-Works-All-Generations-Plan.pdf.

8. Social Security Administration, "Summary of Provisions That Would Change the Social Security Program," October 2013, http://ssa.gov/oact/solvency/provisions/summary.pdf.

9. Ibid.

10. Ibid.

11. Virginia P. Reno and Joni Lavery, "Fixing Social Security: Adequate Benefits, Adequate Financing," National Academy of Social Insurance, October 2009, www.nasi.org/sites/default/files/research/Fixing_Social_Security.pdf.

12. Family and Medical Insurance Leave Act of 2013, H.R. 3712, 113th Cong., 1st Sess., December 12, 2013, www.gpo.gov/fdsys/pkg/BILLS-113hr3712ih/pdf/BILLS-113hr3712ih.pdf; Family and Medical Insurance Leave Act of 2013, S 1810, 113th Cong., 1st Sess., December 11, 2013, www.gpo.gov/fdsys/pkg/BILLS-113s1810is/pdf/BILLS-113s1810is.pdf; Social Security Works, "Current Bills Introduced to Expand Social Security," December 12, 2013, www.socialsecurityworks.org/wp-content/uploads/2013/12/Bills-Introduced-in-the-113th-Congress-to-Expand-Social-Security.pdf.

13. Jane Farrell and Sarah Jane Glynn, "The FAMILY Act: Facts and Frequently Asked Questions," Center for American Progress, December 12, 2013, http://cdn.americanprogress.org/wp-content/uploads/2013/12/FamilyActFactsheet-FAQs1.pdf.

14. Social Security Administration, "National Average Wage Index," 2014, www.ssa.gov/oact/cola/AWI.html; The National Average Wage Index is $44,321.67 for 2012.

15. Nancy J. Altman and Eric R. Kingson, *Social Security Works All Generations Plan*.

16. Social Security Administration, "Summary of Provisions That Would Change the Social Security Program."

17. Nancy J. Altman and Eric R. Kingson, *Social Security Works All Generations Plan*.

18. Ibid.

19. Ibid.

20. Social Security Financing Amendments of 1977, U.S. House of Representatives, *Report of the Committee on Ways and Means to Accompany H.R. 9346, House Report No. 702, Part 1*, (Washington, DC: U.S. Government Printing Office, October 12, 1977), 18; In 1977, Congress indexed Social Security's maximum to average wages. It intended to make the maximum level represent 90 percent of wages nationwide; Social Security Financing Amendments of 1977, U.S. House of Representatives, *Report of the Committee on Ways and Means to Accompany H.R. 9346, House Report No. 702, Part 1* (Washington, DC: U.S. Government Printing Office, October 12, 1977), 1; Because the wages covered by the maximum taxable wage base represented only 85 percent of total wages in 1977, Congress enacted several ad hoc increases to the wage base, over and above the automatic adjustments, so that the base would be restored to covering 90 percent of all wages; U.S. Bureau of the Census, *Income in the United States: 2002, Current Population Reports, Series P60-221*, September 2003, 25, www.census.gov/prod/2003pubs/p60 -221.pdf; The 90 percent level was reached in 1982, but has declined since then because of so much of the wage growth going to those at the top of the earnings scale.

21. Social Security Administration, "Summary of Provisions That Would Change the Social Security Program."

22. Ibid.

23. Nancy J. Altman and Eric R. Kingson, *Social Security Works All Generations Plan*.

24. Ibid.

25. Ibid.

26. Social Security Trustees, *The 2014 Annual Report of the Board of Trustees of the Federal Old-Age and Survivors Insurance and Federal Disability Insurance Trust Funds*, July 28, 2014, www.ssa.gov/oact/TR/2014/tr2014.pdf.

27. Social Security Administration, "Summary of Provisions That Would Change the Social Security Program."

28. Nancy J. Altman and Eric R. Kingson, *Social Security Works All Generations Plan*.

29. Virginia P. Reno and Joni Lavery, "Fixing Social Security: Adequate Benefits, Adequate Financing," National Academy of Social Insurance, October 2009, table 2, www.nasi.org/sites/default/files/research/Fixing

_Social_Security.pdf; This is the latest estimate available, made by the Social Security actuaries based on 2004 data.

30. Developed by authors based on informal conversation with the Chief Actuary of the Social Security Administration.

APPENDIX D: LEADING ORGANIZATIONS WORKING TO EXPAND SOCIAL SECURITY

1. Scholars Strategy Network, "What Is the Scholars Strategy Network?," 2014, www.scholarsstrategynetwork.org/page/what-scholars-strategy-network.

INDEX

PUBLISHING IN THE PUBLIC INTEREST

Thank you for reading this book published by The New Press. The New Press is a nonprofit, public interest publisher. New Press books and authors play a crucial role in sparking conversations about the key political and social issues of our day.

We hope you enjoyed this book and that you will stay in touch with The New Press. Here are a few ways to stay up to date with our books, events, and the issues we cover:

- Sign up at www.thenewpress.com/subscribe to receive up-dates on New Press authors and issues and to be notified about local events
- Like us on Facebook: www.facebook.com/newpressbooks
- Follow us on Twitter: www.twitter.com/thenewpress

Please consider buying New Press books for yourself; for friends and family; or to donate to schools, libraries, community centers, prison libraries, and other organizations involved with the issues our authors write about.

The New Press is a 501(c)(3) nonprofit organization. You can also support our work with a tax-deductible gift by visiting www.thenewpress.com/donate.